WORK ABROAD
THE COMPLETE GUIDE TO FINDING A JOB OVERSEAS

GENERAL EDITOR
Clay Hubbs

CONTRIBUTING EDITORS
Susan Griffith, William Nolting

Transitions Abroad Publishing, Inc.
Amherst, Massachusetts
www.TransitionsAbroad.com

Chapter 1

Introduction

Experiencing a Foreign Culture from the Inside 9

Perspective: Making the Most of Being Overseas

Key Print Resources: Work Abroad Publishers and Organizations 13

Key Web Sites: Work Abroad Publishers and Organizations 14

Chapter 2

International Careers

Work Abroad Preparation: Developing Needed Global Skills 17

Perspective: Finding a Job Abroad 19

Perspective: Working in Western Europe 22

Perspective: Life in the Foreign Service 24

Key Print Resources: International Careers 26

International Job Listings 29

Key Web Sites: International Careers 30

By Profession 32

By Region 34

Chapter 3

Short-Term International Jobs and Internships for Students and Recent Graduates

Work Abroad Overview: Overseas Jobs and How to Find Them 37

Short-Term Work Abroad: Exchange Programs 40

Perspective: Work in Britain 46

Key Print Resources: Worldwide Work and Study Abroad 49

Regional Work and Study Abroad 50

Short-Term Paid Work Abroad 52

International Internships: Cover Expenses, Gain Career Experience 54

Perspective: Work in Washington 58

Key Print Resources: International Internships 60

Directory of Programs: International Internships 62

Best Web Sites: Scholarships and Internships 69

Chapter 4
Short-Term Jobs Abroad

Key Employers by Country 71

Work as an Au Pair in Europe: A Country-by-Country Guide 90

Perspective: Crewing a Boat 95

Best Web Sites: Short-Term Jobs Abroad 96

Chapter 5
Volunteering Abroad

Introduction: Working to Provide for Unmet Needs 99

Selecting the Perfect Opportunity 100

Coping With Potential Problems 101

Perspective: The Cost of Volunteering 103

Perspective: International Monitoring 104

Key Print Resources: Volunteer Work Abroad 107

Directory of Programs: Volunteer Vacations 110

Best Web Sites: Volunteer Work Abroad 117

Chapter 6
Teaching English Abroad

Overview: The Most Accessible Jobs Abroad 119

Preparing to Teach: Pick the Training Course That Best Suits You 121

Work in Europe: Teaching English Offers Most Opportunities 123

Perspective: Teach English in Spain (if You Have *Ganas*) 129

The Eastern Mediterranean: English Teachers in Demand 131

New Destinations: ESL Teaching Jobs in Central and Eastern Europe 133

Perspective: An American at Home in Russia 139

Perspective: Work in Prague 141

Work in Asia: Where and How to Find ESL Jobs 142

Teaching in China: Steps to Finding Your Own Job 151

Perspective: Teaching in The Big Mango 153

Ticket to Latin America: Infinite Possibilities for English Speakers 154

Perspective: Work in Chile 161

Key Print Resources: Teaching English Abroad 162

Directory of Programs: ESL Training and Placement 164

Best Web Sites: Teaching English Abroad 170

Chapter 7

K-12 and University Teaching Abroad

Key Programs and Organizations 173

Recruitment Fairs Are the Places to Get Jobs 175

Perspective: Trade Your Concrete Jungle for a Real One 176

Key Print Resources: K-12 and University Teaching 178

Best Web Sites: Teaching Abroad K-12 179

University Teaching 180

About the Contributors 181

Index 182

Index to Advertisers 186

Reader Response Page 191

Editor's Note

Whether you are a professional planning to relocate, a student preparing for an international career, or a traveler looking to extend your trip, the thing you need most is reliable information. The editors of this book draw on nearly 25 years of experience in compiling and publishing international employment information for the readers of *Transitions Abroad* magazine. They also rely upon the first-hand reports of contributors from around the world.

Almost all of the material in this volume was first published in *Transitions Abroad* magazine. If you would like to read more about a particular kind of work, or what it's like to work in a particular country, you may want to order a copy of our 24-year country and subject index (see order form on page 187).

Please note that contact information changes frequently. All the resource and program directories published here are updated annually and published first in *Transitions Abroad* magazine, then on our web site [www.TransitionsAbroad.com], then in one of our books: *Work Abroad* or the *Alternative Travel Directory* (which covers living and studying as well as traveling overseas). If a contact fails to respond please check the magazine or web site for the most current information.

CHAPTER 1
INTRODUCTION

Any individual with guts and gusto, from students to grandmothers, has the potential to support themselves as they travel to the corners of the globe. Those who have shed their unrealistic expectations are normally exhilarated by the novelty and challenge.

Work Abroad
Experiencing a Foreign Culture from the Inside
By Susan Griffith

I n hopes of soothing the minds of the irresolute, here are some general guidelines to preface the unprecedented amount of specific information and contact addresses included in this third edition of *Work Abroad*.

Motives. Some travelers have future career prospects in view when they go abroad; a few go in search of highly paid jobs. Success is easier for people with acknowledged qualifications such as nurses and pipe-fitters, though cherry pickers and pot washers have been known to earn and save substantial sums. Those on open-ended trips may decide to postpone cashing their last traveler's check by looking around for ways of boosting their travel fund. They may find paid work, or they may decide to volunteer their labor in exchange for a bed and board. Most of the information in this volume concerns short-term work—12 months or less. For help on how to prepare for an international career and find a permanent job, see Chapter 2. Professionals should also consult their own trade's associations and journals.

Advance Planning. The aspiring working traveler either arranges a job before leaving home or gambles on finding something on the spot. Pre-arrangement is especially important for people who have never traveled abroad and who feel some trepidation at the prospect. Jobs can be pre-arranged either through private contacts or with the help of a mediating organization.

Some organizations accept a tiny handful of individuals who satisfy stringent requirements; others accept almost anyone who can pay the fee. Many work schemes and official exchanges require a lot of advance planning since it is not unusual for an application deadline to fall six or nine months before departure.

While it's easy to arrange a job to teach English in the former Soviet Union or work on an Israeli kibbutz, the price you pay for this security is that you commit yourself to a new life, however temporary, sight unseen. Furthermore, a participation fee in some cases can be as expensive as booking a conventional vacation.

The alternative to these packaged arrangements is to wait until after arrival at your destination to explore local job possibilities. In the course of research for my book, *Work Your Way Around the World*, I have come across many examples of fearless travelers who are prepared to arrive in a foreign city with very little money, confident that a means by which they can earn money will present itself. In most cases it does, but not without a few moments of panic and desperation.

Like job-hunting in any context, it will be much easier to contend with the inevitable competition if prospective employers can meet you in the flesh and be assured that you are available to start work the minute a vacancy crops up. For casual work on farms or arranging a passage on a transatlantic yacht, a visit to a village pub frequented by farmers or yachties is worth dozens of speculative applications from home.

The more unusual and interesting the job the more competition it will attract. Less glamorous options can absorb an almost unlimited number of people. International workcamps, for example, mobilize thousands of volunteers from many countries every year who come together to build footpaths, work with disabled persons, etc.

Red Tape. Work permits and residence visas are not readily available in many countries and for many kinds of jobs. In most cases, job-seekers from overseas must find an employer willing to apply to the immigration authorities on their behalf well in advance of the job's starting date, while they are still in their home country. This is easier for nuclear physicists and foreign correspondents than for mere mortals, though in certain countries English teachers are welcomed by the authorities. In organized exchange programs like the ones administered by Council on International Educational Exchange and InterExchange the red tape is taken care of by the sponsoring organization.

Temporary jobs like apple picking and burger flipping will never qualify for a work permit, and unofficial employment can quite often lead to exploitative working conditions.

Improving Your Chances. Preparation will improve your chances of being accepted on an organized work scheme and convincing a potential employer of your superiority to the competition. For example, before leaving home you might take a short course in teaching English, cooking, word processing, or sailing—all skills that have been put to good use by working travelers. If you are serious, you might learn or improve your knowledge of a foreign language.

Even if you are not lucky enough to have friends and family scattered strategically throughout the world, it is always worth broadcasting your intentions to third cousins, pen friends, and visiting Asian professors. The more widely publicized your travel plans, the better your chance of a lead.

If you set off without an address book full of contacts, your fellow travelers are undoubtedly the best source of information on job prospects; most are surprisingly generous with their information and assistance. Youth hostels can be a gold mine for the job seeker. Jobs may even be advertised on the notice board. Any locals or expatriates you meet are a potential source of help. Any skill or hobby, from jazz music to motor car racing, can become the basis for pursuing contacts.

Local English language newspapers like Mexico City's *The News*, the *Bangkok Post*, or *Cairo Today* may carry job advertisements appropriate to your situation, or may be a good place for you to advertise your services. The most effective method of finding a job overseas is to walk in and ask. As in any job hunt, it helps to have a neat appearance and show keenness and persistence. If you want a job for which there appear to be no openings, volunteer. If you prove yourself competent, you will have an excellent chance of filling a vacancy if one does occur.

Seasonal Jobs are most likely to go to itinerant foreigners. In times of recession the number of temporary jobs available may even increase since employers are not eager to expand their permanent staff but will need extra help at busy times. Farmers and hotel/restaurant managers are the best potential sources of employment, and in most cases one setback leads to a success once you are on the track.

Young women and (increasingly) young men who want the security of a family placement and who may also wish to learn a European language may choose to live with a family helping to look after the children in exchange for pocket money. Such positions can be found on the spot by means of advertisements or in advance through agencies, like AuPair Homestay.

English teaching normally requires some experience and a nine-month commitment, though many travelers from Bangkok to Buenos Aires have used the yellow pages to direct them to local language schools willing to employ native speakers of English as conversational assistants.

Volunteering. Paid work in developing nations is rarely available, yet many travelers arrange to live for next to nothing doing something positive. Charities and aid organizations offer a range of volunteer opportunities around the world. Many volunteer agencies require more than a curiosity about a country; they require a strong wish to become involved in a specific project and in many cases an ideological commitment to a cause. Almost without exception, volunteers must be self-funding.

For anyone with a green conscience, conservation organizations throughout the world welcome volunteers for short or long periods in projects ranging from tree planting to gibbon counting. Unfortunately, the more glamorous projects, such as accompanying scientific research expeditions into wild and woolly places, charge volunteers a great deal of money for the privilege of helping.

Whether you set off to work abroad with the help of a mediating organization or with the intention of living by your wits, you are bound to encounter interesting characters and lifestyles, collect a wealth of anecdotes, increase your self-reliance, and feel that you have achieved something. Inevitably there will be some surprises along the way.

Perspective

Making the Most of Being Overseas

By Laura Higgins

You don't want to be just a tourist. You want to get to know the real people to experience what life is really like in this foreign country you've worked so hard and risked so much to live in. But you still feel like an outsider looking in. What can you do?

Accept the fact that you *are* an outsider and enjoy the benefits. When I lived in Tahiti, my light hair, blue eyes, and 5'3" build made it impossible for me to blend in with the black-haired, bronze-skinned, and generally much taller Tahitians. But having grown up where light brown hair, blue eyes, and small size were the most common of features, I enjoyed being "exotic." And I also made lots of friends, all with open minds and a strong interest in learning more about other countries and other cultures, in this case, mine.

Sign up to learn local arts or sports. In Tahiti, the sensual dancing seen in *South Pacific* is unarguably the most vital form of cultural expression for the *Ma'ohi*, as native Polynesians in Tahiti like to call themselves. I had my doubts about joining a class that would require me to bare my midriff and dance publicly in skimpy *pareus*, but by taking the risk I not only learned about but became a part of something quintessentially Tahitian. I also gained self-confidence. Since my return to the U.S. I have been teaching classes in dance to share this confidence and pleasure with others. In Spain I am now learning flamenco—completely different experience yet equally fascinating.

I have also tried outrigger canoeing, drumming, and cooking. For meeting people and learning about a culture, there is nothing like physically participating in something fundamental to that culture.

Intercambios. The word is Spanish, but the idea works everywhere. Meet a native of the country once a week at a café for conversation, alternating between your native language one week and his the next. You not only improve your language ability but the conversations you have can be fascinating and the friendships you develop will endure. I never became as fluent in *Reo Ma'ohi* (Tahitian) as I would have liked, but the fact that I tried led to my being surrounded with friendly, intrigued faces in the market and being invited to families' homes for weekends. Local universities are ideal places to put up notices.

Volunteer. You do it at home, why not abroad? A friend of mine always works with underprivileged children wherever she goes and another involves herself with women's shelters. Volunteering means being part of something that matters.

One nice thing about these "tricks" is that they work even for shy people like me. You live in another country because you are interested in its culture. All you have to do to immerse yourself in it is put a little energy into showing that interest.

Work Abroad Resources
Key Publishers
Selected and Reviewed by William Nolting

L ooking for international work, whether abroad or in the U.S. with an international organization, can be downright frustrating without good resources. There are many useful guides for almost any field in any country, but you won't find them all in your local bookstore. Some of the best guides (including the one you are reading) are made by small publishers that lack mass distribution. The following is a list of the key publishers of work abroad resources, whose web sites and catalogs should be your first stop in your search for a job abroad.

Central Bureau, The British Council, 10 Spring Gardens, London SW1A 2BN, U.K.; 011-171-389-4004, fax 011-171-389-4426; [www.britcoun.org/cbiet/resource]. Publishes guides to working, volunteering, internships, and teaching abroad. Distributed in the U.S. by the Institute of International Education (IIE).

Council (Council on International Educational Exchange), 205 E. 42nd St., New York, NY 10017-5706; 888-COUNCIL, fax 212-822-2699; [www.councilexchanges.org]. Council administers the Council Work Abroad Program and Council Workcamps, as well as study abroad programs.

Global Exchange, 2017 Mission St., #303, San Francisco, CA 94110; 800-497-1994; fax 415-255-7498; info@globalexchange.org, [www.globalexchange.org]. Distributes books on solidarity with developing countries; also organizes "real tours." Add $1.75 ($3 first class) shipping for each book ordered.

Impact Publications, 9104-N Manassas Dr., Manassas Park, VA 20111; 703-361-7300, fax 703-335-9486; info@impactpublications, www.impactpublications.com. The best one-stop source for international career books published by Impact and many other publishers.

Institute of International Education (IIE). IIE Books, P.O. Box 371, Annapolis Junction, MD 20701-0371; 800-445-0443, fax 301-206-9789; iiebooks@pmds.com; [www.iie.org] and [www.iiepassport.org]. Publisher of authoritative directories for study or teaching abroad and financial aid, and distributor of Central Bureau (U.K.) publications on working abroad. IIE also administers several of the Fulbright scholarship programs.

Intercultural Press, P.O. Box 700, Yarmouth,

ME 04096; 800-370-2665 or 207-846-5168, fax 207-846-5181; books@interculturalpress.com, [www.interculturalpress.com]. Numerous publications dealing with cross-cultural issues, moving abroad, dealing with culture shock, and other issues related to working and studying abroad.

John Wiley & Sons, 1 Wiley Dr., Somerset, NJ 08875; 908-469-4400; [www.wiley.com]. Publications on careers.

NAFSA Publications, P.O. Box 1020, Sewickley, PA 15143; 800-836-4994; fax 412-741-0609, [www.nafsa.org]. Essential publications for advisers and administrators in international educational exchange. For membership information, contact NAFSA: Association of International Educators, 1307 New York Avenue, NW, 8th Fl., Washington, DC 20005-4701, 202-737-3699, fax 202-737-3657; inbox@nafsa.org, [www.nafsa.org].

Peterson's, 202 Carnegie Center, P.O. Box 2123, Princeton, NJ 08543-2123; 800-338-3282, outside U.S. 609-243-9111, fax 609-243-9150; [www.petersons.com]. Guides to jobs and careers, study abroad. U.S. distributor for many of the Vacation Work Publications (U.K.).

Reference Service Press, 5000 Windplay Dr., Suite 4, El Dorado Hills, CA 95762; 916-939-9620, fax 916-939-9626; findaid@aol.com, [www.rspfunding.com]. Publisher of numerous directories for scholarships and financial aid.

Seven Hills Book Distributors, 1531 Tremont St., Cincinnati, OH 45214; 513-471-4300, fax 513-471-4311; [www.sevenhillsbooks.com]. U.S. distributor for Vacation Work (U.K.) Publications and Survival Books. Also carries a wide range of travel books and maps from foreign and domestic publishers.

TESOL (Teachers of English to Speakers of Other Languages, Inc.) 700 South Washington St., Alexandria, VA 22314; 703-836-0774, fax 703-836-6447; info@tesol.org, [www. tesol.org]. For orders from TESOL Publications: P.O. Box 753, Waldorf, MD 20604-0753; 888-891-0042, 301-638-4427 or 301-638-4428, fax 301-843-0159; tesolpubs@ tascol.com, [www.tesol.org]. TESOL is the largest professional association for qualified teachers of English as a foreign or second language. TESOL's services include publications, job listings, and conferences.

Transitions Abroad $28/ 6 issues. P.O. Box 1300, Amherst, MA 01004-1300; 800-293-0373, fax 413-256-0373; info@ TransitionsAbroad.com, [www. Transi-

tionsAbroad.com]. Publishes *Transitions Abroad*, the only U.S. periodical which gives extensive coverage to work abroad options, in addition to all other varieties of education abroad. Includes thousands of programs, resources, and first-hand reports.

Vacation Work Publications 9 Park End St., Oxford, OX1 1HJ, U.K; 011-44-1865-241978, fax 011-44-1865-790885; [www.vacationwork. co.uk]. Web site includes forum on work abroad. Publisher of numerous books on work abroad and international careers. Distributed in the U.S. by Peterson's or Seven Hills, depending on the particular book.

VGM Career Horizons a division of NTC/ Contemporary Publishing Group, 4255 West Touhy Ave., Lincolnwood, IL 60712-1975, fax 847-679-2494. Books on careers. Available through bookstores.

Key Work Abroad Web Sites
Introduction and Search Strategies
Selected and Reviewed by William Nolting

These are the best sites we've seen for work abroad and international careers, but for different reasons. Sites designated (I) for *Information* contain lists or databases of work abroad programs, information about working abroad, links to many other work abroad sites, or actual job listings. The (I) sites are some of the best starting places for overseas job hunters.

Sites designated (P) for *Program*, belong to a few selected work abroad programs chosen for their large size, longevity, or other unique qualities—examples include the JET Program, the Peace Corps, and those official work exchange programs in the "Short-Term Paid Work" section.

Sites designated (S) for *Scholarship* provide funding for international exchange or provide information on how to fundraise.

Although the Internet contains enormous amounts of information for finding jobs, volunteer opportunities, and internships, it should be only part of your search. The goal is to find background and contact information for organizations with whom you would like to work and use the online information as a starting place. Find out more about the organization via phone calls, letters, and meetings. Many parts of the world are still not online, so supplement your search by consulting books and newspapers targeted to international opportunity seekers.

Your search will probably proceed in two overlapping stages:

Information Search and Compilation: During this stage, pull together as much information as you can on potential opportunities that interest you. This stage should involve online resources (web search engines, online databases, and discussion lists), as well as international opportunity books and newspapers.

Start out researching as wide as possible and narrow down as you discover opportunities more closely matching your interests. Follow links, search on key words, and generally try to gather as much information as you can handle at first. Then go through it all and sort out what you need. *The most valuable information you can gain for job hunting is a contact name and number.*

Narrowing Down and Networking: Here, you learn more specific details about a small list of organizations that interest you through email and discussion lists, phone calls, letters, and face-to-face meetings.

Email Discussion Lists

Email lists are email groups with many subscribers (sometimes in the hundreds) who share an interest in a specific topic—whether a country, a region, or an issue such as human rights. Once you sign up, don't be afraid to broadcast a question or ask for advice; but follow the list's rules or you will not be very happy with the responses you get. Occasionally, list members will send out information on just what you are looking for, or they may be connected to an organization you want to work with. An excellent database of Internet discussion lists is [**www.liszt.com**]. To find usenet groups specifically, go to [**www.dejanews.com**].

The Best Worldwide Work Abroad Directories on the Web

Web sites in this section are some of the most useful for students and graduates. (For International Careers and International Job Listings, see Chapter 2.) They list internships, volunteer, work abroad, and study abroad programs with or without academic credit. The rating codes are as follows: ***Essential; *Outstanding and of broad interest.*

(I) Informational site with directories or databases listing many programs
(P) Site for a specific work abroad program
(S) Scholarships or fellowships

** (I, P) GoAbroad.com [**www.goabroad.com**] by Troy Peden. A very comprehensive and up-to-date web site with excellent search provisions. Site's design allows continuous updates by program providers. Most listings give extensive information. Search possible by country or subject. Provides addresses, telephone numbers, and email addresses for all programs and links to web sites for some programs. Listings also bring up country-specific travel information. One of the best sites for those looking for a broad range of education abroad options.

** Institute of International Education [**www.iie.org**] The IIE publishes the most comprehensive data on study and work abroad programs for students or recent graduates. Its online versions also offer the best search capabilities. IIE Passport [**www.iiepassport.org**] is a user-friendly search engine

which lets you check off the program characteristics you're interested in, such as location, language of instruction, whether other participants in a program are U.S. students or from the host country, or if the program offers a special "format" such as internships, volunteering, or field research. IIE Passport includes the entire contents of the IIE books *Academic Year Abroad* and *Vacation Study Abroad*. The IIE site also has information about Fulbright teaching and scholarship programs, along with exchange programs in arts, engineering, environment, policy, and other professional areas.

* International Volunteer Programs Association (IVPA) [**www.volunteerinternational.org**] by Christine Victorino. IVPA is a professional association for administrators of international volunteer programs, as well as advisers and students interested in this type of

international experience. The site lists programs for volunteering abroad, some of which offer academic credit, and has extensive links to relevant resources.

** (I) **Studyabroad.com [www.study-abroad.com]** by Mark Landon. Site's databases list approximately 5,000 programs. Has special databases for language courses and experiential programs. Information limited to location and subjects (does not provide cost information, for example). Contains addresses, phone numbers, email addresses. Links to program web sites for only some programs. Search by country, academic subject, or both, but no other variables.

* (I) **The Electronic Embassy** [www.embassy.org] contains links to the home pages of all U.S.-based embassies. Many countries provide cultural and educational exchange information, as well as essential information for travel and work (visas, etc.) on their sites. Note, however, that these sites rarely mention the internship, volunteer, and work exchange programs found in the other resources mentioned here.

** (I) **Transitions Abroad [www.transitions-abroad.com]**. Kurt Carlson, editor. *Transitions Abroad* magazine is unique in its coverage of all education abroad options, from study and work abroad to educational travel. The online version includes annotated guides to resources and country-by-country listings of programs for study, work, internships, volunteering, language study, etc. Includes up-to-date list of short-term employers worldwide. Search functions available for entire site. The major sections of this site include Study Abroad, Work Abroad, International Travel, and Living Abroad Resources.

** (I) **Univ. of California-Irvine, International Opportunities Program** [www.cie.uci.edu/~cie/iop]. Concept by Ruth Sylte, now edited by IOP's Sharon Parks. Extensive directories (not databases) for internships, research, teaching, volunteering and work abroad programs, as well as study abroad and summer programs. Contains links to many useful sites. Information on both academic and nonacademic internships. See also **The World at Your Fingertips** [www.cie.uci.edu/~cie/world], which is not a directory, but an instructional site—how students and advisers can use the Internet to research options for education abroad.

** (I) **Univ. of Michigan, International Center's Overseas Opportunities Office** [www.umich.edu/~icenter/overseas] by William Nolting, Anthony Hand, and students. Not a database, but a collection of articles, annotated links, and print resources for study, work and travel abroad, including in-depth reports on work abroad options—the most singular feature of this site.

** (I) **Univ. of Minnesota, International Study and Travel Center (ISTC)** [www.istc.umn.edu]. Concept by Richard Warzecha. A comprehensive web site with outstanding search provisions. Full contact information including links to web sites and email provided for every listing (where available). Sophisticated and easy-to-use search provisions. Site includes several searchable databases: try using search terms such as "internship," "research," "volunteer," "work," or "teach" in each one of the databases.

** (I, P) **U.S. Department of State** [www.state.gov]. While not a directory of programs, this site provides essential information from the diplomatic branch of the U.S. government for everything from travel safety advisories to crisis assistance for U.S. citizens abroad and contact information for all U.S. embassies and consulates. Also lists foreign embassies and consulates in the U.S. The Department of State offers 1,000 internships annually as well as career positions. Country background notes, travel advisories, and countless other articles make this site one of the most valuable sources of international information on the web. Other frequently consulted parts of this very comprehensive web site include Travel Warnings and Information, Travel Tips for Students, Services for U.S. Citizens Abroad, Passport services, Publications, and Background Notes (country information).

** (I) **Washington and Lee Univ., Office of International Education** [www.wlu.edu/~intled/oiework.htm] by William Klingelhofer. This site, by an expert on work abroad formerly at Harvard Univ., provides an excellent overview of working abroad, including internships, teaching, and volunteering, with links to hundreds of programs. Good section on study opportunities.

CHAPTER 2

INTERNATIONAL CAREERS

There is, literally, a world of opportunity for job seekers who are serious about pursuing an international career. Whether you are an entry-level college graduate or mid-career professional, it is possible to find your niche by thoroughly researching the job market, identifying the relevant skills you already have, and acquiring the skills you may lack.

Preparing for an International Career

Developing Needed Global Skills

By Debra Peters-Behrens

As an international careers adviser, I receive questions daily from people of varied backgrounds who hope to try their luck in the global marketplace. Many job seekers mistakenly believe that they can't begin an international career until their feet are on foreign soil. They overlook their own backyard for resources and training opportunities. Consider the skills most sought after by global employers and the strategies for acquiring them *before* you leave home.

The Most Sought-After Skills

What do international employers really look for in employees and what skills will be needed by professionals to perform successfully in the global marketplace?

A study commissioned by the College Placement Council Foundation surveyed 32 international employers and colleges to determine what international employers seek in prospective employees. They identified the following areas of required knowledge and skills:

Domain knowledge. Colleges in the U.S. are presently preparing their graduates well in domain knowledge, or knowledge in one's academic discipline, although employers expressed concern that increasingly greater demands and higher standards may soon result in inadequately prepared graduates.

The three most important skills were cognitive skills, social skills, and "personal traits." Problem-solving ability, decision making, and knowing how to learn are highly prized generic skills. Social skills were described as the ability to work effectively in group settings, particularly with diverse populations. Personal traits mentioned frequently included flexibility, adaptability, and the capacity to be innovative. Employers often mentioned that colleges do not adequately address this type of skill development.

Cross-cultural competence. Students must make a concerted effort to acquire the knowledge, skills, and traits gained through cross-cultural interaction because we are more geographically and linguistically insulated than most other countries.

On-the-job training and prior work experience. Employers seek applicants who have been successful in applying their domain knowledge or academic studies and generic skills in the workplace. They say that colleges do not place sufficient emphasis on work experience.

Acquiring the Skills

Get Experience. An internship or a stint as a volunteer can be invaluable to recent graduates or career changers. Locate organizations at the local level which have similar goals to those of larger international organizations. Service organizations address issues of health, housing, economic development, and employment—all of which are local as well as global concerns.

For example, one client wanted to find a position in development work in the Third World. I suggested that she research local human service organizations to find an internship that would provide her with opportunities to work with on-going projects. She found an internship as an interagency liaison with a relief organization that distributed medicine, food, and supplies to countries affected by war or natural disasters.

Many job seekers plan to teach English as a second language with little or no experience beforehand. Even a brief stint as a volunteer language assistant can provide insight into the challenges and rewards of the work. Testing a field in familiar settings can make for a smoother transition abroad.

Build Your Resume. Job seekers often do not have the time or the money to pursue a degree program, but in some instances a few courses may sufficiently augment the experience and education you already have. Consult a career counselor to help you assess your skills and identify approaches for strengthening your background. A counselor can also help you determine an optimum strategy for meeting your goals. Investigate extension and continuing education programs offered by local colleges and universities for courses in computer science, graphic design, and foreign languages.

Research the Job Market. Gather information by researching a variety of sources: trade publications, journals, professional associations, and electronic bulletin boards. The public library is a treasure trove of information. Many university libraries will issue a community user card for a nominal annual fee.

After you have a grasp of key issues and trends you may want to get the perspective of people who are active in the field. Use your alumni directory and professional associations as resources for networking and information interviewing. Do not set up an information interview and then ask your informant for a job. People generally resent the imposition. Instead, use the time to ask questions that are not covered in print material, including "If you were me, what would you do next?," "If you had to do it all over again, is there anything you would do differently?," and "What strategies did you use that were most successful?"

With a focused and well-organized approach, you can be on the path to developing skills for a global career.

Go Where the Action Is. Many U.S. cities are becoming global in population and perspective as people with diverse linguistic, national, and cultural backgrounds converge to live and work. Living in these locales can help you acquire cross-cultural competence and find work in fields such as business, cultural exchange, and health and human services with a focus on certain regions of the world. All major cities have world trade centers which support international commerce, as do some mid-sized and smaller cities.

If you're interested in the Asian Pacific Rim, for example, a job with a multinational organization in Seattle, Portland, or San Francisco may be a good starting point. Miami, Houston, and San Diego hold great potential for international trade between the U.S. and Latin America. New York and Los Angeles are centers of international business, diplomacy, and cultural affairs. Washington, DC provides a strong base for finding international employment, particularly in government and nonprofit organizations.

Perspective

Finding a Job Abroad
What You Do Here, You Can Probably Do Overseas

By Bryan J. Estep and Becky Youman

You can land just about any job abroad that you can in the United States; the secret is to go there. While a few lucky souls move with a U.S. contract in hand—including attractive expatriate benefits—most of us go without any guarantee of work on the other side.

The payoffs are worth the gamble. More than likely you will peg in at a higher responsibility level with greater mobility than with your job at home. This doesn't necessarily translate into higher earnings, but nonmonetary benefits include development of language and cross-cultural skills and a global perception.

We are frequently amazed at the positions our friends hold and the activity stemming from their work. The people we know are no different from the people we studied with in college, except that they made the decision to work abroad. The professional community abroad is smaller, the contacts are at higher levels—and things just seem to happen.

Admittedly, the transcontinental jump is a challenge. Pulling up roots, convincing your family to accept a move to a foreign country, then sacrificing part of your savings for airfare and the job hunt is a tough decision. But through adaptability and determination, most of us succeed in making the transition.

Typical Work Arrangements

Work abroad falls into one of three categories: 1) U.S. contract, paid in dollars by a U.S. company, usually with expatriate benefits; 2) national contract, paid in local currency as a resident of the country; and 3) self-employed and freelance.

U.S. Contract. The most desirable situation is to work as a U.S. contracted employee. The company will usually pay for your move and perhaps even include airfare home for the holidays. It may also subsidize rent, buy household appliances, pay foreign taxes, arrange working papers, and provide other expat benefits. Sometimes the most important aspect of the arrangement is payment in dollars, which adds stability in countries with shaky currencies.

Working as a national in a foreign country means being paid in the local currency and in line with similar positions there. In developing countries this usually translates to much less than you would receive in the U.S. for similar work; however, the cost of living is usually lower. In developed countries compensation is usually comparable with similar work in the U.S., but the entry barriers are likely to be higher because of a ready supply of nationals with similar education levels and the difficulty of obtaining a work visa.

The self-employed either start a business in the foreign country or freelance as consultants, journalists, and models. Many have at least a few years of experience in their field and begin generating income immediately.

Targeting Your Country

The first step is picking a deadline six to 12 months down the road to make the move if the stateside search doesn't produce results. In this time you can collect a lot of useful information that will help you choose your target country. Equally important tasks include making contacts in the target country, improving your language skills, and saving money.

Begin with the region that interests you, then narrow down the countries by available opportunities. You can glean macro-economic information from the international sections of periodicals like *Business Week* and the *Wall Street Journal*. As with all secondary research, your web browser and local librarian are your best friends. Personal interests can be as important as macro-ecomonics.

The Search From Home

Interestingly enough, you use the same tools and strategies in an international job search that you would use in a regular job search, the most of important of which is getting the word of your interest out through your personal contacts.

Let's say you've picked Seoul, South Korea as your prospective destination. If in every social occasion you mention off-handedly, "I'm hoping to make a job move to Korea in about six months," you will be amazed at the references you get. The contacts may range from a friend to show you around the city, a prospective host to stay with upon arrival (this is a huge benefit), or perhaps even an employer.

If the referenced person seems worthwhile, you should send a cover letter and resume informing her/him of your goals and requesting an informational interview. If that person doesn't feel responsible for giving you the job, the meeting will probably be more productive.

Internships

Real jobs frequently start with internships. One frequently tried avenue to overseas employment is to look up companies that have operations in the target country and send resumes to their personnel departments. However, the likelihood of this even leading to an interview is small. It is worthwhile, however, to learn all you can about business activity in your target country and to bring along a list of companies to contact upon arrival. (See Krannich and Krannich, *International Jobs Directory*, Impact Publications, under Key Publishers, page 13)

Another route is to take a job in any capacity with a multinational corporation in the U.S. and try to work your way into an international slot from the inside. Many large companies fill overseas positions from within the organization, but there is no guarantee you will be moved abroad.

Making the Move

Few people land a job without first going to their target country, usually on a tourist visa. Working papers are arranged once a job is found. Before you fly into town with nothing more than a couple of suitcases, some savings, and gutsy ambition, try to talk to enough people to know the cost of sustaining a two- to three-month job hunt. Your budget should include roundtrip airfare, initial hotel costs, rent, food, transport, and health insurance.

The first priority is to avoid an expensive hotel stay. Ideally, before leaving you will have lined up a personal contact with whom you can stay for a few days. If not, the first task at hand is to find a place to unpack your suitcases at a monthly rather than daily rate. The English language newspapers often have classified ads from people looking for roommates. You'll also want to check the want ads.

As much as you may want to "go local" immediately and completely immerse yourself in the new culture, meeting other expats is helpful. Look for the watering holes and gyms where they congregate and start the personal networking immediately. This is the most likely way to find a place to live and a job.

Finding the Job

The most efficient onsite job search follows a two-pronged strategy: The first is the direct route of targeting firms in your area of interest and leaving resumes with decision-makers contacted in earlier phone calls. The second is letting as many people as possible know that you are looking for work and eager to get to it. You should be well practiced at this because you did it when you started your search from home.

The American Chamber of Commerce sometimes has a bulletin board of companies that have contacted them looking for bilingual personnel. The member companies themselves are good targets.

Starting out on a student visa in the foreign country is another option for gaining a longer-term legal status. A few manage to transform the study experience into a job experience.

Working for Yourself

The self-employed—entrepreneurs, journalists, consultants, models—follow much the same route as those looking for national contracts. Most are freelancers who live from assignment to assignment and struggle until their business base is established. Their previous experience usually helps them beat down the learning curve a bit. But stubborn determination remains the biggest asset.

Remember that if you are self-employed you have the added challenge of setting up an office. That means wrestling with business taxes, lawyers, and accountants—the same as for entrepreneurs at home, but more difficult in a foreign environment.

The possibility of working overseas is not a pipe dream. In fact, with the globalization of the world's economies, U.S. employers are in a position to benefit from professionals with cross-cultural experience. If you make the move successfully, all the talk about global strategies, trade wars, and common market begins to involve you. Amazingly, you realize that you are one of the actors.

Perspective

Working in Western Europe
Skilled Foreign Workers are in Demand

By Charlie Morris

Western Europe welcomes foreign workers who have skills that are in demand, as long as they play by the rules. Nonresidents workers are required to have a work permit. While thousands work there illegally and some employers may encourage you to work "black" to save them tax money and paperwork, don't do it. If you are caught, you can be hit with hefty fines or even barred from the country. An acquaintance of mine fell afoul of the U.K. immigration authorities because he was honest (or foolish) enough to admit that he was entering the country to work and had no work permit. His passport now sports a "black mark," and he will never be able to enter Britain again without proving that he will only be staying a short while.

Misinformation abounds, and calling the immigration authorities may leave you more confused than before. The best way to get the facts is from a lawyer who specializes in immigration law.

Work permits are generally issued for specific jobs. Technically, you are not allowed to enter a country to look for work, although you can't help it if someone happens to offer you a position while you're on vacation.

In Western Europe, the process usually works this way:

1) An employer agrees to hire you subject to a work permit being approved.

2) The employer applies for a work permit for you; this may be a simple process or very complex, depending on what country the job is in, what country you are from, and what your skills and salary level are.

3) If the permit is approved, you will probably receive a document to take to an official for processing and the payment of a fee.

4) Upon arrival at your place of employment, you may be required to register with the local police and perhaps pay another fee.

If you change jobs you must start the process all over again.

Work Permits for Short-Term Jobs

Perhaps the best place to look for short-term work in Europe is Switzerland (and the other countries that have seasonal tourist industries). Those with special skills, like photographers and ski instructors, have the best chance of success, but I've met Americans behind the bar, in the kitchen, and working the ski lifts. Wages are good, and many jobs include room and board.

Getting a work permit is usually straightforward once you have a job offer. The Swiss Hotel Association (Monbijoustrasse, 130 P.O. Box 3001, Bern, Switzerland; [www.swisshotels.ch]) publishes a directory of hotels every year, a valuable resource for those seeking seasonal work. Send your resume to the larger hotels in resorts like Davos, Klosters, St. Moritz, Zermatt, Grindelwald, and Gstaad. Call the local tourist office verkehrsverein and ask for the numbers of the local ski lift operators.

Generally, a European employer who wants to hire a non-European Union citizen must demonstrate that they can't fill the position with an EU citizen. (Switzerland is not a member of the EU.) Those with valuable skills stand a good chance of getting a permit, while those in lower-paid lines of work will not get one, except possibly for seasonal jobs in resort areas.

The employer does not have to prove that there is not a single qualified person in all of the EU, just that they have made a diligent effort to find one. This usually means that they have to advertise the position in a local newspaper for two to four weeks before the job can be offered to a foreigner.

Immigration law in the U.K. is complex, and much depends on what country you are from. If you are a citizen of a Commonwealth country (including Canada and Australia) and if your grandfather was born in the U.K., then you may not need a work permit. Citizens of non-EU and non-Commonwealth countries need a work permit, and your chances of getting one depend on your skills and salary level. Those seeking unskilled jobs can basically forget about working in the U.K.

Work Permits for Professionals

Even for those in high-paying professions, the paperwork and hassle involved can be a deal-killer. Fortunately, there are agencies that will handle the whole process for a fee. One good one is BCL Immigration Services (43 Berkeley Sq., Mayfair, London W1X 5DB; 011-44-2074-953999; bcl@workpermit.com; [www.workpermit.com].) They will see you through the whole process for around £800 (1999) and offer specific advice for a reasonable fee. Many employers assume that getting a work permit is tougher than it actually is, so knowing about a service like BCL beforehand and mentioning it to your prospective employer can improve your prospects. The employer can make a phone call to the agency and get a good assessment of what your chances are.

I have worked in several European countries and have almost never encountered hostility because of it. But keep in mind this is a controversial issue for some people. Also keep in mind that the U.S. is one of the most restrictive countries in the world in issuing work permits to nonresidents, so you may meet people who resent that you can work in their country but they can't work in yours. Be sensitive.

Work regulations can change often; the above is not the definitive word and certainly not legal advice. You'll have to research your particular situation to make sure you're in compliance. If you make a good-faith effort with your employer to comply with the law, you're unlikely to get in trouble.

Perspective

Life in the Foreign Service
Ideal Career for Adventurous Travelers

By Kelly Bembry Midura

In our 10 years in the Foreign Service, we have experienced some of the best that life abroad has to offier. Bolivia and El Salvador were good places to live, and Guatemala was truly exceptional. On weekends we drove to remote villages that we never would have seen on any guided tour and bargained in the local markets for textiles, paintings, and crafts. We often ate a *tipica* lunch at some hole-in-the-wall place, then drove home to have a carry-out pizza for dinner, with a view of erupting volcanoes from our windows.

Sure, there was a crime problem, but we took reasonable precautions. There was an occasional earthquake and blackouts that lasted for months, but, like most Guatemalans, we took to eating at open-air grills and playing cards by candlelight.

To really connect with local people in a developing country, have a baby. Motherhood is a universally understood experience, and I received fascinating advice. During a full solar eclipse in my last trimester, everyone advised me that I must dress in red, wear a crucifix, and hide under the bed during the eclipse. Otherwise, my baby would certainly be born blind. On local TV a panel of experts, including two astronomers and one obstetretrician, vainly attempted to debunk this myth.

After my blonde blue-eyed daughter was born, we were constantly surrounded by people wanting to hold her, touch her hair, or even "borrow" her for a minute to show to a friend! I am sure that Rachel thought her name was *qué linda* (how pretty) until we left the country.

The Tour from Hell

On the other hand, there are posts that can only be described as "learning experiences." We spent two long years in Zambia, a country bypassed by most travelers for good reason. We expected to find vibrant African art and culture, instead we saw soul-deadening poverty, disease, and cheap mass-produced souvenirs.

The local cuisine was "mealy-meal" (a.k.a. grits, a non-native staple introduced by the former socialist government) and a range of centipedes, grasshoppers, and termites consumed by the protein-starved population. I am all for sampling the native dishes, but I draw the line at bugs.

There was no infrastructure or medical care to speak of, and AIDS was rapidly killing off anyone with youth, energy, or talent. My husband attended the funerals of three of his employees during our stay—all AIDS victims.

Most career diplomats have a story like this. Getting to know the people of a country can be a hard lesson when you are powerless to change the unjust circumstances of their lives.

Has all of this been worth it? Oh yes! I am currently living in the Washington D.C. suburbs surrounded by every material convenience known to man, and I can't wait to get back overseas, this time to the Czech Republic. Sometimes, you end up landing that European tour after all!

Foreign Service Careers

Joining the diplomatic corps offers an unbeatable opportunity to learn about foreign cultures. But there are drawbacks. It is occasionally annoying that the U.S. government controls so much of your life. Simple requests can take weeks or even months to process, and the bureaucracy of the State Department and other foreign affairs agencies has a logic all its own.

Another drawback is that professional level jobs for spouses of foreign service officers are rare; most available jobs are clerical and poorly paid. However, in the digital age, the possibilities for freelancing and telecommunicating are limited only by local telephone service.

For the official line on careers with the United States Department of State, check out their recruitment page at [www.state.gov/www/careers/index.html]. To learn about the Foreign Service exam, the first step to entry into the diplomatic corps, click on "Foreign Service." This section of the site also contains some generic information about the impact of a Foreign Service career on the officer's family.

To get the *unofficial* lowdown on life in the Foreign Service, check out two web sites created by Foreign Service "trailing" spouses:

Foreign Service Lifelines is sponsored by the Associates of the American Foreign Service Worldwide [www.aafsw.org] and features "Tips from the Trenches" and "Perspectives" on current issues written by experienced Foreign Service spouses. "The Cyberspouse," a column on Internet-based employment opportunities (written by yours truly) is a regular feature of the site. Foreign Service Lifelines also details the services provided by the AAFSW, including the Foreign-Born Spouses Network and the Evacuee Support Network, the very existence of which tell you something about life in the Foreign Service.

The Spouses Underground Network [www.thesun.org] is an "edgier" site, which advertises itself as "definitely not endorsed by the U.S. government." It features a small-but-growing collection of "Real Post Reports" on various countries, chat forums on topics relevant to Foreign Service families, and excerpts from its parent publication, the *Spouses Underground Newsletter*. Subscriptions and you can order back issues online as well.

Key Work Abroad Resources
International Careers and International Job Listings
Selected and Reviewed by William Nolting

Looking for international work, with an international organization, whether abroad or in the U.S. can be daunting. Fortunately, some excellent books, organizations, and web sites can provide real help. Here, we separate the best from the rest in several categories:

• **International Careers** resources offer help in planning for a "global" lifetime, which often develops in several stages.

• **International Job Listings** include newsletters specializing in worldwide job openings, but advertised jobs tend to be only a fraction of those actually available.

When address of publisher is not included, see "Key Publishers," page 13.

The rating codes are as follows: **Essential*; *Outstanding and of broad interest.*

INTERNATIONAL CAREERS

Accounting Jobs Worldwide by Ian Collier. 1998. 190 pp. Vacation Work (U.K.). Available for $19.95 from Seven Hills. A guide to accounting and bookkeeping employment opportunities throughout the world.

*The Adventure of Working Abroad: Hero Tales From the Global Frontier** by Joyce Sautters Osland. 1995. 269 pp. $25 from Jossey-Bass, 350 Sansome St., 5th Fl., San Francisco, CA 94104; 800-956-7739. Thirty-five American expatriates assigned abroad tell about the perils and opportunities of working in a new culture. Suggestions for employers and employees for preparation, support, and reentry.

American Jobs Abroad by Victoria Harlow and Edward Knappman. 1994. 882 pp. Gale. $35 from Impact Publications. The only directory, now dated, listing the number of Americans working abroad for specific companies. Most worked for their company in the U.S. before being assigned abroad. Indexes by country and job category.

Building an Import/Export Business by Kenneth D. Weiss. 1997. $19.95 from John Wiley & Sons. Detailed guide to entering the import/export business.

*The Canadian Guide to Working and Living Overseas** by Jean-Marc Hachey. 1998 edition. 970 pp. U.S.$40, CAN$54.40. Save 20 percent on web order. Order by phone 800-267-0105, fax 800-221-9985; [www.workingoverseas. com]. Not only for Canadians, this massive directory provides a comprehensive and up-to-date overview of work abroad and international careers. Profiles tend to focus on Canadian organizations, so U.S. readers should use this book along with one of the U.S. books recommended here. Covers every facet of international work and living overseas. Features 1,870 profiles, 1,670 web sites, and 700 resources in 58 bibliographies, web updates until the year 2002.

*Careers for Foreign Language Aficionados and Other Multilingual Types** by Ned Seelye and Laurence Day. 1992. 128 pp. $14.95 hardcover/$9.95 paperback from VGM Career Horizons. Mainstream and offbeat jobs for those who want to use a foreign language. One of the better books on this topic. Includes profiles of various career fields.

****Careers in International Affairs** edited by Maria Pinto Carland and Michael Trucano. 1997. 6th ed. 282 pp. $17.95 plus $4 and 75¢ shipping for each additional book, $5.75 for UPS and 75¢ shipping for each additional book from Georgetown Univ. Press, P.O. Box 4866, Hampden Station, Baltimore, MD 21211-0866; 800-246-9606, fax 410-516-6998. This is the most up-to-date U.S. overview of international career fields. Provides survey-based specifics on major organizations in all international sectors and first-hand essays by practitioners. Developed by the Georgetown University School of Foreign Service, this is highly recommended for those serious about entering an international career.

Careers In International Business by Edward J. Halloran. 1996. 112 pp. $17.95 hardcover/$13.95 paperback from VGM Career Horizons. Overview of education for international business and types of opportunities, from start-ups to Fortune 500 companies.

Careers in International Law edited by Mark W. Janis. 1993. 229 pp. $19.95 from American Bar Association, ABA Orders and Billing Services, P.O. Box 10892, Chicago, IL 60611; 800-285-2221, [www.abanet.org]. Essays on how to plan for a career in international law by lawyers in the field. Also lists ABA-approved study abroad programs.

**The Complete Guide to International Jobs and Careers by Ronald L. Krannich and Caryl R. Krannich. 1993. 349 pp. $24.95 from Impact Publications. An excellent introduction to strategies and skills for landing an international job in the 1990s, along with listings of resources for researching international employers. Should be used with its companion volume *The International Jobs Directory.*

*Connected: Careers for the Future. This 30-minute video anchored by Charlayne Hunter-Gault in 1997 features on-site interviews with African Americans, Latinos, Asian Americans, and Native Americans who are working in international settings. Available for $75 plus $5 s/h from The Global Center, 1600 Broadway, Suite 700, New York, NY 10019; 212-246-0202, fax 212-246-2677; globaltv@igc.org, [www.globalvision.org/globalvision].

Directory of American Firms Operating in Foreign Countries. 1999. $275 plus $11.50 s/h from Uniworld, 257 Central Park West, Suite 10A, New York, NY 10024-4110; Tel./fax 212-496-2448, fax 212-769-0413; [www.uniworld.com]. Lists 2,450 American companies with 29,500 subsidiaries and affiliates in 190 foreign countries. Check your local library for this and dozens of other expensive specialized international directories beyond the scope of this bibliography. Impact Publications carries this and many more directories.

Directory of International Organizations by Hans-Albrecht Schraepler 1996. 456 pp. $24.95 from Georgetown Univ. Press, P.O. Box 4886, Hampden Station, Baltimore, MD 21211-0866; 800-246-9606, fax 410-516-6998. Comprehensive reference to international organizations.

*The Directory of Jobs and Careers Abroad by Elisabeth Roberts. 2000. 415 pp. Vacation Work Publications. $16.95 from Peterson's Guides. The only career guide with country-by-country (50) coverage of everything from professional fields to short-term and volunteer possibilities. British publication, but usually includes relevant U.S. organizations.

Employment Abroad: Facts and Fallacies edited by Rachel Theus. 1993. $7.50 plus $3 shipping from the International Division of the U.S. Chamber of Commerce, 1615 H St. NW, Washington, DC 20062; 202-463-5460, fax 202-463-3114; [www.uschamber.org/programs/ intl/index.html]. Booklet stresses the realities of international employment.

Global Health Directory 2000: U.S. Based Agencies Working in International Health 2000. 108 pp (oversize). $70 ($35 members) postpaid from Global Health Council, 1701 K St. NW, Suite 600, Washington, DC 20006-1503; 202-833-5900, fax 202-833-0075; ghc@globalhealthcouncil.org, [www.globalhealthcouncil.org]. Lists organizations in international health fields by specialty and location. Includes a listing of those organizations which offer volunteer opportunities abroad. **Career Network** ($120 non-members, $60 members per year) is a job bulletin published by GHC.

The Good Cook's Guide to Working Abroad by Katherine Parry. 1998. Vacation Work (U.K.). Available for $19.95 from Seven Hills. Worldwide opportunities for chefs, servers, etc. in a variety of locales and establishments.

Great Jobs Abroad by Arthur H. Bell. 1997. 378 pp. McGraw-Hill. $14.95 from Impact Publications. Describes strategies for getting hired with corporations based in the U.S., in hopes of being assigned abroad. Tips on research, resumes, interviewing, and using the Internet. Most of book consists of information available elsewhere in directories, such as U.S. corporations with international operations, U.S. embassies and consulates abroad.

Great Jobs for Foreign Language Majors by Julie DeGalan and Stephen Lambert. 1994. 256 pp. VGM Career Horizons. $11.95. Covers careers in all sectors that use foreign languages either directly or as an auxiliary skill. Also discusses career strategies.

Health Professionals Abroad by Tim Ryder. 2000. 256 pp. Vacation Work. Available for $17.95 from Seven Hills. Book provides the first overview (from a British perspective) of working abroad in all areas of health care, from volunteer to career. Professions include doctors, nurses, pharmacists, physiotherapists, and others.

How to Get a Job in Europe: The Insider's Guide by Robert Sanborn and Cheryl Matherly. 4th ed. 1999. 556 pp. $21.95 plus $3 shipping from Surrey Books, Inc., 230 E. Ohio St., Suite 120, Chicago, IL 60611; 800-326-4430, fax 312-751-7334; [www.surreybooks. com]. Names and addresses of over 2,000 companies in 39 countries plus general suggestions on how to conduct an international job hunt.

*Inside a U.S. Embassy: How the Foreign Service Works for America edited by Karen Krebsbach. 1996. 98 pp. American Foreign Service Association. $5 from AFSA, 2101 E St., NW, Washington, DC 20037; 202-338-4045, fax 202-338-6820. In-depth, first-hand descriptions of what foreign service officers do. One chapter provides reports about individual's roles in international crises.

*InterAction Member Profiles 2000-2001. 2000. 400 pp. $60/$50 ($30 members). Up-to-date information on 160 U.S. private voluntary organizations in relief and development work. Details which agencies are doing what in which countries; **Monday Developments.** $65 per year (individuals). Best biweekly job listing in this field. Available from Interaction, Publications Department, 1717 Massachusetts Ave. NW, Suite 801, Washington, DC 20036; 202-667-8227, fax 202-667-8236; publications@ interaction.org, [www.interaction.org].

*International Job Finder by Daniel Lauber. Expected Nov 2000. 200 pp. $19.95 plus $5.50 s/h from Planning/Communications, 7215 Oak Ave., River Forest, IL 60305; 800-829-5220; dl@jobfindersonline.com, [http:// jobfindersonline.com]. Book by a leading career expert promises to provide useful information on the best sources for an international job search, including: specialty and trade periodicals, job hotlines, Internet job and resume databases, job placement services, directories, and salary surveys. Free updates to purchasers of this book available online.

The International Jobs Directory: A Guide to Over 1001 Employers. New edition, formerly entitled The Almanac of International Jobs and Careers by Ronald and Caryl Krannich. 1999. 334 pp. $19.95 from Impact Publications. Companion volume to The Complete Guide to International Jobs and Careers. This is a comprehensive source of hard-to-find information,

tips on other resources including hundreds of web sites, and trends in international employment for Americans. It provides the most up-to-date, comprehensive overview of international employers from a U.S. perspective. Highly recommended.

International Jobs: Where They Are and How to Get Them by Eric Kocher with Nina Segal. 1999. 400 pp. Harper Collins. $16 plus $2.75 shipping from Harper Collins, Direct Mail Dept, P.O. Box 588, Scranton, PA 18512, 800-331-3761; [www.harpercollins.com]. New, revised edition of a classic overview of international career fields and how to prepare for them, by authors associated with Columbia Univ.'s School of International and Public Affairs (SIPA). This is the best one-volume introduction to international careers.

Jobs For People Who Love to Travel by Ronald and Caryl Krannich. 1999. 285 pp. $15.95 from Impact Publications. Information for those who want to work the world before settling down. Explores motivations; 50 myths about jobs involving travel; includes Internet sites, teaching abroad, and internships.

Jobs Worldwide by David Lay and Benedict A. Leerburger. 1996. 374 pp. Impact. $17.95. An overview of career possibilities in the Caribbean, Europe, Africa, Middle East, Asia, and South Pacific. Information about each country including history, culture, recent events, and demographics. A particular strength of this book is its information on technical jobs.

Kennedy's International Directory of Executive Recruiters. 2000. $149. Kennedy Information 800-531-0007, 603-585-6544, fax 603-585-9555; bookstore@kennedyinfo.com, [www.kennedyinfo.com]. Identify recruiters around the globe with this comprehensive source profiling 1,627 firms in 67 countries.

Live and Work in (series): Australia and New Zealand; Belgium, The Netherlands, and Luxembourg; France; Germany; Italy; Japan; Russia and Eastern Europe; Scandinavia; Spain and Portugal; Saudi and the Gulf by Victoria Pybus, Jonathan Packer, Ian Collier, Andre de Vries, and Susan Dunne. Vacation Work (U.K.) 300 plus pages each. Prices $18-$20. Available in the U.S. from Seven Hills. Outstanding British series for long-term stays. Information on employment, residence, home buying, daily life, retirement, and starting a business. More useful for those on overseas assignment than for those looking for a job.

Living and Working in (series): Australia; Britain; Canada; France; London; New Zealand; Spain; Switzerland; U.S. by David Hampshire. Survival Books. $21.95 plus $4 shipping (first book, $1 for additional titles) from Seven Hills. Detailed information on everything from working to buying a house. More useful for those on overseas assignment than for those looking for a job.

NAFSA's Guide to Education Abroad. William Hoffa and John Pearson, eds. NAFSA. 2nd ed., 1997. 494 pp. $45 (nonmembers), $36 (members) plus $5 s/h. An indispensable manual for those working in the field of study abroad advising and administration.

Opportunities in Foreign Language Careers by Wilga Rivers, Maguerite Duffy. 1998. 151 pp. $11.95 paperback from VGM Career Horizons. Harvard professor emerita discusses the use of languages as an auxiliary skill; also covers teaching languages and working as a translator or interpreter.

Opportunities in International Business Careers by Jeffry Arpan. 1996. 160 pp. $11.95 paperback from VGM Career Books. General overview of careers in international business, with discussion of types of international business degrees and specific business schools.

Special Career Opportunities for Linguists/Translators/Interpreters. Free pamphlet from U.S. Department of State, Office of Language Services, Interpreting Division, Room 2212, Washington, DC 20520; 202-647-3492, fax 202-647-3881.

Tax Guide for U.S. Citizens Abroad. (Publication 54.) Free from Forms Distribution Center, P.O. Box 25866, Richmond, VA 23260.

*U.S. Department of State Foreign Service Officer Careers. Free brochure available from Recruitment Division, Department of State, Box 12226, Arlington, VA 22219; 703-875-7490; [www.state.gov/www/careers].

Application for the Foreign Service Officer Exam. Exam date typically in fall. Order info included in application for **Study Guide.**

*Work Worldwide: International Career Strategies for the Adventurous Job Seeker by Nancy Mueller. 2000. 231 pp. $14.95. John Muir Publications (available in bookstores). An in-depth look at strategies for finding

international jobs. Covers topics such as researching, networking, resumes and job applications, interviewing, working abroad, and readjustment upon returning home. From an American perspective.

Working with Animals: The U.K., Europe, and Worldwide by Victoria Pybus. 1998. Vacation Work (U.K.). Available for $19.95 from Seven Hills. Opportunities for individuals to work with animals in zoos, nature preserves, and out in the wild.

Working with the Environment by Tim Ryder. 2000. 271 pp. Vacation Work. Available for $17.95 from Seven Hills. This new book provides the first survey of international environmental work possibilities, from volunteer to career. Intended for a British audience, it provides in-depth coverage of Great Britain and Ireland, but also includes organizations (including U.S.-based ones) offering placements worldwide.

*The World on a String: How to Become a Freelance Foreign Correspondent by Alan Goodman and John Pollack. 1997. 198 pp. Henry Holt. $12.95 from most bookstores. Two experienced American freelancers based overseas give lots of first-hand advice on how to break into the field and survive financially.

INTERNATIONAL JOB LISTINGS

*The Guide to Internet Job Searching by Margaret Riley Dikel and Frances E. Roehm. 2000. 344 pp. $14.95 from VGM Career Horizons. The best book on job search resources on the Internet, by the author of the respected web site *The Riley Guide* [www.rileyguide.com]. Book includes 30 pages on international jobs web sites.

International Career Employment Weekly. Weekly listings of 500 international job openings (about 70 percent located overseas) organized by career fields: international education, foreign policy, international commerce, environment, development, program administration, health care. Main listings are for professionals, typically asking for two to five years or more experience. One section in each issue covers internships (nearly all in U.S). Subscriptions available from 6 issues ($26 individuals) to 49 issues ($149 individuals, $195 institutions) from International Employment Weekly, Carlyle Corporation, 1088 Middle River Rd., Stanardsville, VA 22973; 804-985-

6444, fax 804-985-6828; Lisa@internation-aljobs.org, [www.internationaljobs.org].

International Employment Gazette. Each biweekly issue includes more than 400 overseas job openings by region and field. Good for private-sector business and technical jobs, although many of these require extensive experience, as well as teaching and volunteer positions. Subscriptions available from $40 for 3 months (6 issues); $75 for 6 months (13 issues); $95 for 1 year (26 issues) from International Employment Gazette, 423 Townes St., Greenville, SC 29601; 800-882-9188, fax 864-235-3369; intljobs@aol.com, [www.intemployment.com]. Also publishes **The International Directory of Employment Agencies and Recruiters,** which contains information on nearly 200 international recruiters, including complete contact information as well as the occupations and geographic regions for which they recruit. Available for $29.95.

*International Employment Hotline. Subscriptions available from $21 for 3 months to $129 for 2 years from International Employment Hotline, Carlyle Corporation, 1088 Middle River Road, Stanardsville, VA 22973; 800-291-4618, fax 804-985-6828; Hotline@internationaljobs.org, [www.internationaljobs.org]. Monthly reports on who's hiring now in private companies, government, and nonprofit organizations. Lists entry-level and mid-career openings. Jobs located overseas and in the U.S.

Job Registry, NAFSA: Association of International Educators. 10 issues a year for $30 ($20 members) from NAFSA Job Registry, 1875 Connecticut Ave. NW, Suite 1000, Washington, DC 20009-5728; 202-462-4811, fax 202-667-3419, inbox@nafsa.org, [www.nafsa.org]. Email version also available for $25 ($18 members). The best job listing for those interested in the field of international educational exchange.

The Key Web Sites

International Careers and International Job Listings

Selected and Reviewed by William Nolting

Web sites in this section list mainly career positions, most of which require previous experience. These sites rarely include listings of exchange programs for work abroad, internships, volunteering, or teaching abroad of most relevance to students and recent graduates. ***Essential; *Outstanding and of broad interest.*

(I) Informational site with directories or databases listing many programs
(P) Site for a specific work abroad program
(S) Scholarships or fellowships

INTERNATIONAL CAREERS

(I) The Canadian Guide to Working and Living Overseas [www.workingoverseas.com] by Jean-Marc Hachey. Essentially a promotional site for his book (see Print Resources above). You'll have to buy the book to benefit from the hundreds of web sites listed therein.

* (I) Career Mosaic [www.careermosaic.com]. Links to thousands of international jobs, virtually all requiring previous experience. Engineering and business jobs predominate.

(I) Career Web [www.cweb.com] lists thousands of professional, technical and managerial jobs in the private sector, virtually all requiring previous experience.

(I) Career Office of Brandeis Univ. [www.brandeis.edu/hiatt] includes sections for internships and international jobs.

** Wall Street Journal [www.careers. wsj.com]. An outstanding site, though most jobs are in business and require previous experience. Check the "Working Globally" section for excellent articles about international careers.

* (I) **Chronicle of Higher Education** [thisweek.chronicle.com] is the best source of job listings for the well-qualified academicians. Much of site accessible only to subscribers. Also check with discipline-specific professional associations.

(I) **College Grad Job Hunter** [www.college-grad.com] is a well-designed site with lots of listings of internships, entry-level jobs, and jobs for those with experience; few if any overseas positions.

** (I) **Dave's ESL Café** [www.eslcafe.com], ESL Cafe's Web Guide: Jobs [www.eslcafe.com/search/Jobs] by Dave Sperling. Site has a staggering amount of well-organized information about teaching and other types of work abroad; links to hundreds of job databases of particular interest to teachers, college students, and liberal arts graduates. A highly recommended resource for anyone interested in working abroad.

* **Dickinson College, Web Guide to International Employment,** [www.dickinson.edu/career/international.htm] by Dr. Kate Brooks. One of the few sites on the web to provide an overview of international careers and how to plan for one.

** **Escape Artist, Escape from America Overseas Jobs Pages** [www.escapeartist.com/jobs/overseas1.htm] by Roger Gallo. This site is one of the best overall for those looking for overseas jobs. It links to hundreds of job bank sites listed by country and region. There's also lots of other useful information for anyone working, studying, or living abroad, with one of the best online bookstores for this purpose.

** (I) **Impact Publications** [www.impactpublications.com] by Ronald and Caryl Krannich. This publisher carries one of the most extensive selections of books on working abroad and international careers. The Krannichs' own *International Jobs Directory* lists hundreds of web sites and gives an outstanding overview of international jobs and careers.

** (I) **International Career Employment Center (Carlyle Corporation)** [www.internationaljobs.org]. Not a jobs web site, this nonprofit organization publishes 2 of the best listings of international jobs: *International Career Employment Opportunities* (weekly) and *International Employment Hotline*. The site gives examples of their listings but does not list current openings.

(I) **IRS: Tax Information for Aliens and US Citizens Living Abroad,** [www.irs.ustreas.gov/prod/tax_edu/faq/faqg.html]. Essential information from the U.S. Internal Revenue Service for anyone working abroad.

(P, I) **JETAA Job Guide** [cheno.com/job]. Site by alumni of the JET (Japan Exchange and Teaching) Program, one of the largest of all work abroad programs, includes a guide to international career issues and links to job web sites listed by country.

Job Source Network [www.jobsourcenetwork.com/intl.html] includes links to job web sites and businesses offering employment in many countries; most positions require previous experience.

Jobtrak [www.jobtrak.com]. This site is associated with hundreds of U.S. college and university career offices (access by password), so may be useful for students and alumni.

* (I) **Jobweb (National Association of Colleges and Employers)** [www.jobweb.org]. One of the more useful sites for college students and recent graduates, has sections for international jobs [www.jobweb.org/catapult/interntl.htm] and internships and summer jobs, [www.jobweb.org/catapult/jintern.htm].

(I) **The Monster Board** [www.monster.com]. Jobs by international location: [http://international.monster.com]. Links to job databases for specific countries. Thousands of jobs listed, most for engineers or managers and virtually all requiring previous experience.

(I) **Overseas Jobs Express** [www.overseasjobs.com]. British-based site claims to list vacancies that are open to non-citizens of the target country. It has databases of career positions for specific countries or regions.

(I,P) **Peace Corps Career TRACK** [www.peacecorps.gov/rpcv/careertrack]. Even if you're not int erested in the Peace Corps, this web site has lots of information about international work and careers.

** (I) **Purdue Univ.'s Center for International Career Opportunities** [www.cco.purdue.edu/student/InternInternational.html]. Two outstanding sets of links to web site job banks arranged by country or region. Check both sites, since they are not entirely identical.

** (I) **The Riley Guide: Resources for International Job Opportunities** [www.dbm.com/jobguide/internat.html], Alternative Work and Career Options [www.dbm.com/jobguide/misc.html] by Margaret Dickel. Classic guide provides an excellent country-by-country compilation of employment resources on the web.

PROFESSION-SPECIFIC SITES

All Professions

** (I) The Riley Guide [www.dbm.com/jobguide/jobs.html] by Margaret Dickel. An excellent compilation of profession-specific resources on the web. See "Resources for Specific Industries and Occupations."

Academia

** (I) Chronicle of Higher Education [http://thisweek.chronicle.com/jobs]. The best source of job listings for well-qualified academians (most positions require a PhD or professional degree). Much of site accessible only to subscribers. Also check with discipline-specific professional associations.

Arts, Architecture

(I, S) Arts International [www.artsinternational.org]. Grants, events, and an excellent region-by-region compilation of arts web sites worldwide.

(I) National Endowment for the Arts [www.arts.endow.gov/partner/International.html]. The NEA's International Partnerships Office site has links to organizations that may consider applications for internships or may offer funding for international activities.

Business

Most overseas job sites list plenty of business jobs, though most require experience.

** (P) AIESEC-USA [www.us.aiesec.org]. AIESEC (from the French acronym for the International Association of Students in Economic and Business Management) is an international student-run organization which offers approximately 5,000 paid internships each year in business and other fields in over 80 countries. Site has links to chapters worldwide. Note that application for AIESEC internships is possible only through campus chapters. Students who have no AIESEC chapter at their university should see the programs listed in "Worldwide Short-Term Paid Work Abroad Programs," all of which have great opportunities for those interested in business.

** (I) Working Globally (Wall Street Journal) [www.careers.wsj.com]. An outstanding site for those interested in business. Most jobs require previous experience.

* U.S. Chamber of Commerce: International Division [www.uschamber.com/International]. Not a jobs site, but an essential organization for anyone interested in international trade.

Engineering and Computer Science

Most overseas job sites list plenty of engineering and computer science jobs. Students of engineering and computer science should definitely look into the overseas internship programs of the following organizations (see International Internships, Directory of Programs (page 62) for more information):

** (P) American-Scandinavian Foundation [www.amscan.org/training.htm]

** (P) CDS International [www.cdsintl.org]

** (P) IAESTE [www.aipt.org/iaeste.html]

** (P) International Cooperative Education Program [www.icemenlo.com]

Environment and Natural Resources

* (I) Envirolink: The Online Environmental Community [www.envirolink.org]. Site has links to hundreds of environmental organizations. There are good links for finding jobs and internships; however, the site does want you to sign up and become a member before using their resources.

* (I) SD Gateway (Sustainable Development) [http://sdgateway.net]. Not only environmental, this outstanding site will be of interest to people in a number of fields, from policy and international relations to development and nongovernmental organizations. Searches using "internship" or desired location bring up plenty of internationally-related positions.

Health: Dentistry, Medicine, Nursing, Public Health, Social Work

* (I) American Medical Student Association [www.amsa.org/gh.html]. AMSA's site lists overseas internship and volunteer programs, including options for premed and other health sciences—see International Health Opportunities section. Site includes an excel-

lent online guide to fundraising, *Creative Funding Guide*, useful for all students.

* (I) Global Health Council (formerly National Council for International Health) [www.globalhealth.org/]. NCIH is one of the main professional associations for U.S. organizations working in international health. It publishes (in hard copy only) *The Directory of Global Health* which lists the health fields and locations in which each organization is active, and *Internship and Volunteer Opportunities*. Web site includes an online article on "Career Opportunities in Global Health" (see Publications section), information for students and internships, and extensive links to member organizations.

(P, S) Minority International Research Training Grant (MIRT) [www.nih.gov/fic/programs/mirt.html]. Program of the Fogarty International Center, National Institutes of Health, sends minority undergraduates and medical students abroad to do health-related research.

* (I) Social Work and Social Services Jobs Online, Washington Univ., George Warren Brown School of Social Work [http://gwb-web.wustl.edu/jobs] by Carol Doelling. This outstanding site has specific job listings and automatic links to other job web sites. Search provisions make it easy to find jobs by type of work or location, including a good number of overseas listings.

Information and Library Science

(I) Human-Computer Interaction Resources Network [www.hcirn.com]. A top resource for students and professionals in user interface design, usability and other HCI-related fields. Job bank includes some international jobs and site links to other international HCI employment sites.

* (I) Library Job Postings on the Internet, Bridgewater State College [webhost.bridgew.edu/snesbeitt/libraryjobs.htm] by Sara Nesbitt. Best meta-site for library jobs is viewable by regions, including good international links. Well-organized and up-to-date.

International Educational Exchange

* NAFSA: Association of International Educators [www.nafsa.org]. The largest and most helpful professional association for those interested in careers in international educational exchange. NAFSA publishes a hard-copy

Job Bulletin, and also announces jobs through email lists which can be subscribed to from their web site.

* (I) Overseas Teachers Digest & Expat Exchange For Americans [www.overseasdigest.com]. This site contains valuable information for Americans working abroad. Be sure to see the Better Business Bureau article made available by this site, "Overseas Job Scams," [http://overseasdigest.com/scams.htm].

International Relations, International Organizations, Public Policy

* (I) APSIA (Association of Professional Schools of International Affairs) [www.apsia.org]. These are some of the top graduate schools offering advanced degrees in preparation for international careers. Web site links to these schools, but offers little information about international work—try the Career Services offices of the individual schools.

** (I, P) U.S. Department of State [www.state.gov/www/careers]. How to work for the U.S. diplomatic services. The State Department offers 1,000 internships annually, student work programs, and special fellowship/internship programs such as the Foreign Affairs Fellowship and Fascell Fellowship. Site also shows how to apply for career positions.

(I) UN and International Organization Employment Information (site of the U.S. Department of State) [www.state.gov/www/issues/ioemployment.html]. An extensive overview of employment with the UN and other multigovernment international organizations, with links and job announcements.

(I) The WWW Virtual Library: International Affairs Resources [www.etown.edu/v/]. While not designed as an employment site, this web site has the most comprehensive set of links for international relations.

(S, P) Woodrow Wilson International Fellowship Foundation [www.woodrow.org/public-policy]. Information on several multi-year scholarship-internship programs for students, especially women and minorities, interested in careers in international affairs.

Law

* (I, P) American Bar Association, Section of International Law [www.abanet.org/intlaw]. The ABA's site offers an extraordinary number

of links, as well as the International Legal Exchange Program.

(I, P) International Law Students Association [www.ilsa.org]. ILSA administers an internship abroad program for law students. Site has many useful links.

(I) Legal Study Abroad Headquarters [www.studylaw.com]. Comprehensive guide to study abroad and internships for law students.

Nongovernmental and Volunteer Organizations

** (I) Idealist [www.idealist.org]. This site's claim of tens of thousands of organizations "under one roof" says it all. Excellent search provisions give useful results using "internship" or "volunteer." Also has lists of volunteer, internship and job opportunities. Search possible by country, type of work, and many other variables. The "browse by country" section lists organizations according to their work focus. Site includes organizations worldwide, not only U.S.-based ones.

(I) InterAction: American Council for Voluntary International Action [www.interaction.org]. InterAction is a coalition of over 150 private, U.S.-based voluntary organizations engaged in international humanitarian efforts, including disaster relief, sustainable development, refugee assistance, advocacy, and education. Their web site includes links to their members and an online *Guide to Volunteer Opportunities* (most of which require professional skills). InterAction also publishes in hard copy *Global Work* (organizations seeking volunteers), *InterAction Member Profiles*, and *Monday Developments* (biweekly job announcements).

REGION-SPECIFIC SITES

Africa and Middle East

(I) Africa South of the Sahara, African Studies Association [www-sul.stanford.edu/depts/ssrg/africa/guide.html]. Karen Fung, ed. Site is not intended primarily for study and work abroad, but offers a huge number of links to web sites of organizations concerned with Africa, arranged by topics such as development, health, human rights. Try a search using "work," "internship," "volunteer," or "research."

(I) African Studies, Univ. of Pennsylvania [www.sas.upenn.edu/African_Studies/AS.htm l]. Ali Ali-Dinar, ed. Site is not intended primarily for work abroad, but offers a huge number of links for information about Africa. Look on the Bulletin Board for the Job and Grant Opportunities section. A search on the main site using "internship" or "volunteer" produces useful results.

* (I) AMIDEAST's Guide to Study Abroad [www.amideast.org]. Nonprofit site provides complete listing of study abroad and internship programs throughout the Middle East. AMIDEAST may consider applications for internships at its overseas offices.

* (I) National Consortium for Study in Africa (based at Michigan State Univ.) [www.isp.msu.edu/NCSA/volteer.htm]. Includes a section on volunteer, research and work in Africa.

** (P, I) Peace Corps [www.peacecorps.gov/countries/africa.html]. More U.S. citizens work in Africa through the Peace Corps than through any other organization.

* (I) World Zionist Organization [www.wzo.org.il], **Complete Guide to the Israel Experience** [www.israelexperience.org]. Directories of study and volunteer opportunities in Israel, along with offices in the U.S. that can provide information and advice.

Latin America and Canada

*(P) AIPT [www.aipt.org/prog_cde.html]. Nonprofit AIPT's Career Development Program can assist university graduates who find their own position abroad with work permits for up to 18 months in Mexico.

** (P) COUNCIL Work in Canada and Costa Rica Programs [www.ciee.org]. Work exchange program for students and recent graduates issues work-permits and provides job search assistance.

(I) HISPANIC Online, Career Links [www.hisp.com/carlinks.html] by Hispanic magazine. Lots of information about jobs and careers for Spanish speakers, though this site's job bank lists few overseas positions.

* (P) International Cooperative Education program [http://www.icemenlo.com]. ICEP and Foothill College offer paid summer internships in Argentina, Brazil, or Chile for students and recent graduates who have studied Spanish or Portuguese. Apply by January.

* (P) IIE Internship in Mexico City [www.iie.org/latinamerica/admin.html]. The

Institute of International Education (IIE) offers 3-month paid internships at its advising center in Mexico City. Email to iie@profmex-is.sar.net for details.

(I) LatPro: Latin America's Professional Network [www.latpro.com]. Positions in Latin America and the U.S. for professionals who are bilingual in Spanish or Portuguese. All positions require previous experience.

** (P, I) Peace Corps [www.peacecorps.gov/countries/americas.html]. More U.S. citizens work in Latin American and the Caribbean through the Peace Corps than through any other organization.

* (I) South American Explorer's [www.samexplo.org]. Nonprofit organization produces a guide to volunteering in South America (hard copy only, but inexpensive). Site includes links to volunteer organizations as well as employment opportunities.

* (I) Univ. of Pittsburgh, Center for Latin American Studies [www.pitt.edu/~clas/english/finassist.htm]. This Center's "Guide to Financial Assistance and Internships" has good information for graduate students and graduates, though few overseas listings.

Asia

(P) AIPT [www.aipt.org/prog_cde.html]. Nonprofit AIPT's Career Development Program can assist university graduates who find their own position abroad with work permits for up to 18 months in Japan and Malaysia.

* (I) Asia-Net [www.asia-net.com] lists internships and professional jobs for people who speak Japanese, Chinese, or Korean as well as English. Has search categories for internships and first full-time positions.

* (I) Association for Asian Studies [www.aasianst.org]. Professional association web site includes sections on employment listings, study abroad, and grants and fellowships. Comprehensive links to other sites on all regions of Asia.

** (P, I) JETAA Job Guide [www.jet.org/job]. Site by alumni of the JET (Japan Exchange and Teaching) Program, one of the largest of all work abroad programs. Site includes a guide to international career issues and links to job web sites listed by country.

* (P) International Cooperative Education program [http://www.icemenlo.com] offers internships in Japan, Singapore and Malaysia for students and recent graduates who have studied Japanese or Chinese.

** (P, I) Peace Corps [www.peacecorps.gov/countries/asia.html], [www.peacecorps.gov/countries/pacific.html]. More U.S. citizens work in Central, South and Southeast Asia and the Pacific through the Peace Corps than through any other organization.

(I) Singapore Economic Development Board [www.sebd.com.sq/index1.html]. The Singapore government's site for career jobs in Singapore lists positions mainly for engineers and managers.

Australia and New Zealand

(I) Australian Job Search [http://job-search.dewrsb.gov.au]. Government site lists jobs by occupational category. "Traineeships" indicate entry-level or internship positions.

** (P) BUNAC Work in Australia and New Zealand Program [www.bunac.org]. Work exchange program for students and recent graduates issues work-permits and provides job search assistance.

** (P) Camp Counselors USA, Outbound Program [www.campcounselors.com/americans.html]. Work exchange program for students and non-students issues work permits and provides job search assistance for Australia and (students only) New Zealand.

** (P) COUNCIL Work in Australia and New Zealand Programs [www.ciee.org]. Work exchange program for students and recent graduates issues work-permits and provides job search assistance.

(I) Employment Opportunities in Australia [www.employment.com.au]. Jobs mostly for experienced professionals, except for "graduates" section—where most listings specify Australian residents.

Central and Eastern Europe and the Former USSR

(P) AIPT [www.aipt.org/prog_cde.html]. Nonprofit AIPT's Career Development Program can assist university graduates who find their own position abroad with work permits for up to 18 months in Hungary and the Slovak Republic.

(I) American Association of Teachers of Slavic & East European Languages [http://clover.slavic.pitt.edu/~aatseel].

Professional association web site includes internships, scholarships and career information related to Central and East European Studies.

* (I) Indiana University, Russian & East European Institute—Employment Resources [www.indiana.edu/~reeiweb/indemp.html]. Site has extensive section on employment, as well as sections on academic programs (both in the U.S. and abroad), language programs, scholarships, and links to dozens of centers for Russian and East European studies.

** (P, I) Peace Corps [www.peacecorps.gov/countries/europe.html]. More U.S. citizens work in Central and Eastern Europe, Russia, and the NIS through the Peace Corps than through any other organization.

* (I) Univ. of Washington, Center for Civil Society [http://solar.rtd.utk.edu/~ccsi/announce.htm], [http://solar.rtd.utk.edu/~ccsi/jobs]. Site has extensive listings of internships, volunteer, and career positions throughout Russia and the Newly Independent States (i.e. entire former USSR) and facilitates NGO development throughout the region.

Western Europe

** (P) AIPT [www.aipt.org/prog_cde.html]. Nonprofit AIPT's Career Development Program assists university graduates who find their own position abroad with work permits for up to 18 months in Austria (11 months max.), Britain (12 months max.), Finland, France, Germany, Ireland, Sweden,and Switzerland. Current students have access to these and other countries through the AIPT/IAESTE Student Exchanges program.

* (I, P) American-Scandinavian Foundation [www.amscan.org/work.htm]. Web site includes a comprehensive directory of study, language, and work abroad programs throughout Scandinavia. ASF offers placements for technical internships and teaching English. ASF can also provide work permits

for those who find their own internships.

** (I) British Information Services [www.britain-info.org]. British government site provides official information on employment options for foreigners in Britain, with links to work and internship programs.

** (P) BUNAC Work in Britain Program [www.bunac.org]. Work exchange program for students and recent graduates issues work-permits and provides job search assistance.

** (P) Council Work in Ireland, France, and Germany Programs [www.ciee.org]. Work-exchange program for students and recent graduates issues work-permits and provides job search assistance.

* (P) CDS International [www.cdsintl.org]. Government supported nonprofit organization offers paid study-internship programs in Germany for students, graduates, and professionals. Site provides program information and listings of current internship openings, plus links for information about Germany.

(I, S) German Academic Exchange Service (DAAD) [www.daad.org/]. Deutscher Akademischer Austauschdienst (DAAD) site provides official information about study abroad (direct enrollment), degree study, and scholarships for Germany. Site also has information about the Deutscher Bundestag/Humboldt Univ. of Berlin Internship Program and an internship program for law graduates.

** (P) International Cooperative Education program [http://www.icemenlo.com]. ICEP offers paid summer internships in Switzerland, Germany, Belgium, or Finland for students and recent graduates who have studied the appropriate language: German, French, Italian, Finnish, Dutch, Japanese, or Chinese. Apply by January.

** (P) InterExchange [www.interexchange.org]. Nonprofit organization offers low-cost placements for internships and work abroad in several Western and Eastern European countries.

CHAPTER 3

SHORT-TERM JOBS AND INTERNSHIPS FOR STUDENTS AND RECENT GRADUATES

The best time to seek work overseas and to prepare for an international career is while you are a student (or soon after graduation). Numerous special work abroad programs are available only to undergraduate and graduate students, and to recent graduates up to around age 30.

Work Abroad Overview
Overseas Jobs and How to Find Them

By William Nolting

Y ou may be considering an overseas work experience for many reasons: an adventure, a chance to gain in-depth knowledge of another culture and of yourself, an inexpensive way to improve foreign language proficiency, or as preparation for an international career.

Keep in mind what you want from working abroad: Will an unpaid internship working with Americans in a U.S. embassy do as much for your French as working in an ice cream shop in Paris? Or would the State Department internship be the best choice if your long-term goal is an international career?

Also, keep in mind how extraordinarily difficult it is to be hired into a career position abroad unless you have a scarce skill and professional experience.

Visas and Work Permits

One major obstacle to working abroad is the law. All countries require special permission for foreigners to either work or reside for long periods of time. Whereas short-term tourists sometimes do not need a visa and student visas are granted relatively easily, work permit visas are normally available only through application by an employer who has offered you a job. The employer must show that you have unique skills and abilities not possessed by local citizens.

This is expensive and time-consuming to prove, so most employers, who are subject to heavy fines if they hire illegally, will not offer a job to a foreigner who does not possess a work permit. Work exchange programs are one of the few legal ways around this. Note: it is also possible to work illegally; i.e., without a work permit. Such jobs may turn up in restaurants and agriculture as well as in teaching English. We cannot recommend working illegally because it puts you at risk of immediate deportation, possible fines, lowest wages (or no wages at all), and lack of legal protection or health insurance in case of injury or illness.

Study, Work, and the Cost of Living Abroad

Study abroad programs provide logistical assistance and a structured learning environment, which can be especially valuable if you are going abroad for the first time. They provide the quickest way to achieve fluency in a foreign language, a prerequisite for many international careers. For those interested in working abroad, the study abroad program can also provide a secure base from which to explore job possibilities and make contacts with potential employers. Credit towards your degree is available as long as you check with the proper offices before going. Disadvantages: Cost ranges from about the same to considerably more than the cost of study at home. If you don't need the academic credit towards a degree, study abroad might simply be impractical.

Scholarships for undergraduate study abroad are fairly rare. Even fewer scholarships support work abroad (except for graduate students), and students report more success with fundraising through family, friends, and hometown associations (such as Rotary, Kiwanis, etc.).

Work abroad can be combined with study (before, during, or after), helping you to defray the cost and gain experience in a very different environment from academia. But two caveats:

1. **Do not expect to finance study with part-time work.** At best, it can provide extra spending money. Savings can usually be accumulated more quickly by working in the U.S.

2. **You must carefully investigate whether and under what circumstances work is allowed for American students in a particular country.** Most countries do not allow students to work and may deport those who work without a work permit. However, student work-permit programs for some popular European destinations allow work in combination with study. You have to enter the country with a special work permit provided by the work exchange program, which can only be obtained by applying in advance. Finally, a few countries (e.g., Australia and some locales in Germany) permit part-time work for students who are directly enrolled in local universities. Other countries (e.g., Britain and France) will generally not allow students to work unless they participate in a special student work exchange program.

Study and Work Abroad After Graduation

Fulbright, Rotary, and other scholarships are available to support a year of overseas study (not necessarily for a degree) after graduation. These prestigious awards and the contacts they open up are often stepping stones to international careers.

Direct enrollment in a foreign university is another postgraduate possibility.

Tuitions for direct enrollment are low in some countries, but high in Britain, Ireland, and Australia. Student status may allow you to work part time or during vacations in some countries. However, the main disadvantage of attempting to "work your way" through an overseas university is that you may find yourself marking time, neither making headway towards a degree nor progress in a career. You also want to be sure that a degree earned from an overseas university would be recognized as well in the U.S. as one from a U.S. university.

Types of Work Abroad Programs

Numerous special programs offer placements in specific jobs (paid or unpaid) along with a work permit or assist you in procuring a short-term work permit and help with a job search once overseas. Work abroad programs are limited in duration, lasting from two weeks for short-term volunteer programs, to a summer or six months, or as long as one or two years for programs for teaching abroad or long-term volunteering such as the Peace Corps. There are four types of work abroad programs.

1. International Internships. Internships offer the most direct connection to international careers. Available in a wide range of locations and disciplines, internships are equaled in this respect only by volunteer options. Internships for academic credit are plentiful (they charge tuition); paid internships are rare. "International" internships may be located abroad or in the U.S. with international organizations. Typical duration is one semester.

2. Short-Term Paid Work Abroad. Typical types of short-term paid work abroad include restaurant work, temping, childcare (au pair) and farm work, though enterprising students do find work of a professional nature. (For a list of employers for short-term jobs and au pair placements, see Chapter 3.) Short-term work abroad programs for students or recent graduates offer the best chance for you to earn your way abroad; however, there are up-front costs for program fees, airfare, and initial spending money. Programs are located primarily in Europe, with a small number of other locations. The typical duration is up to six months.

3. Volunteering Abroad. Volunteers usually work and live together with ordinary local citizens. Types of work range from archaeology digs to social services in locations worldwide. Volunteering is excellent career preparation for those interested in work in developing countries or careers with non-governmental organizations. (See Chapter 5.)

4. Teaching Abroad. Teaching English as a Foreign Language (TEFL or ESL) is one of the most accessible options for long-term (one to two years) work abroad. (See Chapter 6.) A college degree is required by most programs. Jobs are typically in Asia or Eastern Europe (few such jobs are available in Western Europe for Americans). Experience in tutoring or teaching is recommended. Additional teaching abroad options are available for those with teaching qualifications at the K-12 or university level. (See Chapter 7.)

Work Abroad Calendar: When to Apply

Internships. September-November for study abroad internships for winter term. This is also the best time to contact organizations if you are lining up your own job. **November 1:** Deadline for U.S. State Department internships. **December:** IAESTE, American-Scandinavian Foundation (engineering and sciences), CDS Congress-Bundestag Program (Germany). **January-April:** deadlines for study abroad internships for spring, summer, fall terms. **March 1:** Deadline for State Department internships for fall semester. **July 1:** Deadline for State Department internships for winter semester.

Short-Term Paid Work Abroad. Apply in the fall term for International Cooperative Education Program paid summer internships. Apply three to four months in advance for InterExchange and other placement programs. Apply one month in advance for BUNAC and CIEE Work Permit programs.

Volunteering Abroad. Apply at least nine months in advance for Peace Corps and other long-term volunteer programs; apply in March-May for short-term "work-camps."

Teaching English Abroad. Apply at least nine months in advance for Peace Corps; September-October for Fulbright English Teaching Assistantship positions; December for major TESL programs in Asia, including JET, Princeton-in-Asia, Earlham College; January-March for various other TESL programs, but best to apply early.

Short-Term Paid Work Abroad

Exchange Programs for Students and Recent Graduates

By William Nolting

The bad news about working abroad is that you can't just hop a plane to any country and start looking for a paid job. To work would be illegal without a permit, which you cannot acquire without a job offer, and—Catch 22—very few employers will offer you a job if you don't already have a work permit. The good news is that a number of organizations can help you cut the red tape and acquire a legal work permit or place you in a job.

If you're looking for an inexpensive way to experience total cultural immersion, or to simply earn your way through an adventure abroad, here's a good place to start. The emphasis is on exchange, since your participation in most of these programs enables someone from abroad to have the equivalent experience in the U.S.

The two main program types are 1) **the Council and BUNAC Work Abroad exchanges**, which enable students to get a work permit in advance, then look for a job on site with assistance from overseas offices, and 2) **overseas job placement** programs offered by a number of U.S.-based work exchange organizations.

Work Permit Programs for Students

Over 6,000 U.S. students and recent graduates work abroad each year in programs administered by the Council on International Educational Exchange (Council) and BUNAC, the most popular option for working abroad and one of the few which does not require applying far in advance. You can get a work permit without a job offer, you can work at any job you find, and the application process is non-competitive.

BUNAC or Council can get you a work permit—otherwise virtually impossible for Americans to obtain—any time of the year for Australia, Britain (BUNAC only), Ireland, France, Canada, Germany, and Costa Rica (Council only). Without a work permit, you could only work illegally, seriously limiting your options. The cost of the program ranges from $225 (for Britain) to $500.

To be eligible, you must be a U.S. citizen (or permanent resident) and an undergraduate or graduate student of any age studying in the U.S. and taking at least eight credit hours. (Student status as defined by the program continues for one semester after you leave school: spring and summer graduates have until the following December 31 to enter the country in which they will work, and December graduates have until June 30.) Participants in the France, Germany, and Costa Rica programs must have had two years' study of the appropriate language.

This is a do-it-yourself program—you find your own job and apartment using listings provided by the overseas program office. The average time for finding jobs is around one week, depending upon the country. The initial investment includes the program fee, roundtrip airfare, and enough money ($800-$1,000), to tide you over until you get the first pay check. Most students report that they can cover their expenses and save money, although this is not likely in Costa Rica (low wages) or Australia and New Zealand (high airfares).

The typical Council/BUNAC job is in restaurant, hotel, clerical, or sales work— but even these ordinary jobs provide a total immersion experience in the daily life of another culture, resulting in cross-cultural insights, friendships, and personal growth.

According to BUNAC and Council, less than a quarter of their participants arrange for a job or an interview in advance—not necessary for ordinary jobs such as pub and temp work, but a good strategy for getting a career-related internship.

As explained elsewhere, internships are available through special organizations such as EAIESEC or IAESTE (see below), as well as universities, but these are competitive, have early deadlines, or require paying tuition in the case of "academic" credit-granting internships.

Rather than paying for someone else to place them, many students use their own initiative, combined with work permits from BUNAC or Council, to find a career-related job. You can write to firms well in advance to request an interview upon your arrival. Try to be neither too general nor overly specific in your work objective. Send a one-page resume outlining your education, work experience, computer skills or organizational talents, and interests. Include a cover letter clearly stating that you will arrive with a valid student exchange work permit. Even if you have been unable to arrange for an interview or job in advance, contact the company again by phone just before or after you arrive and try again—chances are good that your persistence will be rewarded.

Come prepared. Bring your resume and references from previous employers or professors and a suit for interviews.

For applications and more information, contact: **Council Work Abroad**, 205 E. 42nd St., New York, NY 10017-5706; 888-COUNCIL; info@councilexchanges.org, [www.councilexchanges.org/work]. **BUNAC USA,** P.O. Box 430, Southbury, CT 06488; 800-GO BUNAC or 203-264-0901, fax 203-264-0251; wib@bunacusa.org, [www.bunac.org].

Accommodations. Take advantage of optional room reservation services offered by most programs. Otherwise, reserve a youth hostel ($15-$30 per night) in advance. Contact the **American Youth Hostel** headquarters 202-783-6161; hiayhserv@hiayh. org, [www.hiayh.org] to find out how. You should find an apartment after you get your job to minimize commuting time. Some jobs include housing.

Insurance. Most programs require you to have your own health insurance. The Council International Student ID card, available from Council Travel 888-COUN-CIL, [www.councilexchanges.org] for $20, provides travel discounts and minimal health insurance. We recommend everyone get one. More comprehensive coverage is available from special agencies starting at $60 per month, essential if you have no other health insurance. Agencies include Council Travel, John Hancock (800-767-0169), Hinchliff (607-257-0100), and Wallace & Co. (800-237-6615).

Study and Work. If you are going on a study abroad program, you may be able to combine it with a BUNAC or Council permit, allowing work before, during, or sometimes after studying. However, don't expect to finance your studies this way. Since 1999 American students studying in Britain for more than six months are officially allowed to work part-time during the term and full-time during vacations. Those studying for only one semester still need the BUNAC work permit to work legally. In Britain you can only work before or during study abroad (i.e. during the first six months when you are in the country), ever after.

Getting a work permit overseas. This is nearly impossible unless you already have a job offer. Get the work permit before you leave, or use one of the job placement programs below which also arrange for work permits.

Other Work Permit Programs

The BUNAC/Council work permits cannot be extended or renewed, but the following organizations may be able to assist with a different permit—if you already have a job offer.

The Association for International Practical Training (AIPT, Work Exchanges, 10400 Little Patuxent Pkwy., Columbia, MD 21044-3510; 410-992-3924; iaste@aipt. org, [www.aipt.org]). AIPT can get you a permit for up to 18 months for college graduates to work in dozens of countries—ask for Jeff Lange.

Work permit and placement programs are also offered by the **American-Scandinavian Foundation** and CDS (see below).

Placement Programs

If you would you rather be placed in a job than find your own, or if you want a certain type of job, these programs may make it easier. Agencies should be willing to furnish you with names and telephone numbers of past participants.

American-Scandinavian Foundation (725 Park Ave., New York, NY 10021; 212-879-9779, fax 212-249-3444; training@amscan.org, [www.amscan.org]). Offers placements in Finland for teachers of English as a foreign language to students of all age levels for 2 months to an academic year. Eligibility: U.S. citizens, age 21-30, with English as their native language who have completed at least their junior year in college. Salary: FIM4,000-5,000 per month ($775-$975); housing is arranged, participants responsible for rent ($200-$300 per month). Application deadline: February 1. Application fee $50; refundable deposit $200. ASF also offers placements for engineering, business, and agriculture students throughout Scandinavia (apply by January 1). ASF can also assist with work permits for those who have a job offer.

Camp Counselors USA (Outbound Program, 2330 Marinship Way, Suite 250, Sausalito, CA 94965; 800-999-2267, fax 415-339-2744; outbound@ campcounselors.com, [www.camp-counselors.com]). "Educational work-travel program" in camps and orphanages all across the former Soviet Union. New work-abroad programs also available in Australia, New Zealand, and Venezuela. Placement in camp with full room and board and a symbolic stipend (not enough to cover program fee). Minimum requirements include experience with children, knowledge of the appropriate foreign language, and teaching/coaching experience. Fee of $1,500 includes roundtrip airfare from New York, visa, travel insurance, orientations (not training) in New York and Moscow, and support during the 4- or 8-week program. Application deadline: April 1. Usually about 100 applicants for 50-75 placements.

CDS International, Inc. (871 United Nations Plaza, 15th Fl., New York, NY 10017-1814; 212-497-3500, fax 212-497-3535; info@cdsintl.org, [www.cdsintl.org]). Offers 3 paid programs in Germany, including programs for those in mid-career. At least some knowledge of German is a prerequisite. Check their web site for updated listings of specific internships posted year round.

Center for Interim Programs (INTERIM, P.O. Box 2347, Cambridge, MA 02238; 617-547-0980, fax 617-661-2864; info@interimprograms.com, [www. interimprograms.com]). Matches client's interests with a database of over 3,000 structured opportunities worldwide from internships to volunteering, for people between the ages of 16 and 70. Basic $1,500 fee.

InterExchange (161 6th Ave., New York, NY 10013; 212-924-0446, fax 212-924-0575; interex@earthlink.net, [www.interexchange.org]). Nonprofit organization founded in the early 1970s offers placements in a variety of jobs abroad. For both students and nonstudents. Present programs:

• **English Teaching in Bulgaria, Costa Rica, Czech Republic, Hungary, or Poland.** Bachelor's degree required as well as some experience teaching or tutoring English as a foreign language. Application deadline: April 15 ($350-$450 fee).

• **Internships in Germany** for marketing, trade and tourism, museums, and business. Intermediate German required. Application deadline is 4 months before preferred starting date (fee approx. $700).

• **Agricultural work in Norway.** Work 2 to 3 months year round on family-run farms. Stipend provided. Apply at least 4 months before preferred starting date ($300 fee). Apply by March 1.

• **Au Pair in Austria, France, Germany, Italy, Spain, and Switzerland** for those with some knowledge of the language of the host country. No foreign language necessary for placements in Holland, Norway, and Switzerland. Men may apply to the France, Holland, Germany, Norway, and Swiss programs (otherwise women only). Summer placements for France, Italy and Spain or for at least 6 months in all countries. Apply at least 3 months prior to desired starting date (fees from $300-$400).

International Cooperative Education Program (Guenter and Ellen Seefeldt, 15 Spiros Way, Menlo Park, CA 94025; 650-323-4944, fax 650-323-1104, icemenlo@aol.com, [http://members.aol.com/icemenlo]). In existence since 1971, this program places some 450 students each summer in paid internships of 2 to 4 months in Belgium, Finland, Germany, Japan, Singapore, and Switzerland. Applicants must have good working knowledge of German, French, Italian, Dutch, Finnish, Chinese, or Japanese, or study it for the full academic year preceding the internship; U.S. or Canadian students 18-30. The program offers entry level or advanced internships in department stores, hotels/restaurants, agricultural, offices, hospitals, banks, and engineering and computer science jobs. After initial interview, $200 fee for extensive application process; additional $600 fee when placed. Airfare, health insurance, and $800 reserve are the participant's responsibility. Apply in fall or no later than February.

Internships International, LLC Internships International, P.O. Box 480, Woolrich, ME 04579-0480; 207-443-3019, fax 207-442-7942; intintl@aol.com, [http://rtpnet.org/~intintl]. Offers placements for college graduates into unpaid internships worldwide. May be possible to obtain part-time jobs on the side. Fee of $700 ($800 for London) refunded if placement not found.

Taking Off (Gail Reardon, Director, P.O. Box 104, Newton Highlands, MA 02461; 617-630-1606, fax 617-630-1605). This is a consulting service which works with students and graduates aged 17-25 to match interests with around 3,000 opportunities worldwide (which are unpaid or self-supporting). Basic consultation fee of $1,000 or $150 hourly.

Short-Term Volunteer Projects ("Workcamps")

Volunteer projects known as workcamps, which last two to four weeks, usually in the summer, and "pay" only room and board, provide invaluable opportunities for international experience. Hundreds are available, located in most European countries, as well as a few in Africa, Asia, and Latin America. You can work for social causes—unlikely as a paid job. And workcamps are group experiences, often with nearly every participant coming from a different country. The best time to apply is in early April, when you'll have the greatest choice. Student status not required. Registration fees are typically around $200-$300 but much more for locations in Africa or Asia. Americans can register for workcamps through:

● **Council International Volunteer Projects,** 205 E. 42nd St., New York, NY 10017-5706; 888-COUNCIL; info@ciee.org, [**www.ciee.org**]. Over 600 projects in more than 20 countries. Fee typically $300.

● **Operation Crossroads Africa,** 475 Riverside Dr., Suite 1366, New York, NY 10027; 212-870-2106; oca@igc.apc.org, [**www.igc.org/oca**]. Seven-week volunteer projects in Africa and Brazil; $25 application fee, $3,500 program fee (includes airfare), which many participants fundraise.

● **SCI-IVS,** 5474 Walnut Level Rd., Crozet, VA 22932; 804-823-1826, fax 804-823-5027; sciivsusa@igc.apc.org, [**www.wworks.com/~sciivs**]. Fee typically $125.

● **Volunteers for Peace** (VFP), 43 Tiffany Rd., Belmont VT 05730, 802-259-2759, fax 802-259-2922; vfp@vfp.org, [**www.vfp.org**]. Over 1,200 projects offered in more than 65 countries. Fee typically $200.

For further exploration of short-term work abroad options, see back issues of *Transitions Abroad* and Susan Griffith's classic book, *Work Your Way Around the World* (available from Peterson's Guides, 800-338-3282.)

Work Abroad Checklist

To help ensure a succesful job search, follow this checklist compiled by Jane Cary for her students at Amherst College.

Before Leaving

● Make a list of alumni living in the city and country where you'll be.

● Talk with students who are back from your future study site. Did any work or perform an internship while there? How did they arrange it?

● Read the sections of all work abroad books that mention the country or city where you'll be.

● Read back issues of *Transitions Abroad* magazine.

While Abroad

● Maintain a "contacts" notebook. Include the name, address, phone number, email address of every interesting professional you meet.

● Contact alumni. Meet them at their place of business or socially. Express your interest in staying on after your program of study ends, or your interest in returning after graduation.

● Check the local Yellow Pages and the daily paper want ads for future reference.

● Look for schools that teach in English. What qualifications do their teachers have?

● If in a homestay, take every opportunity to meet the family's friends and extended family. Network.

● Practice, the local language. Meet the "natives" in all walks of life, constantly. Read the local and national papers and periodicals.

● Introduce yourself to older Americans living locally. Learn about where they are or were employed and how they obtained their positions.

● Pay attention to living costs of the country and figure out how much money you would need.

● Have a standby friend at home pick up and save summer job and internship information for you.

● If graduate study in that country is an option, get information while you're there.

After Returning

● Visit your Career Center early and often to learn about its services for job-hunting seniors; attend all relevant job-seekers workshops.

● Find out if firms with offices abroad recruit on campus. Don't be distressed to learn that you might have to work in the U.S. first.

● Ascertain whether you will need a higher degree to obtain the job you want. What graduate entrance exams are required? Where in the U.S. or abroad can that degree be earned? Make time to gather and pursue short-term and more permanent work-abroad resources.

● Prepare your resume. Make sure it describes your experience abroad and all the skills you acquired, including language competency.

● Keep in touch with all the contacts you gathered abroad. Write to them, stating your serious interest in returning to work in that country after graduation (if you are serious).

- Investigate short-session programs that teach the Teaching of English as a Second Language. Do they help with job placement?

- Assess your financial situation. How much money must you earn before you go? How long can you afford to live abroad?

- Find a friend to job hunt with. Two heads are better than one: you can share leads and contacts.

Perspective

Work in Britain

A Veteran's Tale of the BUNAC Program

By Lori Cloutier

During the summer following my college sophomore year, my friend and I wanted to go overseas. The problem was age-old—money. How were we to fund a whole summer abroad and survive? The answer was BUNAC, The British Universities North America Club, which provides British work visas for students from the U.S. for up to six months.

The visa made it legal for me to work anywhere in Britain. The administrative cost of $225 was very reasonable. Planning to leave for Britain in mid-May, we applied for the work permits in March and received them in mid-April. BUNAC also sent us a whole packet of prep materials to help us get ready.

Preparations: We attended an information session about BUNAC and heard tips from past participants and what their trips and jobs entailed. We bought International Student Identification Cards that offer basic insurance and allowed us to get a great discount on a flight from Council Travel. The BUNAC handbook also listed a few hostels that could guarantee a place to stay for BUNACers but you must call about a week ahead.

Settling Down in London: My friend and I said a tearful goodbye to our families and were off on our journey. We rounded up our luggage at Gatwick airport and somehow got a train to Victoria Station. Never had I felt so free—an ocean away from home, all my belongings with me, and able to go anywhere. It was the best.

The city was beautiful and strange: black "cabbies," as taxis are called in Britain, double decker busses, uniform townhouses, and drivers on the left. We had so much to discover and a whole summer to do it! We settled into our hotel and went out to look for a flat. We found that most apartments charge rent by the week, and some wanted a month plus the first week's rent down as a deposit. If the flat was 100 pounds per week ($150—average to inexpensive), that would have been 400 pounds ($600) down, plus the first week which would be a total of 500 pounds ($750) just for the first payment. As a flat proved to be far too expensive for us, we decided to look for work with housing included, like some pub or hotel jobs.

Finding a Job and Housing: At the BUNAC orientation the next day, we learned how to register with the Jobcentre and a few other simple things to make sure we were legal to work. There were about 20 other students at the orientation, all BUNACers, all as jobless and homeless as we were. It was comforting to meet others in the same situation. The BUNAC office had many listings of employers wanting to hire BUNACers and of available apartments. We called dozens of places for jobs, mostly pubs and restaurants. Some positions were already filled; others wanted us to bring them a resume and they would conduct a short interview. After the interviews, they kept our resumes and wanted to call us back. We quickly learned that you need a stable contact number during the job search.

After calling and interviewing at about four more places, we were both offered jobs at a pub located near the London Bridge. It was exactly what you would think of as a traditional English pub. Our manager, his wife, and their two small children had come over from Ireland and they lived above the pub. My friend and I would share a room in their apartment, and essentially become part of the family. We could move in and start immediately. The entire job and house search process took us about five days.

Working in Britain: Our manager wanted my friend and I to run the pub together during the day and then alternate working at night with another bartender. On our first day they put me behind the bar and told me to just do my best and ask lots of questions. Everything was fine until in came the lunch-time crowd. All I remember is loud music, many voices, and people throwing orders at me through the noise and in various accents. But I made it without any major problems, and it took only about a week of on-the-job training before I felt comfortable in my bartender's job and could really start to enjoy it.

As we settled into our jobs and new home, we found more time to go out and see the great city of London. I benefitted so much from the museums, historical sights, and cultural events because I could enjoy them at a slow pace due to my long stay in the city.

As the summer went on, we found it a bit difficult to travel because we worked almost every day, so my friend and I decided to quit work two weeks early. At the beginning of May, we traveled to Paris and then went on a tour all over Scotland. Finally, we had three more days in London which we spent taking our last admiring impressions of the wonderful city we called home for three months.

Work Abroad vs. Study Abroad: I learned many things by being a part of the British work force. I have studied abroad as well, and in comparing the two experiences, I felt I learned more factual information from study abroad, but I gained better insight into the country's culture and social system by working overseas.

I was immediately aware of a larger division between the social classes in Britain compared to the U.S. This also translated to the workplace where people are very formal when speaking to their superiors. One man who had just started working for an American company said he was absolutely astounded when the American boss came right up to him, introduced himself, and asked him all kinds of friendly, casual questions. His comment was, "This would never happen in Britain. You can't be that casual with your company superiors if they even speak to you at all."

There was also the famous British reserve that I noticed right away. People were less apt to begin a conversation, but I found every British person with whom I did speak to be incredibly polite and friendly. The British are also less likely to complain about customer service. My boss said that from a British perspective, complaining, even though the service may be really bad, is seen as rude and inappropriate. Even as a novice bartender I never had one complaint.

The British people I met were curious about America and asked many questions. I found that a few of them had quite strange views of American culture, associating the U.S. with Hollywood and the Old West. I also found that the British get a lot of American talk shows, and I was asked many times if our society is really that corrupt. I tried to give everyone the most accurate perspective possible, which is all part of the learning experience. I found I learned not only about British culture, but also much about myself, how others view my culture, and why I do things the way I do. This all came from being in another culture and seeing the world from a different perspective. Working in London really changed me and widened my view of the world. It was a priceless experience.

Contact: BUNAC USA, P.O. Box 430, Southbury, CT 06488; 800-GO-BUNAC or 203-264-0901, [www.bunac.com]; BUNAC UK, Incoming Programmes, 16 Bowling Greene Ln., London, ECIR OBD, England; 011-44-171-251-2472, fax 0215; bunac@easynet.co.uk, [www.bunac.org].

International Jobs For Students and Recent Graduates

The Key Print Resources

Selected and Reviewed by William Nolting

The following resources focus on casual work abroad that is often, though not always, for students and recent graduates. The positions are generally not career-related and last from a summer to six months. Typical locations are Western Europe. Look into these a few months before traveling.

**Essential; *Outstanding and of broad interest.

For ordering information, if not included below, see Key Publishers, page 13.

WORLDWIDE WORK AND STUDY ABROAD

**Academic Year Abroad edited by Sara J. Steen. 2000 (revised annually). 690 pp. Institute of International Education (IIE). $44.95 plus $6 shipping from IIE (See Key Publishers). Also available free as a searchable document on IIE's web site at [www.iiepassport.org]. The most comprehensive and authoritative directory of semester and academic year programs abroad for college students and adults. Lists over 2,600 programs offered by U.S. and foreign universities and private organizations. Indexed for fields of study and location, with special indexes for cost; graduate, professional, teacher and adult courses. More than 800 programs include work or practical experience, and are listed under indexes for internships, practical training, student teaching, and volunteer/service (or see "format" category in web site search). Companion volume to *Vacation Study Abroad*. Found in most college libraries and study abroad offices.

*Advisory List of International Educational Travel & Exchange Programs. Annual. $15 from: Council on Standards for International Educational Travel, 212 Henry St., Alexandria, VA 22314; 703-739-9050, fax 703-739-9035; [www.csiet.org]. The most valuable resource listing programs for high school students that adhere to CSIET's standards.

*The Back Door Guide to Short Term Job Adventures by Michael Landes. 2000. 496 pp. Ten Speed Press. $19.95 plus $3.50 s/h from Ten Speed Press, P.O. Box 7123, Berkeley, CA 94710, 800-841-2665, fax 510-559-1629; [www.backdoorjobs.com]. A guide to internships, "extraordinary experiences," seasonal jobs, and volunteering for everyone from college students through senior citizens. Most listings are in the U.S., but one section lists 200 programs and resources for overseas work and educational travel.

**The Canadian Guide to Working and Living Overseas by Jean-Marc Hachey. 1998 edition. 970 pp. U.S.$40, CAN$54.40. Save 20 percent on web order. Order by phone 800-267-0105, fax 800-221-9985; [www.workingoverseas.com]. Not only for Canadians, this directory provides the most comprehensive and up-to-date overview of work abroad and international careers. Profiles focus on Canadian organizations, so U.S. readers should use this book along with a U.S. book recommended here. Features 1,870 profiles, 1,670 web sites, and 700 resources in 58 bibliographies, web updates until the year 2002. Indispensable for students, recent graduates, managers, and world travelers.

*Charting a Hero's Journey by Linda A. Chisholm. 2000. 300 pp. $25.90 postpaid from Partnership for Service Learning, 815 2nd Ave., Suite 315, New York, NY 10017; 212-986-0989, fax 212-986-5039; pslny@aol.com, [www.studyabroad.com/psl]. Based on the work of Joseph Campbell and using excerpts from journals of famous authors, this is a guide to the writing of a journal for college students engaged in study abroad, off-campus study, and/or service learning. Not a directory of opportunities (for program listings, see the IIE and Peterson's publications).

*Council's Bowman Scholarship. Covers air-fare costs for undergraduates to study, work or volunteer in less-traditional countries (most countries outside Western Europe, Australia, New Zealand) through any organization's programs, individual projects too. Contact Council for applications (see Key Publishers) or see web site: [www.ciee. org/study/scholarships/bowman.htm].

Directory of Grants for Study Overseas by Susan Offerman. 1999. 280 pp. $65. From Overseas Academic Opportunities, 72 Franklin Ave., Ocean Grove, NJ 07756; Tel./fax 732-774-1040. Grants, scholarships, and fellowships for graduate study overseas.

Directory of International Organizations by Hans-Albrecht Schraepler 1996. 456 pp. $24.95 from Georgetown Univ. Press, P.O. Box 4886, Hampden Station, Baltimore, MD 21211-0866; 800-246-9606, fax 410-516-6998. Comprehensive reference to international organizations.

Fellowships in International Affairs: A Guide to Opportunities in the United States and Abroad by Women in International Security. 1994. 196 pp. $10 plus $3.50 s/h from Lynne Rienner Publishers, 1800 30th St., Suite 314, Boulder CO 80301; 303-444-6684; [www.rienner.com]. Well-researched directory of fellowships and grants. Most are for grad students, postdoctorates, or professionals. Indexes for level of study and geographic specialization.

**Financial Aid for Research and Creative Activities Abroad 1999-2001 edited by Gail Ann Schlachter and R. David Weber. 1999 (revised every 2 years). 480 pp. $45 plus $5 shipping from Reference Service Press. Lists over 1,400 funding sources available to support research, professional development, teaching assignments, or creative activities. Most useful for graduate students, postdoctorates, and professionals. Relatively few funding opportunities (ca. 50) listed for high school and undergraduate students. Indexes for level of study, location, and subject. Available online to AOL subscribers—keyword RSP—at [www.rspfunding.com].

**Financial Aid for Study and Training Abroad 1999-2001 edited by Gail Ann Schlachter and R. David Weber. 1999 (revised every 2 years). 350 pp. $39.50 plus $5 s/h from Reference Service Press. Lists 1,100 funding sources available to support formal educational programs such as study abroad, training, internships, work-

shops, or seminars. Sources for high school, undergraduate and graduate students, post-doctorates, and professionals. Indexes for level of study, location, and subject. Available online to AOL subscribers (keyword RSP) and at [www.rspfunding.com].

**Financial Resources for International Study: A Guide for U.S. Nationals edited by Marie O' Sullivan and Sara Steen. 1996. 300 pp. $39.95 plus $6 shipping from IIE. Available free as a searchable document on IIE's web site, at [www.iie.org/help/search]. Comprehensive and authoritative directory of almost 700 funding sources based on a survey of over 5,000 organizations and universities in the U.S. and abroad. Lists funding sources available to support undergraduate, graduate, postdoctorate, and professional learning abroad, from study and research to internships, training and teaching. Indexes for level of study, subject, and organization.

A Handbook for Creating Your Own Internship in International Development by Natalie Foster and Nicole Howell (Just Act: Youth Action for Global Justice, 333 Valencia St., #101, San Francisco, CA 94110; 415-431-4204, fax 415-431-5953; sahar@justact.org, [www.justact.org]). Includes practical advice and a workbook to help evaluate your skills, motivations, and learning objectives.

**Impact Press Catalog: Great International Job and Travel Resources. Free from Impact Publications. Catalog of hard-to-find books on international jobs and careers which can be ordered from Impact.

**Intercultural Press Catalog. Updated quarterly. Free from Intercultural Press. Catalog of practical books on cross-cultural issues, moving abroad, dealing with culture shock, and other issues related to working and/or studying abroad.

*Peterson's Study Abroad. Peterson's. 2000 (Annual). 1,141 pp. $29.95 plus shipping from Peterson's. Detailed information on over 1,700 semester and academic year study abroad programs worldwide for college students, of which about 500 offer internships, listed in a special index. Includes essays on credit, financial aid, nontraditional destinations, internships and volunteering, and traveling. Indexes for field of study, host institutions, and internships.

*Peterson's Summer Study Abroad. Peterson's. 2000 (Annual). 622 pp. $29.95 plus shipping from Peterson's. Detailed information on over 1,400 summer and short-term (up to 6 weeks) study abroad programs worldwide of which about 200 offer internships, listed in a special index. Other indexes for field of study and host institutions.

*Study Abroad: A Parent's Guide by William A. Hoffa. 1998. 112 pp. $15 from NAFSA. The only guide to respond to parents' questions and concerns about safety, academic credit, financial aid, program evaluation, travel documents, insurance, banking, and other issues related to study abroad. Not a directory of programs.

**Transitions Abroad. Bimonthly magazine. P.O. Box 1300, Amherst, MA 01004-1300; 413-256-3414, fax 413-256-0373; info@TransitionsAbroad.com, [www.TransitionsAbroad.com]. $28/6 issues. Also available in bulk at reduced price for educators. This is the only U.S. periodical that gives extensive coverage to work abroad options, in addition to all other varieties of education abroad.

**University of Michigan International Center web site, [www.umich.edu/~icenter/overseas]. By Transitions Abroad contributing editor William Nolting, this web site provides articles on working and studying abroad, as well as annotated and rated links to around 200 related web sites.

**The Unofficial Guide to Study Abroad by Ann M. Moore. 2000. 512 pp. $14.95. Arco/IDG Books, 800-762-2974. This book provides an excellent introduction to all aspects of studying and working abroad. Not a directory of programs (for program listings, see the IIE and Peterson's publications).

**Vacation Study Abroad edited by Sara J. Steen, 2000 (Annual). 512 pp. IIE. $44.95 plus $6 shipping from IIE. Also available free as a searchable document on IIE's web site, at [www.iiepassport.org]. This is the most comprehensive and authoritative directory of summer and short-term (less than a semester) programs abroad for college students and adults. Lists over 2,200 programs offered by U.S. and foreign universities and private organizations, of which nearly 500 include work or practical experience. See full description for companion volume, Academic Year Abroad. Can be found in most college libraries and study abroad offices.

What in the World is Going On? A Guide for

Canadians Wishing to Work, Volunteer or Study in Other Countries by Alan Cumyn. 2000. 250 pp. Canadian Bureau for International Education. CAN$19.99 plus shipping from CBIE Resources, 220 Laurier Ave. West, Suite 1100, Ottawa, ON, K1P 5Z9, Canada; 613-237-4820, fax 613-237-1073, [www.cbie.ca]. Includes a comprehensive listing of work abroad possibilities, organized according to location and level of skills and education required. Invaluable for Canadians.

*A World of Option edited by Christa Bucks. 3rd ed., 1997. 658 pp. Mobility International USA. $30 (members), $35 (nonmembers), $40 (member organizations) $45 (non member organizations) from MIUSA, P.O. Box 10767, Eugene, OR 97440; 541-343-1284 (v/tty), fax 541-343-6812; info@miusa.org, [www.miusa.org]. A comprehensive guide to international exchange, study, and volunteer opportunities for people with disabilities.

REGIONAL WORK AND STUDY ABROAD

*After Latin American Studies: A Guide to Graduate Study and Fellowships, Internships, and Employment by Shirley A. Kregar and Annabelle Conroy. Revised ed. 2000. $10 (check payable to Univ. of Pittsburgh) post-paid from: Center for Latin American Studies (CLAS), 4E Posvar Hall, Univ. of Pittsburgh, Pittsburgh, PA 15260; 412-648-7392, fax 412-648-2199; clas@ucis.pitt.edu, [www.ucis.pitt.edu/clas]. An essential resource for anyone with career or scholarly interests in this region, but few listings for overseas opportunities. Extensive bibliography. Also available on the CLAS web site: *A Guide to Financial Assistance for Graduate Study, Dissertation Research and Internships for Students in Latin American Studies. 1996.

*Complete Guide to the Israel Experience. Annual. Available free from Israel Experience, Inc., 111 8th Ave., Suite 11E, New York, NY 10011-5201; 888-99-ISRAEL, info@israelexperience.org, [www.israelexperience. org]. A comprehensive listing of study, volunteer, and travel programs in Israel for high school, college students, and other young adults. Also listed are offices in the U.S. that can provide information and advice. Full text also on the web site.

*The Directory of Work and Study In Developing Countries by Toby Milner. 1997. 256 pp. Vacation Work (U.K.). $16.95 from Seven Hills. Comprehensive guide to employment, voluntary work, and academic opportunities (with over 400 organizations) in developing countries. Chapters on Work, Voluntary Work, and Study, with subsections about specific professional fields and geographic areas. Intended primarily for a British audience, it omits some organizations of interest to Americans.

*Living in China: A Guide to Teaching and Studying in China Including Taiwan by Rebecca Weiner, Margaret Murphy, and Albert Li. 1997. 284 pp. $19.95 from China Books and Periodicals, Inc., 2929 24th St., San Francisco, CA 94110; 415-282-2994, fax 415-282-0994; info@chinabooks.com, [www.chinabooks.com]. Comprehensive advice on topics such as "Adjusting: How Not to be a Foreign Barbarian." Has extensive directories of schools and colleges as well as organizations which offer study abroad or teacher placement.

*Living, Studying, and Working in France: Everything You Need to Know to Fulfill Your Dreams of Living Abroad by Saskia Reilly and Lorin David Kalisky. 1999. 304 pp. $14.95. Owl Book, Henry Holt and Co., 115 West 18th St., New York, NY 10011; 212-886-9268, fax 212-647-1874; academic@hholt. com. The only book on this topic from an American perspective provides useful, very comprehensive advice for anyone wishing to study, work or live in France. Includes nearly 80 pages on working, though for Americans paid jobs will be difficult to find (see AIPT and Council work permit programs for France in "Short Term Paid Work," page 53).

*Living, Studying, and Working in Italy: Everything You Need to Know to Fulfill Your Dreams of Living Abroad by Travis Neighbor and Monica Larner. 1998. 340 pp. $14.95. Owl Book, Henry Holt and Co., 115 West 18th St., New York, NY 10011 ; 212-886-9268, fax 212-647-1874; academic@hholt.com. The only book on this topic from an American perspective provides useful, very comprehensive advice for anyone wishing to study, work or live in Italy. Includes nearly 100 pages on working, though for Americans paid jobs will be very difficult to find.

*Overseas Summer Jobs edited by David Woodworth and Ian Collier. 2000 (revised annually.) 271 pp. Vacation Work (U.K.). $16.95 from Peterson's. Lists more than 30,000 temporary jobs, paid and volunteer, in over 50 countries: who to contact, pay rates, how and when to apply. Valuable information on work permit requirements.

**The Peace Corps and More: 175 Ways to Work, Study, and Travel at Home and Abroad by Medea Benjamin and Miya Rodolfo-Sioson. 1997. 126 pp. $8.95 from Global Exchange, 2017 Mission St., # 303, San Francisco, CA 94110; Book orders 800-497-1994, 415-255-7296, fax 415-255-7498; [www.globalexchange. org]. Describes 175 programs that allow anyone to gain Third World experience while promoting the ideals of social justice and sustainable development. Chapters on Working in the Third World, Working in the U.S. and Canada, Study Opportunities, and Socially Responsible Travel. Includes an index listing locations and fields of study or work.

*The Post-Soviet Handbook: A Guide to Grassroots Organizations and Internet Resources in the Newly Independent State by M. Holt Ruffin, Joan McCarter, and Richard Upjohn. 1999. 416 pp. Univ. of Washington Press. $19.95 plus $4 shipping from Center for Civil Society International, 2929 N.E. Blakely St., Seattle, WA 98105; 206-523-4755, fax 206-523-1974; ccsi@u.washington.edu, [www.friends-partners.org/~ccsi]. The best guide to independent, non-governmental ("third sector") organizations in Russia and the NIS. Up-to-date source for organizations, both U.S.-based and local, that may welcome volunteers. Includes listings of U.S. study abroad programs and academic area studies centers. CCSI's web site and listserv (CivilSoc) are the best sources for announcements of jobs located in this region.

*Summer Jobs Britain edited by David Woodworth and Kate George. 2000 (revised annually). 270 pp. Vacation Work (U.K.). $16.95 from Peterson's. Lists more than 30,000 jobs, ranging from internships ("traineeships") to casual jobs to farming and hotel work to volunteering. Each listing includes wages, qualifications, and contact information. U.S. citizens need a work permit—contact BUNAC or AIPT.

*Working in Asia by Nicki Grihault. In Print Publishing Ltd. (U.K.). 1996. 488 pp. $16.95 from bookstores. The only book that gives an overview of all work options, from volunteer to teaching to career opportunities, throughout Asia—from the Indian subcontinent to Southeast Asia to Northern Asia. Includes specifics on U.S. and other organizations.

SHORT-TERM PAID WORK ABROAD

U.S. citizens need work permits to work legally in other countries. The officially recognized work exchange programs listed here can help.

** AIPT/IAESTE Work Abroad Programs. (See Internships section below). IAESTE can assist U.S. students who have found their own internships with work permits in over 60 countries. AIPT can assist U.S. college graduates with work permits for up to 12-18 months in Finland, France, Germany, Ireland, Japan, Malaysia, Mexico, Slovakia, Sweden, Switzerland, the U.K. and possibly others—contact AIPT / IAESTE for specifics. Also offers internship programs.

*American-Scandinavian Foundation. (See Internships.) Can assist U.S. citizens who have found their own internships with work permits for the Scandinavian countries.

The Au Pair & Nanny's Guide to Working Abroad by Susan Griffith and Sharon Legg. 1997. 304 pp. Vacation Work (U.K.). $16.95 from Seven Hills. Practical, insightful advice on how to prepare for and find a child care job in another country.

*The British Council: Internships/Work Experience in the UK; Students and Employment in the U.K. Free from The British Council, 3100 Massachusetts Ave., NW, Washington DC 20008-3600; 202-588-7830, fax 202-588-7918; [www.studyintheuk. org]. Information on work regulations and work-exchange programs.

**BUNAC Work Abroad Programs (for Britain, Australia, or New Zealand). Application from BUNAC USA, P.O. Box 430, Southbury, CT 06488; 800-GO-BUNAC or 203-264-0901, fax 203-264-0251; [www. bunac.org]. Nonprofit organization provides a work permit and job-hunting assistance. Program fee of $225 or more. U.S. college students and recent grads (within one semester) eligible for Britain. Non-students aged 18-30

eligible for Australia and New Zealand. The invaluable **BUNAC Work in Britain Participant's Handbook may be requested by study abroad and career offices; otherwise for program participants only (not for sale).

Camp Counselors USA Work Abroad Programs. Application from Camp Counselors USA Outbound Program, 2330 Marinship Way, Suite 250, Sausalito, CA 94965; 800-999-2267, fax 415-339-2744; [www.camp-counselors. com]. Offers work permit programs in Australia and New Zealand (similar to those of BUNAC and Council), as well as volunteer placements in Russia for camp counselors.

*CDS International (See Internships.) Can assist U.S. citizens who have found their own placements with work permits in Germany.

**Council Work Abroad Programs. Application from Council Work Abroad, 205 E. 42nd St., New York, NY 10017-5706; 888-COUNCIL; [www.councilexchanges.org/ work]. Nonprofit work exchange program provides a work permit and job-hunting assistance in Australia, Canada, Costa Rica, France, Germany, Ireland, and New Zealand. Program fees from $300 up, depending on the country. U.S. college students and recent grads (within 1 semester) eligible.

*The Directory of Overseas Summer Jobs. edited by David Woodworth and Ian Collier. 2000. (revised annually.) 271 pp. Vacation Work (U.K.). $16.95 from Peterson's. Lists more than 30,000 temporary jobs, paid and volunteer, in over 50 countries: who to contact, pay rates, how and when to apply. Valuable information on work permits required by each country.

*The Directory of Summer Jobs in Britain edited by David Woodworth and Kate George. 2000 (revised annually.) 270 pp. Vacation Work (U.K.). $16.95 from Peterson's. Lists more than 30,000 jobs, ranging from internships ("traineeships") to casual jobs to volunteering. Each listing includes wages, qualifications, and contact information. U.S. citizens need a work permit—contact BUNAC or AIPT (above).

*French Cultural Services: Employment in France for Students. Free information from French Cultural Services, 972 5th Ave., New York, NY 10021; 212-439-1400, fax 212-439-1455; [http://info-france-usa.org/culture/ education/index.html]. Work regulations and work possibilities. Also free: **Teaching Assistant Program; Au Pair Work in France**.

How to Get a Job with a Cruise Line by Mary Fallon Miller. 2000. 258 pp. $18.95 ($28 foreign) from Ticket to Adventure, Inc., P.O. Box 41005, St. Petersburg, FL 33743; 800-929-7447 or 727-822-5029; cruisechooser@yahoo.com, [www.cruisechooser.com]. Detailed information on how to apply plus tips from cruise line employees.

* **Working Abroad** (InterExchange). Free brochure from InterExchange, Inc., 161 6th Ave., New York, NY 10013; 212-924-0446, fax 212-924-0575; info@interexchange.org, [www.interexchange.org]. Nonprofit program offers placements for work abroad, internships, English teaching, and au pair.

*International Cooperative Education Work Abroad Program. (See Internships section below). Program offers paid internship placements in Europe and Asia.

Work Your Way Around The World by Susan Griffith. 1999. 532 pp. Vacation Work (U.K.). $20 from Peterson's Guides. The authoritative (and only) guide to looking for short-term jobs while abroad, by *Transitions Abroad* Work Editor Susan Griffith. Extensive country-by-country narratives include first-hand reports.

*Working Holidays. Updated annually. Central Bureau (U.K.). $18.95. 384 pp. from IIE (See Key Publishers). Thoroughly researched information on 101,000 paid and voluntary work opportunities in over 70 countries. Written for a British audience, it sometimes omits organizations relevant to Americans, such as the work exchange programs mentioned in this section.

Working in Ski Resorts—Europe and North America by Victoria Pybus. 1997. 304 pp. Vacation Work (U.K.). $16.95 from Seven Hills. Available jobs plus reports from resorts.

Working in Tourism: For Seasonal and Permanent Staff by Verite Reily Collins. 1999. 320 pp. Vacation Work (U.K.). $16.95 from Petersons. How to find jobs in tourism, country-by-country listings, and a directory of travel companies with staff requirements.

International Internships
Cover Expenses, Gain Career Experience
By William Nolting

Why do you want an international internship—to live and work abroad, or to gain specific career-related work experience? If the former, many other work abroad opportunities may be easier to get or less expensive. These include short-term paid work abroad programs, teaching English abroad, or volunteering abroad.

Where. Many internships related to international careers, especially ones with international organizations, are actually located here in the U.S.—especially in centers of international activity such as Washington or New York. But it is often possible to combine an international internship with an overseas location.

How. *Tuition-based* study abroad internships sponsored by universities provide credit towards your degree. Financial aid can usually be used to help meet expenses. Tuition costs range widely. If living costs are high at the location, tuition may be as expensive.

Volunteer positions abroad sometimes provide room and board, which can make them less expensive than unpaid internships. The Peace Corps pays well, although this is a two-year commitment. Repayment of educational loans can often be deferred during volunteer work (check with your lender and the volunteer agency). Volunteer positions may be the best option for those interested in careers having to do with developing countries.

Paid internships are somewhat rare abroad and are available mainly in applied fields such as business and engineering. See the resource section of this chapter for a directory of internships.

When to Apply. For summer internships, it's best to apply in the fall. Some programs, such as the U.S. State Department, have deadlines as early as November 1. IAESTE and others have deadlines in early December. Study abroad internships usually have application deadlines the semester before the term of the internship.

Types of Internships and International Organizations

1. Study Abroad Internships. Hundreds of overseas internships are sponsored by universities and for undergraduates are the most easily available option. Advantages include credit, applicability of financial aid, and a variety of subjects and locations. Disadvantages are cost and sometimes unpredictability of placement.

2. Internship Exchange/Work Permit Programs. A few reciprocal exchange programs offer paying internships in applied fields. If you find your own internship abroad, these organizations can also assist in obtaining a work permit.

AIESEC (80-plus countries), a student-run international organization with chapters on many campuses, offers business-related internships open to all majors. AIESEC members have preference in getting these internships. See AIESEC's web site. The Council and BUNAC work abroad programs are the only ways to get a work permit without a job offer. The programs are available for Britain, Ireland, France, Germany, Canada, Costa Rica, Australia, and New Zealand. (See page 53.)

IAESTE (60 plus countries) and the **American-Scandinavian Foundation** (Scandinavian countries) have placements in engineering and natural sciences, while AIPT offers hotel and culinary programs.

CDS (Germany) has several programs in business and technical fields for undergraduates, graduates, and professionals. Applicants must know German. These organizations accept applications directly from students. (See page 53.)

3. Internship Placement Programs. The International Cooperative Education Program (ICEP) is one of the few paid internship programs available to liberal arts majors and also offers placements in engineering, business and other fields. Knowledge of a foreign language is usually required (e.g., German, French, Spanish, Dutch, Japanese, Chinese). (See page 60.) Internships International, the Center for Interim Programs, and others offer low-cost placements in unpaid internships. (See page 61.)

4. Internships Directly with International Organizations. Some organizations in international sectors offer internship programs with a centralized formal application process. Many do not have formal internships but often respond positively to applications from individuals who propose their own "internship." In general, the larger and better-known the organization, the more competitive the application process for internships will be. Smaller and more locally-based organizations, often overlooked by applicants, may offer some of the best internship experiences.

Government. The U.S. State Department and other federal agencies overseas and in the U.S. offer internships (usually unpaid) for undergraduates and graduate students. Application is competitive. Apply by November 1 for summer, March 1 for fall, July 1 for winter. State and city governments have many internship possibilities, often overlooked by applicants, in their international trade offices. Internships with members of Congress who sit on international committees are also possible. For addresses of state and local international commerce offices.

A **U.S. State Department Internship** is a great way to see if a career in diplomacy is for you. Most are unpaid, but free housing may be provided. Eligibility: U.S. citizens who are undergraduates (junior or senior) or graduate students who will continue as students. Application deadlines are November 1 for summer internships, March 1 for fall internships. Contact: Intern Coordinator, U.S. Department of State, Recruitment Division, SA-1, 2401 E St., NW, 5th Fl., Washington DC 20522; 202-261-8912; [www.state.gov/www/careers/rinterncontents.html].

The U.S. Foreign Service includes the Department of State (diplomacy), which recently incorporated the U.S. Information Agency (cultural and educational exchanges). To apply you simply take the Foreign Service Exam, which is similar to the GRE, and includes a test of English expression and usage, a section on international "job-related" knowledge, a biographic information questionnaire section, and an essay to test general writing skills. The free test is given once a year. Most people take it more than once before passing. Eligibility: U.S. citizens at least 20 years old who are willing to be assigned anywhere worldwide.

You can order the booklet "Study Guide for the 2000 Foreign Service Officer Written Examination and Assessment Procedure" for $15-$25 depending on type of shipment from: ACT Customer Services (68), P.O. Box 1008, Iowa City IA 52243-1008; 319-337-1429, fax 319-337-1578; or downoaded from the State Department website.

The State Department also has some career positions as foreign service specialists that do not require the Foreign Service exam. See [www.state.gov/www/careers].

The **U.S. Peace Corps** is possibly the best (and best-paying) entry-level job for anyone interested in grassroots development work overseas. Unlike in a State Department job, you live and work with ordinary local people. Eligibility: U.S. citizens, generally for those with at least a bachelor's degree; two-year commitment. Peace Corps pays all expenses plus over $6,000 ("resettlement allowance") at the end of service. Full training and support is provided. Educational loans can be deferred and some partially canceled. Some tuition support is available for later graduate study. Contact Peace Corps, P.O. Box 948, Washington DC 20526; 800-424-8580; [www.peacecorps.gov].

The **Woodrow Wilson Foundation** administers several scholarship/internship programs for which women and minorities are especially encouraged to apply. Most of these scholarships fund several years of study and include summer institutes and internships. Applicants must apply as sophomores (for three-year scholarships) or as seniors (for graduate school scholarships, for a shorter period of time). The three major programs are:

● Department of State Foreign Affairs Fellowship Program. A 3-year scholarship for students interested in careers in diplomacy with the U.S. State Department, leading to a masters degree and a position with the State Department.

● Institute for International Public Policy (IIPP). A 3-year scholarship for students interested in public service.

● Department of Commerce/Ronald H. Brown Commercial Service Fellowship Program Award. A 3-year scholarship for those interested in international trade, leading to a masters degree and a position with the Department of Commerce.

For the most up-to-date information and applications, see the Woodrow Wilson website, [www.woodrow.org/public-policy]. Other U.S. government departments that offer international internships and career positions include the **U.S. Agency for International Development** (USAID) and the **U.S. Department of Commerce**.

Public Multinationals. Multi-government giants like the United Nations, the European Community and the World Bank offer internships. They are often unpaid and highly competitive (paid positions are usually reserved for graduate students), and most positions for Americans are in the U.S. Most internships in the "Key Resources" list that follows have information on internships with these organizations. Some organizations are designated as officially recognized international organizations. Work permits for these employers are easier to get.

Private Enterprise. Organized international internship programs are sponsored by Proctor & Gamble, Coca-Cola, and others. These are sometimes restricted to students in MBA programs. Many undergraduates, however, have arranged overseas internships with U.S. or host-country companies, especially by using the Council or BUNAC programs. Most internships with private industry pay enough to cover basic living expenses, though usually not the cost of transatlantic airfare.

Non-Government Organizations (NGOs), typically nonprofit, include humanitarian or human-rights watchdogs lkike Amnesty International, health care providers like CARE, research institutes like the Bermuda Biological Station, and organizations supporting international educational exchange such as the Institute of International Education or the Academy for Educational Development. NGOs typically welcome interns in their U.S.-based offices and sometimes by direct application to overseas offices. Internships with NGOs are often unpaid.

Educational Organizations. Teachers are needed worldwide. Positions fall into two categories: Teaching English as a foreign language, for which no other credential than a bachelor's degree is usually needed, and teaching K-12 in overseas schools taught in English, for which teaching certification is usually required. Most teaching positions require a commitment of at least one academic year. Teaching at the university level nearly always requires an advanced degree. See Chapters 6 and 7 for specific organizations.

Private Voluntary Organizations (PVOs) offer many overseas placements and are one of the only possibilities for work in developing countries. Positions are typically designated as "volunteer" or service positions, rather than internships. These range from secular organizations, such as Amigos de las Americas or Los Ninos, to religious-sponsored groups. While some religious groups insist on affiliation, others, such as the Brethren or the American Friends Service Committee, do not. Short-term placements (of less than one year) will often charge fees, or at best provide room and board. A few long-term placements provide for all the expenses of the volunteer, most notably the Peace Corps. Again, "volunteer" positions offer the substantial benefit of deferring educational loan repayments during the volunteer assignment. For more information see Chapter 5.

Perspective

Work in Washington

International Education Internships Lead to Careers

By Heather Powers

The average job search after graduation lasts six months, long enough to erode the confidence of any qualified candidate. But while the job market in your area may be depressed, Washington, DC continues to offer internships and entry-level job opportunities in the field of international education. With planning and persistence, you may land an internship that will get you started in your desired career.

College graduates sometimes dismiss internships because a steady income is needed to pay off accumulated debt—student loans, car payments, or credit cards. But when job leads are scarce, an internship may provide the experience that will help you break into the field while giving you the opportunity to get to know the players. An internship also lets an organization learn what you have to offer, and as an internal candidate you get first crack at job openings. Other benefits of an internship are the ability to openly conduct a job search, after-hours use of computers and printers to produce cover letters and resumes, and work experience that will immediately be recognized by other not-for-profits in DC.

The Search

So how do you begin? Some nonprofits, like the Institute of International Education and Meridian International Center, try to reach prospective interns through flyers sent to career placement offices. I discovered NAFSA *Job Registry*, a bimonthly publication of job openings, in my alma mater's international center. This opened my eyes to the wide range of positions available in international education—from credentials evaluation to international student advising to grant administration.

Two sources that will reveal the wealth of potential employers awaiting you in Washington are *International Education Career Information*, produced by NAFSA (NAFSA Item #1680; 800-836-4994, $10 plus s/h), and the *International Exchange Locator: 2000 Edition* published by IIE New York (IIE Books; 800-445-0443, $19.95

plus $6 s/h, [www.alliance-exchange.org/store]). The first is an excellent introduction to the field of international education, with an overview of the qualifications required. Also listed are career resources to assist you with informational interviewing and networking in DC. *The Exchange Locator* contains overviews of organizations involved in international educational exchange. While not all-inclusive, it does provide information critical to a job search, such as the organization's mission, branch offices if any, and the number of staff.

Not-for-profit organizations such as Youth for Understanding, NAFSA, and the Institute of International Education welcome interns and rely on volunteers to meet their objectives. Personalize your resumes and cover letters to convince human resource personnel they have a good match. Call to determine to whom your resume should be sent, if writing samples and transcripts are required, and if there is a hiring cycle for interns. A bachelor's degree, demonstrated interest in international education, and writing samples are usually all that is required to secure an internship.

Compensation ranges from nothing to stipends of $500 per month. Your survival during this time requires careful budgeting. Once you obtain your internship, contact your student loan provider about a temporary hardship deferment; it won't affect your credit rating and the six-month deferment of payments on the principal will help you pay your bills.

Getting the Job

Only 20 percent of job vacancies are advertised, so networking is the key to success. This is especially true of international nonprofits where position descriptions are distributed to similar organizations. Asking your colleagues to keep their eyes open is important. Your chances of getting the job increase enormously when you have a contact or you are an internal candidate. Typical minimum requirements are a BA, foreign language study, experience abroad, and good communication skills. Computer skills are recommended. Salaries in the field are low and there is no overtime, but most organizations offer excellent benefits: health insurance, retirement, sick leave, and ample paid vacation time.

The circle of international educational exchange in Washington is relatively small; after a year in the city you will recognize names and begin to run into familiar people. Participating in career roundtables, after-work happy hours, office sports leagues, and an occasional embassy reception will give you sufficient opportunity to mingle with your colleagues and advance your new career.

International Internships
The Key Print Resources
Selected and Reviewed by William Nolting

Like the international careers they can help open up, internships may be either located in the U.S. with international organizations or overseas. They are often unpaid. Start your search early, as applications can be due three to nine months in advance.

**Essential; *Outstanding and of broad interest.*
For ordering information, if not included below, see Key Publishers, page 13.

**Academic Year Abroad & Vacation Study Abroad. (See Worldwide Overviews section.) This is the most comprehensive and authoritative directory of study abroad programs. Indexes for internships, practical training, volunteering, and student teaching list over 1300 programs, most of which charge tuition and give academic credit. Available free online at [www.iiepassport.org].

*American-Scandinavian Foundation: "Study in Scandinavia." 2000 (annual). 54 pp. Free from ASF, 15 E. 65th St., New York, NY 10021; 212-879-9779, fax 212-249-3444; [www.amscan.org]. Booklet and site list study and work programs. This nonprofit organization offers paid internships in Scandinvia in engineering, teaching English, business, and agricultural fields. Apply for internships by late Dec. Fee $50. (If accepted a $200 refundable deposit is required to hold position). ASF also assists with obtaining work permits for Scandinavia.

**Association for International Practical Training (AIPT)/International Association for the Exchange of Students for Technical Experience (IAESTE). Information and applications available from AIPT/IAESTE, 10400 Little Patuxent Pkwy., Suite 250, Columbia, MD 21044-3510; 410-997-2200, fax 410-992-3924; aipt@aipt.org; [www.aipt.org]. Nonprofit organization provides paid internships in over 60 countries in engineering and science (apply by Jan 1), and in tourism and hotel and restaurant management. They can also assist in obtaining work permits for career-related practical training in most fields.

*CDS International, Inc. Free booklet and applications available from CDS, 871 United Nations Plaza, 15th Fl., New York, NY 10017-1814; 212-497-3500, fax 212-497-3535; info@cdsintl.org, [www.cdsintl.org]. Nonprofit organization offers several paying internship programs (deadlines as early as December) in Germany in fields ranging from business to engineering. Programs for college students and professionals. Some knowledge of German usually required. The CDS web site lists internship placements which become available year round. CDS also assists with obtaining work permits for Germany. Most programs have fees from $200-$400.

**Directory of International Internships: A World of Opportunities edited by Charles A. Gliozzo and Vernicka K. Tyson. 1998. 4th edition. 162 pp. Michigan State Univ. Career Services and Placement. $25 postpaid from Michigan State Univ., Career Services and Placement, Attn: Directory of International Internships, 113 Student Services Bldg., East Lansing, MI 48824; 517-355-9510 ext. 146, fax 517-353-2957, [www.isp.msu.edu/InternationalInternships]. This is the most comprehensive directory of both academic and non-academic internships abroad. Describes experiential educational opportunities offered through educational institutions, governmental, and private organizations—for academic credit, for pay, or simply for experience. In-depth profiles of more than 200 internship programs offered by over 160 organizations. Very useful cross-indexes by subject and country.

A Handbook for Creating Your Own Internship in International Development by Natalie Foster and Nicole Howell (Just Act: Youth Action for Global Justice, 333 Valencia St., #101, San Francisco, CA 94110; 415-431-4204, fax 415-431-5953; sahar@justact.org, [www.justact.org]). Includes practical advice and a workbook to help evaluate your skills, motivations, and learning objectives. For a directory of opportunities, contact Just Act about their new publication.

*International Cooperative Education Work Abroad Program. Free information from ICE, 15 Spiros Way, Menlo Park, CA 94025; 650-323-4944, fax 650-323-1104; ICEmenlo@ aol.com, [www.icemenlo.com]. Organization offers 450 paid summer internships for students with knowledge of foreign languages (German, Finnish, French, Italian, Chinese, Japanese) in Europe and Asia. U.S. or Canadian citizens preferred. Apply by February. Fee of $800.

International Health Electives for Medical Students. American Medical Student Association. $15 from AMSA Resource Center, 1902 Association Dr., Reston, VA 20191; 800-767-2266 fax 703-620-5873; amsa@www.amsa. org, [www.amsa.org] (see "International Health" section.) Overseas internships for third- or fourth-year medical students. Related titles, **A Student's Guide to International Health** ($8), **Cross-Cultural Medicine: What to Know Before You Go** ($8), and **Creative Funding for International Health Electives** ($5) also available from AMSA. Most publications available free on AMSA web site.

*The Internship Bible by Mark Oldman and Samer Hamadeh. 2000 (Annual). 641 pp. $25. Princeton Review, distributed by Random House, available through Velarde Publicity; 212-572-2870, fax 212-572-6026; [www. review.com]. Directory describes in detail paid and unpaid internships offered by nearly 900 mostly non-academic organizations. Around 120 of these organizations have overseas branches, listed in an index for location, though it's often not made clear which of these actually offer internships abroad. Other indexes for field, benefits, level of study, minority programs, and deadlines.

*Internships International, P.O. Box 480, Woolrich, ME 04579-0480; 207-443-3019, fax 207-442-7942; intintl@aol.com, [http://rtpnet.org/~intintl]. Organization offers unpaid, not-for-credit internship placements in all fields for college graduates (or seniors who need an internship for graduation) in London, Paris, Dresden, Florence, Dublin, Melbourne, Budapest, Santiago, Glasgow. Fee of $800 ($1,000 for Dublin).

LEAPNow: Lifelong Education Alternatives & Programs. Download brochure available from web site or available from LEAPNow, P.O. Box 1817, Sebastopol, CA 95473; 707-829-1142, fax 707-829-1132; info@leapnow.org, [www.leap-now.org]. LEAPNow is a leading source for low-cost internships, volunteers positions, work exchanges, and experiential academic programs in 129 countries and the U.S. Over 20,000 options and 20 years experience tailoring custom programs for people of all ages and backgrounds. Academic credit available for all programs.

*Peterson's Study Abroad & Summer Study Abroad. (See Worldwide Overviews section). These directories of study abroad programs list over 700 internships in a special index. Most are for academic credit.

*U.S. Department of State Student Intern Program. Free brochure and application from U.S. Department of State, Intern Coordinator, Recruitment Division, Box 9317, Arlington, VA 22219; (703) 875-4884; [www.state.gov/ www/careers]. Nearly 1,000 mostly unpaid internships in international relations annually, in Washington and abroad. Only for currently-enrolled undergraduate and graduate students who will continue studies after the internship. Competitive. Deadlines: Nov 1 (Summer), Mar 1 (Fall), Jul 1 (Spring).

Workplace: The Complete Guide to Work Experience and Work Placements edited by Thom Sewell and Lindsey Smith. 1997. 224 pp. Central Bureau (U.K.), distributed in the U.S. by IIE. $18.95 from IIE (See Key Publishers). Intended for a British audience, this thoroughly-researched book is a guide to work placements for internships and practical training. Index for type of work but not for location. Unfortunately, it omits some organizations of interest to U.S. students or omits relevant U.S. addresses.

A Year Between: The Complete International Guide to Work, Training, and Travel in a Year Out edited by Lindsey Smith and Lorraine Rodgers. 1997. 352 pp. Central Bureau (U.K.), distributed in the U.S. by IIE. $18.95 from IIE. Intended for a British audience, this thoroughly-researched book describes over 100 internships, teaching, and volunteer possibilities of up to 1 year, primarily in Britain and Europe. Unfortunately, it omits some organizations of interest to U.S. students or omits the relevant U.S. addresses.

International Internships
Directory of Programs

By Transitions Abroad Editors

For the most up-to-date information on international internship programs check the *Transitions Abroad* web site [www.TransitionsAbroad.com], or contact the program directors. Please tell them you read about their program in this book. Programs based in more than one country or region are listed under "Worldwide."

WORLDWIDE

AIPT Exchanges

Founded in 1950, AIPT is the foremost provider of worldwide on-the-job training programs for students and professionals seeking international career development and life-changing experiences. AIPT arranges workplace exchanges in hundreds of fields, bringing employers and trainees together from around the world. AIPT is the U.S. affiliate of the IAESTE program, which provides international training opportunities and work permits for university students in technical fields.
Dates: Year round. **Cost:** A nonrefundable application fee must be submitted with each application. Cooperating organizations in some countries require additional application and/or program fees. Please contact AIPT for details. **Contact:** Sally Keller, Customer Service Representative, Association for International Practical Training, 10400 Little Patuxent Pkwy., Suite 250, Columbia, MD 21044-3510; 410-997-2200, fax 410-992-3924; aipt@aipt.org, [www.aipt.org].

Boston Univ. International Programs

Students enroll in 3 academic courses in conjunction with an academic internship. Students choose from internships in advertising and public relations, arts administration, business and economics, health and human service, hospitality administration, the media (journalism, film, and television), politics, and prelaw. The internship experience allows students to explore organizations from multinational corporations to local businesses, from hospitals to community service centers, from major magazine publishers or film production studios to local radio or advertising agencies. Academic credit offered. Prerequisites: good academic standing, 3.0 GPA; language depending on site. Application materials: 2 references, transcript, essays, academic approval, interview for upper-level language programs.
Dates: Fall, spring, and summer (length varies). Application deadline: Mar 15 (fall); Oct 15 (spring); Mar 1 (summer). **Cost:** $5,160-$16,575. Application fee: $45. **Contact:** Boston Univ., International Programs, 232 Bay State Rd., 5th Fl., Boston, MA 02215; 617-353-9888, fax 617-353-5402; abroad@bu.edu, [www.bu.edu/abroad].

Directory of Int'l Internships

The Directory is a comprehensive guide to international internships sponsored by educational institutions, government agencies, and private organizations. The Directory consists of 170 pages which includes subject and location indexes, international internship opportunities, and a bibliography.
Dates: Up-to-date, 4th ed., revised in late 1998. **Cost:** $25 includes s/h. **Contact:** Charles Gliozzo, Michigan State Univ., Rm. 209, International Center, E. Lansing, MI 48824; 517-353-5589, fax 517-353-7254; gliozzo@pilot.msu.edu, [www.isp.msu.edu].

Global Campus—Study Abroad

Select from a growing list of programs in Costa Rica, Ecuador, England, France, India, Kenya, Mexico, Senegal, and Venezuela. Curriculum may include language, culture, area studies, international development, and much more with integrated classroom options. Internships are available for credit at many sites. Open to all students and professionals.
Dates: Academic year, semester, quarter, and summer options. Academic year, semester, quarter, and summer options. **Cost:** From $2,900-$16,900. Includes tuition, study abroad, and reg-

istration fees, room and board, and excursions. **Contact:** Global Campus, Study Abroad, Univ. of Minnesota, 230 Heller Hall, 271 19th Ave. S, Minneapolis, MN 55455; 612-626-9000, fax 612-626-8009; UMabroad@umn.edu, [www.UMabroad.umn.edu].

Global Service Corps

Service-learning, cultural immersion in Costa Rica, Kenya, or Thailand. Live with a village family while assisting grassroots organizations on community service and development projects. Project areas: rainforest conservation, sustainable agriculture, HIV/AIDS awareness, clinical health care, women's groups, classroom teaching. Experience the challenges of developing countries from the inside out. Includes orientation, training, and excursions. University credit available.
Dates: Year round. Contact GSC office or check the web site for specific starting dates. **Cost:** $1,795-$1,995 for 2-4 week project trips; $595 per month for 2-6-month long-term extensions $2,815-$3,145 for summer and semester internships. Includes extensive pre-departure preparation and in-country expenses (hotel and homestay room and board, orientation, training, project expenses, transportation, excursions). Airfare not included, discount rates available. **Contact:** Global Service Corps., 300 Broadway, #28, San Francisco, CA 94133; 415-788-3666 ext. 128, fax 415-788-7324; gsc@earthisland. org, [www.globalservicecorps.org].

Internship Programs (Nicaragua, Bolivia, Tanzania)

Volunteers intern with local nonprofit groups, live with host families, and work in various areas of community development: women's issues, youth development, health, environment, economics, business, human rights, etc. Complete immersion, extensive support network.
Dates: Summer programs: 8-10 weeks beginning in June, other programs available year round. **Cost:** Starts at $1,200, depends on length and program. **Contact:** Alicia Robb, Director, Foundation for Sustainable Development, 5547 Miteham Ct., Springfield, VA; fsd@interconnection.org, [www.interconnection.org/fsd].

Internships International

Quality, nonpaying internships in London, Paris, Dublin, Dresden, Santiago, Budapest, Melbourne, Bangkok, and Glasgow. Internships in all fields, from 8 weeks to 6

months. Open to college graduates and seniors requiring an internship to graduate.
Dates: Based on individual's needs. **Cost:** $800 program fee for all cities except Dublin ($1,000). **Contact:** Judy Tilson, Director, **Internships International,** P.O. Box 480, Woolrich, ME 04579-0480; 207-443-3019, fax 207-442-7942; intintl@aol.com, [http://rtpnet.org/~intintl].

Marist International Internships

Internship and study abroad programs in Sydney, Australia; Leeds, England; Dublin, Ireland; Florence, Italy; Madrid, Spain. Programs combine internships, homestays, and course work at host institutions.
Dates: Fall and spring semesters and full academic year. **Cost:** Average program fee is $11,000. **Contact:** Carol Toufali, Marist College, 290 North Rd., Poughkeepsie, NY 12601; 914-575-3330, fax 914-575-3294; international@marist.edu, [www.marist.edu/international].

Australian Internships

Interns are placed with research teams, Australian employers, political administrations, etc., for periods ranging from 6 weeks to a year. Positions are unpaid, homestay (or other) accommodations are included. Placement is arranged to suit the individual provided 4 months notice is given. Most placements are in Queensland or New South Wales. Fields: marine and wildlife biology, business, etc. No academic credit. Unlimited internships. Prerequisites: a) High School Graduates, b) Professional Development for Graduates and Junior/Senior college students.
Dates: Year round. Application deadline: Four months before start date. **Cost:** $2,455 (includes room and board) for 6-week program. Application fee: $500. **Contact:** Dr. Maurice A. Howe, Education Australia, P.O. Box 2233, Amherst, MA 01004; 800-344-6741, fax 413-549-0741; edaust@javanet.com.

BELIZE

Internships in Belize

Interns live with host families. Following a 1-week orienion, participants work full time in various non-governmental agencies. Must be self-starters. Journals and written projects are submitted at the end of program for assessment. Academic credit offered: 15 to 16 credits per semester. Required: 2.5 cumulative GPA, strong performance in major, maturity, and adaptability; junior or senior status. **Dates:** Fall and spring, 17 weeks each. **Cost:** $4,400 includes room and board, health insurance, local transportation, international airfare, and orientation. **Contact:** Office of International Programs, Box 2000, SUNY Cortland, Cortland, NY 13045; 607-753-2209, fax 607-753-5989; studyabroad@cortland.edu, [www.studyabroad.com/suny/Cortland].

COSTA RICA

Learn Spanish While Volunteering

Assist with the training of Costa Rican public school teachers in ESL and computers. Assist local health clinic, social service agencies, and environmental projects. Enjoy learning Spanish in the morning, volunteer work in the afternoon/evening. Spanish classes of 2 to 4 students plus group learning activities; conversations with middle class homestay families (1 student or couple per family). Homestays and most volunteer projects are within walking distance of school in small town near the capital, San Jose. **Dates:** Year round, all levels. Classes begin every Monday (except Apr 17-21 and Dec 18-29), volunteer program is continuous. **Cost:** $345 per week for 23 hours of classes and group activities plus Costa Rican dance and cooking classes. Includes tuition, 3 meals per day, 7 days per week, homestay, laundry, all materials, weekly 3-hour cultural tour, and airport transportation. $25 1-time registration fee. **Contact:** Susan Shores, Registrar, Latin American Language Center, PMB 123, 7485 Rush River Dr., Suite 710, Sacramento, CA 95831-5260; 916-447-0938, fax 916-428-9542; lalc@madre.com.

CZECH REPUBLIC

Penn-in-Prague

For students interested in Czech and central European culture, this program, located amidst the fairy tale beauty of Prague and affiliated with Charles Univ., offers an insight into the rich history and urgent contemporary problems of this important region, as well as an opportunity to learn beginning and intermediate Czech. **Dates:** Jul 3-Aug 11. **Cost:** Tuition $3,190; housing and activities $350. **Contact:** Penn Summer Abroad, College of General Studies, Univ. of Pennsylvania, 3440 Market St., Suite 100, Philadelphia, PA 19104-3335; 215-898-5738, fax

215-573-2053; sdanti@sas.upenn.edu, [www.sasupenn.edu/CGS].

ECUADOR

Academia Latinoamericana

Proud to be the friendliest Spanish school you have ever known. Family owned and operated. The program offers language study at 9 levels, for complete beginners through advanced. Experienced staff, native Ecuadorians. Carefully selected host families within walking distance of school. Exclusive "SierrAzul Cloud Forest and Galápagos" extension program, volunteer program. U.S. college credit available. **Dates:** Year round. **Cost:** $230 per week. Includes 20 hours of lessons, 7 days with host family, 2 meals per day, transfer, services at the school, and teaching material. **Contact:** Suzanne S. Bell, Admissions Director, USA/International, 640 East 3990 South, Suite E, Salt Lake City, UT, 84107; 801-268-4608, fax 801-265-9156; academia@juno.com, [delco@spanish.com.ec].

Internships in Latin America

Emphasis on community participation for social change. Students work 3 days a week in an internship, also meet together for core seminar and internship seminar, and carry out independent study project. Wide range of internship opportunities in community development, health, environment, youth concerns, and women's issues. Family homestay, field trips, Latin American faculty. Full semester credit, U.S. transcript provided. All majors, 2 years Spanish language required. **Dates:** Early Feb-mid-May. **Cost:** $9,450 (spring 2001). Includes tuition, internship placement and supervision, room and board, field trips. **Contact:** Rebecca Rassier, Director of Student Services, HECUA, Mail #36, Hamline Univ., 1536 Hewitt Ave., St. Paul, MN 55104-1284; 612-646-8832 or 800-554-1089; info@hecua.org, [www.hecua.org].

EUROPE

¿?don Quijote Spanish Schools

Spanish language courses in 6 schools in Spain and 5 partner schools. Courses (standard, intensive, business, D.E.L.E., tourism, flight attendants and refresher for teachers) are year round, from 2 weeks on. Students can combine different cities and schools. Academic credit is available.

Dates: Year round—fall, spring, winter, and summer, 2 weeks to a full year of study. **Cost:** Email or check web site for details. **Contact:** ¿?don Quijote In-Country Spanish Language Schools, calle/Placentinos n°2, Salamanca 37008, Spain; 011-34-923-268860, fax 011-34-923-268815; amusa@donquijote.org, [www.donquijote.org].

Internship Program

CCI's Discovery Abroad Internship Program gives students (18-28) the opportunity to participate in a volunteer internship in 1 of 7 countries. Internships provide exciting opportunities for language and cross-cultural immersion and work experience. Participants live with a host family for the duration of the program and will be placed in an internship related to their course of study.
Dates: Year round. **Cost:** 1 month approx. $1,800, 2 months approx. $2,500, 3 months approx. $3,200. **Contact:** Outbound Department, Center for Cultural Interchange, 17 N. 2nd Ave., St. Charles, IL 60174; 888-ABROAD1, fax 630-377-2307; karen@cci-exchange.com, [www.cci-exchange.com].

Internships in Europe/E.P.A.

The Univ. of Rochester and Educational Programs Abroad sponsor programs in London, Bonn, Brussels, Madrid, and Paris that combine coursework with unpaid internships for academic credit. Fields include politics, law, business, health science, and the arts. Available to juniors, seniors, and recent graduates. Requirements: 3.0 GPA or better, and at least 2 years of college-level language study where appropriate.
Dates: Sep-Dec, Jan-Apr; 2 summer terms of 8 weeks each. **Cost:** Semester programs range from $6,700-$9,650; summer $5,290. **Contact:** Jacqueline Levine, Director, Center for Study Abroad, Univ. of Rochester, Rochester, NY 14627; 716-275-7532, fax 716-461-5131; abroad@mail.rochester.edu, [www.rochester.edu/college/study-abroad/europe].

FRANCE

French Language Courses

Founded in 1995, LSF specializes in all-inclusive French language vacation courses in Montpellier, Paris, and Bayonne. In 1997 opened a year-round school for adults in the heart of Montpellier's old town. Students follow a wide range of French language programs—general and business French, DELF and DALF exam preparation classes, teacher training, and internships.
Dates: Year round. **Cost:** From FF1,120. **Contact:** Langues Sans Frontières, 3 Impasse Barnabé, Montpellier 34000, France; 011-33-467-91-31-60, fax 011-33-467-91-31-61; info@lsf.fr, [www.lsf.fr].

Penn-in-Compiègne

For students with some proficiency in French who are interested in international relations, sociology, economics, or business. The program, affiliated with The Université de Technologie de Compiègne, also offers a 2-week internship in a French enterprise. Students live with local families.
Dates: May 27-Jul 6; with internship: May 27-Jul 20. **Cost:** Tuition $3,190; room and board, and activities $900 (study only) or $1,200 (full program). **Contact:** Penn Summer Abroad, College of General Studies, Univ. of Pennsylvania, 3440 Market St., Suite 100, Philadelphia, PA 19104; 215-898-5738, fax 215-573-2053; sdanti@sas.upenn.edu, [www.sas.upenn.edu/CGS].

GERMANY

Learn German and Discover Berlin

GLS, one of the leading institutions teaching German as a foreign language in Germany, offers various levels of German all year round (age 16 and up), preparation for all language certificates, business German, German for bankers and lawyers. Special feature: internships in German companies. GLS has accreditation with some U.S. universities.
Dates: Year round. **Cost:** Price example: $1,080 standard 4-week course and apartment share.
Contact: GLS Sprachenzentrum, Barbara Jaeschke, Managing Director, Kolonnenstrasse 26, 10829 Berlin, Germany; 011-49-30-780-08-90; fax 011-49-30-787-41-92; deutschkurse@gls-berlin@.de, [www.gls-berlin.com].

INDIA

Penn-in-India

For students interested in South Asian studies, performing arts, religion, and traditional medicine, PSA's newest program offers students a survey of both India's rich cultural history and its burgeoning industrial life. The program is located in Pune, a cosmopolitan city of 4,000,000 which is a thriving arts center, a hub of scholarship, and a growing economic presence. Students will live with Indian families in the area and be involved in community projects.

Dates: Jun 6-Jul 21. **Cost:** Tuition $3,190; program $1,790. **Contact:** Penn Summer Abroad, College of General Studies, Univ. of Pennsylvania, 3440 Market St., Suite 100, Philadelphia, PA 19104; 215-898-5738, fax 215-573-2053; sdanti@sas.upenn. edu, [www.sas.upenn.edu/CGS/].

LATIN AMERICA

Internship Positions

In Costa Rica, Mexico, Guatemala, Ecuador, Argentina, Peru, Bolivia. Positions in health care, education, tourism, ESL, business, law, marketing, administrative, environmental, and social work. Additional customized options available. Four weeks to 6 months. Inexpensive lodging in homestays or dorms. Some positions provide free room and board. **Dates:** Year round. Flexible start dates. **Cost:** $350 placement and application fee. Travel insurance and pre-departure preparation included. Lodging costs depend on location. **Contact:** AmeriSpan Unlimited, P.O. Box 40007, Philadelphia, PA 19106; 800-879-6640, fax 215-751-1100; info@amerispan.com, [www.amerispan.com].

MEXICO

El Bosque del Caribe, Cancun

Take a professional Spanish course 25 hours per week and enjoy the Caribbean beaches. Relaxed family-like atmosphere. No more than 6 students per class. Special conversation program. Mexican cooking classes and excursions to the Mayan sites. Housing with Mexican families. College credit available. **Dates:** Year round. New classes begin every Monday. Group programs arranged at reduced fees. **Cost:** Enrollment fee $120, $185 per week. One week with a Mexican family $160. Book included. **Contact:** Eduardo Sotelo, Director, Calle Piña 1, S.M. 25, 77500 Cancún, Mexico; 011-52-98-84-10-38, fax 011-52-98-84-58-88; bcaribe@mail.cancun-language.com.mx.

POLAND

Penn-in-Warsaw

For students interested in Polish history and culture, as well as international relations, economics, and other business disciplines. Taught in English, this program will acquaint students with the political and economic changes occurring in Poland and provide insight into the conditions for doing business in a changing economy. Short-term internships with Polish or joint-venture institutions will complement class instruction.

Dates: Jun 24-Jul 28. **Cost:** Tuition $3,190; housing $250. **Contact:** Penn Summer Abroad, College of General Studies, Univ. of Pennsylvania, 3440 Market St., Suite 100, Philadelphia, PA 19104-3335; 215-898-5738, fax 215-573-2053; sdanti@sas.upenn.edu, [www.sas.upenn.edu/CGS/].

RUSSIA

ACTR Business Russian Language and Internship Program

This program combines a curriculum focusing on the language of Russian business communication with a 20-hour per week internship in a U.S. or Russian business, NGO, or government agency. The program emphasizes speaking and reading skills for business communications, commercial document preparation, and reading the Russian business press. **Dates:** Summer term, academic year, fall and spring. **Cost:** Summer $5,000, fall/spring terms $7,250, academic year $12,450. **Contact:** Graham Hettlinger, Gabriel Coleman, or Terrence Graham, ACTR, 1776 Massachusetts Ave., NW, Suite 700, Washington, DC 20036; 202-833-7522, fax 202-833-7523; hettlinger@actr.org, [www.actr.org].

SPAIN

Acento Español

Spanish tailored to your needs. Eight levels, small groups (maximum 8 students per class). We provide accommodations for our students and organize a wide range of cultural and social activities. **Dates:** Courses start every Monday year round, for beginners every second Monday. **Cost:** Fifteen hours per week PTS64,000, 4 weeks; 20 hours per week PTS76,000, 4 weeks. **Contact:** Acento Español, Calle Mayor, 4- 6º, 9, Madrid 28013, Spain; 011-34-91-521-36-76, fax 011-34-91-531-71-12; acentoes@teleline.es, [www.acentoespanol.es].

International Program in Toledo

Great location with its historical and artist heritage. Participants with 2 years of Spanish select from a variety of Spanish language and courses taught in Spanish. New internship options available for credit. Summer term requires 1 year of Spanish. Monday-Thursday classes enhanced by excursions. Housing available in historic residence or with Spanish families. Univ. of Minnesota accredited.

Dates: Fall and/or spring semester, summer term. **Cost:**$8,665 (fall or spring), $3,775 (summer). Includes tuition, study abroad and registration fees, room and board, and 1-day excursions. **Contact:** Global Campus, Study Abroad, Univ. of Minnesota, 230 Heller Hall, 271 19th Ave. S, Minneapolis, MN 55455; 612-626-9000, fax 612-626-8009; UMabroad@umn.edu, [www.UMabroad.umn.edu].

Seville Internship Option

Three- or 6-credit internship available to students attending the CC-CS academic program during fall or spring semester. Applicants must have completed 1 advanced college-level Spanish course. Internships are unpaid and not guaranteed. Many potential areas available. An internship application must be requested in addition to the program application.

Dates: Spring: Jan 25-May 24. Fall: Aug 30-Dec 19. **Cost:** Semester $7,995. Includes tuition, double occupancy room and full board, laundry, study visits, orientation, health insurance, enrollment, activity and computer fees including email account. **Contact:** Dr. Judith Ortiz, Director U.S., Center for Cross-Cultural Study, 446 Main St., Amherst, MA 01002; 800-377-2621, fax 413-256-1968; cccs@crocker.com, [www.cccs.com].

UNITED KINGDOM AND IRELAND

AIFS Int'l Internship in London

A 1-semester program awarding 12 to 18 credits for an unpaid internship in London. Placements are in international business, finance, marketing, international relations, education, media, museums and galleries, art and design firms, theater and entertainment. Individual attention given to clarify and set goals, support during placement.

Dates: Sep-Dec; Jan-May. **Cost:** $11,000 includes tuition, housing, most meals and one-way flight to London from any of 28 U.S. cities. **Contact:** AIFS, River Plaza, 9 West Broad St., Stamford, CT 06902-3788; collegeinfo@aifs.com, [www.aifs.com/college/css/intern/intern.htm].

AIU London Internship Program

AIU offers undergraduate and graduate students the opportunity to gain international work experience within an academically supervised format. Based upon the program students choose, they are able to earn up to 10 quarter hours, 6 semester hours of academic credit for their internship placement.

Dates: Five regular academic quarters: fall (Oct-Dec); winter (Jan-Mar); spring (Mar-May); summer I (Jun or Jul); summer II (Aug-Sep). **Cost:** Part-time $1,450; full-time $2,900. **Contact:** American InterContinental Univ., 6600 Peachtree-Dunwoody Rd., 500 Embassy Row, Atlanta, GA 30328; 800-255-6839, fax 404-965-8006; studyabroad@aiuniv.edu, [http://studyabroad.aiuniv.edu].

Internships in Dublin

Interns live with families or in apartments. Two programs available: 6-credit internship plus 9-credit classwork in Irish Studies through the Institute of Public Administration or full-time (15-16 credits) internship. IPA placements may be in Parliament, municipal government, health care administration, radio/TV, and at the *Irish Times*. Full-time placements available in social services, communication, film, advertising and others. Fields: public administration, parliamentary internships, political science, technology, finance, health and communications. Prerequisites: 2.5 GPA for traditional internships, 3.0 for IPA internships. Adaptability and maturity. Strong performance in major. Junior or senior status. Application materials: SUNY application.

Dates: Fall: early Sep-mid-Dec (application deadline Feb 1); spring: early Jan-late Apr (application deadline Sep 1); summer: early Jun-mid-Aug (application deadline Feb 1). **Cost:** (2001): IPA $5,730 per semester, Dublin internships $4,855 per semester, Dublin internships summer $3,650 (IPA not available). Estimates include full-day orientation before departure, application fee, room and board, food allowance, health and accident insurance, roundtrip airfare from N.Y., bus pass. SUNY tuition not included. **Contact:** Office of International Programs, Box 2000, SUNY Cortland, Cortland, NY 13045; 607-753-2209, fax 607-753-5989; studyabroad@cortland. edu, [www.studyabroad.com/suny/Cortland].

London Internship Program

A pioneer of supervised work experience, Middlesex Univ. offers one of the widest range of internships in the U.K. Year-long opportunities are available to gain experience in business, politics, community, and health, amongst others. All internships are project-based, academically supervised, and carry academic credit. Internships can be taken alongside other university courses.

Dates: Fall, spring, or summer semester. Cost: Approx. $1,950 (tuition and internship). Contact: Valdev Chaggar, Registry Admissions, Middlesex Univ., White Hart Ln., London N17 8HR, U.K.; 011-44-203-362-5782, fax 011-44-208-362-5649; admissions@mdx.ac.uk.

Study in Great Britain

Thirty-one program opportunities in England, Scotland, and Wales. University study and special subject area, including internships, for fall, spring, academic year and summer. Program provides a full range of services including predeparture advising, orientation, homestay, and guaranteed housing. Need-based scholarships available.

Dates: Fall, spring, academic year. Summer semester and terms. Cost: Varies. Call for current fees. Contact: Beaver College Center for Education Abroad, 450 S. Easton Rd., Glenside, PA 19038-3295; 888-BEAVER-9, fax 215-572-2174; cea@beaver.edu, [www.beaver.edu/cea].

Univ. of North London

SUNY Cortland celebrates its 28th year at UNL. Over 400 courses are offered. Fields of study include education, natural sciences, humanities, communications, social sciences, business, health, theater arts, and others. Direct enrollment with British students. Credits per semester: 12-16. Pre-arranged housing in flats in the Bayswater district. Full- and part-time internships available.

Dates: Spring: end-Jan-mid-May. Cost: Estimates: spring 2001: $7,350 per semester; academic year: $13,000. Estimates include full-day orientation in the U.S., application fee, pre-arranged apartment rental, meals, commuter ticket on underground, London tour and Thames cruise, insurance, roundtrip airfare from N.Y., transportation from airport to downtown London upon arrival, passport, books and supplies, various cultural activities, administrative fees. SUNY tuition and spending money not included. Contact: Office of International Programs, Box 2000, SUNY Cortland, Cortland, NY 13045; 607-753-2209, fax 607-753-5989; studyabroad@cortland.edu, [www.studyabroad.com/suny/Cortland].

UNITED STATES

Masters for International and Intercultural Management

The School for International Training (SIT) is recognized around the world for providing students with the competencies required to teach, manage, and advocate for a just and sustainable world. Academic curriculum is integrated with field-based practice, reflection, and application and includes a period of professional practice. As a result, students acquire the cross-cultural, language, management, and teaching skills to be effective leaders in their fields throughout the world. SIT offers master's degrees in Teaching (ESOL, French, Spanish), Intercultural Relations, International Education, Sustainable Development, Organizational Management, and a self-design option. SIT also offers professional certificates in a variety of areas, as well as undergraduate semester abroad programs in over 45 countries.

Dates: Call for details. Cost: Call for details. Contact: Admissions, School for International Learning, P.O. Box 676, Kipling Rd., Brattleboro, VT 05302; 800-336-1616, 802-257-7751, fax 802-258-3500; info@sit.edu, [www.sit.edu].

The National Council on U.S.–Arab Relations

This organization offers a variety of internships that allow students in the fields of International Business, Relations, Finance, or Governance to explore their areas of interest while developing tangible skills desired by today's employers. Full-time and part-time internship opportunities exist for those students desiring to work in the contextual region of the Middle East.

Dates: Ongoing recruitment. Cost: Call for information. Contact: National Council on U.S.-Arab Relations, 202-293-0801; internship@ncusar.org.

The Best Web Sites

Internet Resources for Finding Scholarships and Internships

Selected and Reviewed by William Nolting

Scholarships for undergraduates and for nonacademic work abroad are relatively rare; funding for graduate students, postdocs, and professionals tends to be more readily available. For other options, fundraising through job savings, family, friends, hometown organizations such as Rotary, Kiwanis, Optimist, and religious organizations may be more effective than scholarships. The sites of AMSA and WorldTeach have "non-traditional" fundraising suggestions useful for anyone.

**Essential; *Outstanding and of broad interest.
(I) Informational site with directories or databases listing many programs
(P) Site for a specific work abroad program
(S) Scholarships or fellowships

* (I) American Medical Student Association [www.amsa.org/gh.html] lists overseas internship and volunteer programs, including options for premed and other health sciences—see International Health Opportunities section. Site includes an excellent online guide to fundraising, *Creative Funding Guide*, useful for all students.

** (S) Council Bowman Scholarship [www.ciee.org/study/scholarships]. CIEE's undergraduate scholarship funds the cost of airfare and can be used for study, work, volunteering, or research in developing countries (i.e. excluding Australia, Canada, Europe, Israel, Japan, Korea, New Zealand, Russia, Singapore). Students at CIEE member institutions, participants in CIEE programs, and students at institutions which sell ISIC cards are eligible. Application deadlines are twice a year, typically in October and March or early April.

** (S) Fulbright scholarships and teaching programs [www.iie.org/fulbright]. All the Fulbright programs—official exchange programs for teaching, study or research—are described here; Fulbright Student programs (including scholarships and English Teaching Assistantships) are for graduating seniors, graduate students, and alumni; Fulbright Scholar programs are for university faculty and international education administrators. The Fulbright Teacher Exchange is for cur-

rently employed K-12 and community college teachers.

** (I, S, P) Institute of International Education [www.iie.org], Financial Resources for International Study and Funding for United States Study, Marie O'Sullivan and Sara Steen, editors. IIE publishes of some of the best hard-copy directories of scholarships for overseas opportunities, which include grants for all levels of students as well as for postdoctorates and professionals. IIE's databases are available on its site. Search terms "work," "internship," "practical," "teach," "research" all yield a good number of listings. Full texts are available only to those at IIE member institutions with password provided by IIE (for password, send email to: membership@iie.org). Or, use the search with book in hand; most college libraries have these books.

* (I) National Association of Financial Aid Administrators [www.finaid.org]. Site of the main U.S. professional association for financial aid administrators. Search using terms such as "study abroad" or "work abroad."

(S, P) Minority International Research Training Grant (MIRT) [www.nih.gov/fic/programs/mirt.html]. Program of the Fogarty International Center/National Institutes of Health sends minority undergraduates and medical students abroad to do health-related research. Apply through one of the centers listed.

** (I) Reference Service Press, Financial Aid for Study and Training Abroad and Financial Aid for Research and Creative Activities Abroad [www.rspfunding.com]. RSP publishes of some of the best hard-copy directories of scholarships for overseas opportunities, which include grants for all levels of students as well as for postdoctorates and professionals. Its databases are available online to America Online subscribers (keyword RSP), or through some university libraries to their own students.

** (S) Rotary Foundation Ambassadorial Scholarships [www.rotary.org]. The Rotary Foundation provides the largest single U.S. scholarship program for study abroad. Scholarships are available for all levels of study, from highschool, undergraduate, and graduate students to alumni and professionals. Generally not for use with study abroad programs sponsored by U.S. institutions. Application possible only through local Rotary Clubs. Deadlines (locally-determined) may be as much as one and one-half years in advance. Web site provides scholarship information and lists Rotary clubs worldwide.

** (I) Univ.of Minnesota, International Study and Travel Center Scholarships Database [www.istc.umn.edu/study/scholarships.html]. An excellent, free online database of scholarships. Search categories include study, research and internships as well as location and other variables.

* (S) U.S. State Department "International Information Programs" [www.usinfo.state.gov] in the Bureau of Educational and Cultural Affairs [http://exchanges.state.gov]. Official information about Fulbright and other US-sponsored programs for study, research, and teaching abroad.

* (I) U.S. Department of Education: Student Financial Assistance Programs, [www.ed.gov/offices/OSFAP/Students] and The Student Guide to Financial Aid [www.ed.gov/prog_info/SFA/StudentGuide]. The federal government's official guide to financial aid (which can be used only for academic study, including study-internship or study-volunteer programs).

* (I) WorldTeach [www.worldteach.org/funds.html]. Contains ideas for non-traditional fundraising.

(S) Woodrow Wilson International Fellowship Foundation [www.woodrow.org/public-policy]. Information on several multi-year scholarship-internship programs for students, especially women and minorities, interested in careers in international affairs.

Also From *Transitions Abroad*

Alternative Travel Directory: The Complete Guide to Living, Study, and Travel Overseas

The only comprehensive resource for travelers interested in alternatives to mass tourism. Use this highly acclaimed travel guide to start your next adventure.
"Of enormous assistance to those who want to strike out on their own. Highly recommended" (**Library Journal**). *"A nigh-well indispensable resource"* (**Arthur Frommer**). See page 187 for ordering information.

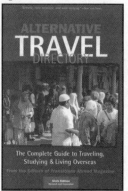

Transitions Abroad, P.O. Box 1300, Amherst, MA 01004; **800-293-0373;** **www.TransitionsAbroad.com.**

CHAPTER 4

SHORT-TERM JOBS ABROAD

The major fields of temporary employment abroad are tourism and agriculture, au pairing, English teaching, and volunteer work in exchange for room and board. The more you research before you go abroad the better; however, available information is often misleading. Remain determined in the face of discouragement and use the reliable resources compiled each year by Bill Nolting and published in the September/October issue of Transitions Abroad and on [www.TransitionsAbroad.com] to clarify what you want to do and determine what is possible.

Key Employers
Short-Term Jobs Abroad

Compiled by Susan Griffith

As a first step in finding short-term work, contact the embassy or consulate and the tourist office of the countries in which you want to work to find out the official line on visas, etc. In the old days, some job-seekers visited embassy libraries or reading rooms to check the "situations vacant" columns of national and preferably) local newspapers or to consult the telephone directories and yellow pages for lists of English language schools or other potential employers in their field. Increasingly, this information is available on the Internet.

If you are searching for a specific kind of job you might get leads by consulting the specialist press. Professionals should consult their own associations and journals. For example, teachers should look at *The International Educator*, P.O. Box 513, Cummaquid, MA 02637; [www.tieonline.com].

WORLDWIDE JOBS

AFS USA, 310 SW 4th Ave., Suite 630, Portland, OR 97204-2608; 800-AFS-INFO; [www.afs.org/usa]. Students aged 18-29 spend 6 or 12 months in 1 of 10 countries (in Latin America, Africa, Thailand, Russia, or France) living with a family and working voluntarily on a social project. Participants must fundraise before program begins.

Agriventure (International Agricultural Exchange Association), 1000 1st Ave. S, Great Falls, MT 59401; 406-727-1999; [www.agriventure.com/usa]. Farm placements of agricultural trainees in many European countries plus Japan, Australia, and New Zealand. A separate agricultural and horticultural work exchange exists between the U.S. and most European countries and elsewhere.

AIESEC (International Association for Students in Economics and Business Management), 135 W. 50th St., 17th Fl., New York, NY 10020; 212-757-3774, fax 212-757-4062; aiesec@us.aiesec.org, [www.us.aiesec.org]. Business-related jobs available in over 80 countries. Highly qualified interns must apply through an AIESEC chapter in the U.S.

AIFS (American Institute For Foreign Study), 38 Queen's Gate, London SW7 5HR, England; 011-44-171-590-7474. U.S. office: River Pl., 9 West Broad St., Stamford, CT 06902; tmdepartment@acis.com, [www.acis.com/contact/tourmanagers/index.asp]. One hundred tour managers needed to lead educational tours of Europe for North American students.

Alliances Abroad, 702 West Ave., Austin, TX 78701; 888-6-ABROAD; info@alliances-abroad.com, [www.alliancesabroad.com]. Range of programs include teaching in Mexico, Africa, and the Far East; unpaid internships and volunteer work in many countries including Ireland, Germany, Jamaica, Guatemala, and Ecuador. Fees vary; samples are $1,200 for up to 5 months of teaching in Mexico, and for 2-month internship in Dublin.

Amity Volunteer Teachers Abroad (AVTA), 10671 Roselle St., Suite 101, San Diego, CA 92121-1525; 858-455-6364; mail@amity.org, [www.amity.org]. Voluntary teaching in Latin America, Africa (Senegal and Ghana), and France while living with local families.

Association for International Practical Training, 10400 Little Patuxent Pkwy., Suite 250, Columbia, MD 21044-3510; 410-997-2200, fax 410-992-3249; aipt@aipt.org, [www.aipt.org]. Short- and long-term placements in over 60 countries through the International Association for the Exchange of Students for Technical Experience (IAESTE) available to students in science, engineering, math, agriculture, or architecture. Runs hotel and culinary exchanges to Austria, Finland, France, Germany, Ireland, Netherlands, Switzerland, U.K., Australia, and Japan, and career development exchanges for candidates who can find their own employer overseas.

Au Pair in Europe, P.O. Box 68056, Blakely Postal Outlet, Hamilton, ON L8M 3M7, Canada; 905-545-6305; aupair@princeent. com, [www.princeent.com/aupair]. Au pairs placed in

21 countries including Australia. Airfare reimbursement plan operates in Holland, Sweden, and Iceland. Administrative fee $425.

CCUSA/Work Experience Outbound, 2330 Marinship Way, Suite 250, Sausalito, CA 94965; 415-339-2728; outbound@workexperienceusa.com, [www.workexperienceoutbound.com]. Work programs in Russia (summer camp counselling), Brazil (4 to 12 weeks conservation volunteering), Australia, and New Zealand.

CDS International, 871 United Nations Plaza, 15th Fl., New York, NY 10017-1814; 212-497-3500, fax 212-497-3535; info@cdsintl.org; [www.cdsintl.org]. Arranges 3- to 6-month paid internships in Germany, Switzerland, Singapore, and Austria for students or recent graduates in business, engineering, and other technical fields. Longer placements of 12-18 months also available.

Communicating for Agriculture Exchange Program, 112 East Lincoln Ave., Fergus Falls, MN 56537; 218-739-3241; [http://ca.cainc.org/outbound]. Work abroad program in 23 countries from Chile to Latvia for people aged 18-28 with at least 1 year of experience in agriculture, horticulture, equine husbandry or oenology.

Council Exchanges, 633 3rd Ave, 20th Fl., New York, NY 10017-6706; 888-COUNCIL (268-6245); [www.councilexchanges.org]. Coordinates a working holiday program for U.S. college students to Ireland, France, Germany, Canada, New Zealand, Australia, and Costa Rica. The participation fee ranges from $300 to $425. Participants receive work documentation and access to job-finding assistance in the destination country. The Canadian equivalent is the Student Work Abroad Program (SWAP) administered by the Canadian Federation of Students, 45 Charles St. E., Suite 100, ON, M4Y 152, Canada.

ELS International Inc., 400 Alexander Park Dr., Princeton, NJ 08540; 609-514-9650. international@els.com, [www.els.com]. International chain of language schools. U.S. office is a clearinghouse of recruitment for ELS's 50 overseas franchises. Berlitz at the same address has frequent EFL teacher vacancies in Latin America, Korea, and Europe. Berlitz teachers must be university graduates and willing to be trained in the Berlitz method.

Explorations in Travel, 1922 River Rd, Guilford, VT 05301; 802-257-0152; explore@volunteertravel.com, [www.volunteertravel.com]. Volunteer environmental work placements and internships for students and adults in Australia, New Zealand, Belize, Costa Rica, Mexico, Ecuador, Puerto Rico, and Nepal. Placement fee $750-$950.

Global Routes, 510-848-4800; [www.global-routes.org]. Places volunteerswith families in rural communities in Costa Rica, Ecuador, Thailand, India, Kenya, Ghana, and the Navajo Nation to teach in local schools. Training, support, and adventure travel are integral parts of the program. Information on scholarships, fundraising, and academic credit is available. Program fee is $3,950 for summer semester, and $4,250 for fall and spring semesters.

Horizon Cosmopolite, 3011 Notre Dame Ouest, Montréal, Quebec, H4C 1N9, Canada; 514-935-8436; info@horizoncosmpolite.com, [www.horizoncosmopolite.com]. Maintains database of 1,500 opportunities abroad. Tries to match clients with suitable placements. Enrollment fee of CAN$345 guarantees placement.

Institute for Cultural Ecology, 758 Kapahula Ave., #500, Honolulu, HI 96816; 808-782-6166; reply@islandtime.org, [www.island-time.org/intern1.html]. Unpaid internships in Fiji, Thailand, and Hawaii working in villages or for environmental organizations for 4, 8, or 12 weeks. Sample fees: $1,900 for 4 weeks; $3,850 for 12 weeks.

InterExchange Program, 161 6th Ave., New York, NY 10013; 212-924-0446; info@interexchange.org, [www.interexchange.org]. Work placements for students in Germany and anyone 18-30 in France, Scandinavia, Switzerland, and Eastern Europe. Also au pair placements in Austria, Finland, Netherlands, Italy, Norway, and Spain. Teaching English in Russia, Ukraine, Bulgaria, and Poland. Fees are $400-$600.

Interlocken International, RR 2, Box 165, Hillsboro, NH 03244; 603-478-3166; fax 603-478-5260, kim@interlocken.org, [www.interlocken.org/jobs.htm]. Experienced leaders needed for small group travel programs for teens worldwide. Minimum age is 24. Ten-day orientation held in June.

International Cooperative Education, 15 Spiros Way, Menlo Park, CA 94025; 650-323-4944; info@icemenlo.com, [www.icemenlo .com]. Arranges paid summer work for 2-3 months in Germany, Switzerland, Belgium, Finland, Singapore, Japan, and Luxembourg. Jobs include retail sales, hotels and restaurants, agri-

culture, offices, etc.; most require knowledge of relevant language. Placement fee is $600 plus application fee of $200.

International House, 106 Piccadilly, London W1V 9NL, U.K.; 011-44-207-518 6970; [www.ihlondon.com[. With 120 schools in 30+ countries, IH is one of the largest English teaching organizations in the world. The Human Resources Department (address above) does much of the hiring of teachers-who must have an EFL certificate after completing a 4-week Cambridge CELTA or Trinity College London course.

International Schools Services, 609-452-0990, fax 609-452-2690; edustaffing@iss.edu, [www.iss.edu]. Applicants for overseas teaching positions in private American international-al schools are able to interview in the states at U.S.-based International Recruitment Centers. Applicants must have a Bachelor's degree and 2 years of current K-12 teaching experience.;

Internships International, P.O. Box 480, Woolrich, ME 04579-0480; 207-443-3019, fax 207-442-7942; intintl@aol.com, [http://rtp-net.org/~intintl]. Internships (unpaid) arranged in London, Glasgow, Dublin, Paris, Dresden, Florence, Budapest, Santiago, Bangkok, Shanghai, and Melbourne. Must be college senior or graduate. Application fee from $700.

i-to-i, 1 Cottage Rd., Headingley, Leeds LS6 4DD, U.K.; 0870-333 2332, fax 011-44-113 274 6923; info@i-to-i com, [www.i-to-i.com]. TEFL and voluntary placements in Africa, Latin America, Asia, and Australia.

People to People International, 501 E. Armour Blvd., Kansas City, MO 64109-2200; 816-531-4701; internships@ptpi.org. Two-month unpaid internships in Brazil, Denmark, England, Ireland, Spain. Interns can receive 6 hours of academic credit.

Taking Off, P.O. Box 104, Newton Highlands, MA 02161; 617-630-1606; tkingoff@aol.com, and Center for Interim Programs, P.O. Box 2347, Cambridge, MA 02238; 617-661-2864. Consulting services aimed primarily at pre-university and university students looking to arrange a worthwhile experience abroad, including paid and voluntary work.

Teaching & Projects Abroad, Gerrard House, Rustington, W. Sussex BN16 1AW, U.K.; 011-44-1903 859911; [www.teaching-abroad.co.uk]. Short-term unpaid teaching and other voluntary positions in Ukraine, Moscow, St. Petersburg and Siberia, Ghana, Mexico, Brazil, China, and India; expanding to Peru. Togo, Thailand and Zimbabwe. Fees from about £800-£1,300 (not including travel).

Travellers, 7 Mulberry Close, Ferring, West Sussex BN12 5HY, U.K.; Tel./fax 011-44-1903 502595; info@travellersworldwide.com. Volunteers can teach conversational English and other subjects in a growing range of countries including India, Nepal, Sri Lanka, Russia, Cuba, Ukraine, and Malaysia. Sample charge for 2- to 3-month stay in India and Sri Lanka is £925 excluding airfares.

Wall Street Institute International, Sylvan Learning Systems, Rambla de Catalunya 2-4, 08007, Barcelona, Spain; 011-34-93-412-0014, fax 011-34-93-412-3803; [www.educate.com]. Chain of 164 commercial language institutes for adults that employ approximately 350 full-time EFL teachers in Europe and Latin America. In some countries such as Spain the "Master Center" acts as a clearinghouse for teacher vacancies.

Willing Workers on Organic Farms-WWOOF, P.O. Box 2675, Lewes, Sussex BN7 1RB, England; [www.welcome.to/wwoof]. Connects members with organic farmers around Britain (annual membership £10). Irish equivalent is WWOOF Ireland, Harpoonstown, Drinagh, Co. Wexford, Ireland (membership $15).

YMCA Go Global, International YMCA, 71 West 23rd St, Suite 1904, New York, NY 10010; 212-727-8800/888-477-9622; ips@ymcanyc.org. Range of outbound programs lasting up to 3 or 6 months worldwide. Most consist of teen leadership, English teaching or camp counseling.

AFRICA

Travelers sometimes negotiate teaching contracts in East Africa and casual tutoring in Cairo on the spot. It may also be possible to join conservation or scientific research trips for a fee. Additional contacts include:

American Language Center, 4 Zankat Tanja, Rabat, 10000 Morocco; 011-212-7-761269/766121, fax 011-212-7-767-6255; alcrabat@mtds.com. The largest of 7 ALCs in Morocco, which hires EFL teachers for 1 year.

American Universities Preparation Institute, P.O. Box 14842 Westlands Road, Chiromo Lande), Nairobi, Kenya; aupi@africa-online.co.ke. TEFL teachers needed for a year.

APARE/GEC, 41 cours Jean Jaurès, 84000 Avignon, France; 011-33-490-85-51-15; apare@apare-gec.org. Runs volunteer work-camps at historic sites in Tunisia and Morocco (as well as France and Europe).

Care of the Needy (COTN), P.O. Box 2247, Mwanza, Tanzania; 011-255-811-218364; cotn@raha.com. NGO working with homeless children uses volunteers, including on Lake Victoria environmental project.

Cross-Cultural Solutions, 47 Potter Ave., New Rochelle, NY 10801; 800-380-4777; info@crossculturalsolutions.org, [www.cross-culturalsolutions.org]. Volunteer vacations in eastern Ghana (as well as India, Peru and China). Volunteers spend 3 weeks teaching, providing skills training, and direction in arts, and recreation. Program fee is $1,950.

Frontier Conservation Expeditions, 77 Leonard St., London EC2A 4QS, England; 011-44-207-613-2422; enquiries@frontier.mail-box.ac.uk, [www.frontierprojects.ac.uk]. Carries out environmental surveys in Tanzania, Mozambique, and Madagascar (also Vietnam) that use paying volunteers for 10 weeks.

Global Citizens Network/Harambee 130 N Howell St., St. Paul, MN 55104; 651-644-0960; gcn@mtn.org, [www.globalcitizens.org]. Sends paying volunteers for 3 weeks to rural Kenya (among other countries worldwide). $1,650 plus airfare.

Greenforce, 11-15 Betterton St., Covent Garden, London WC2H 9BP, U.K.; 011-44-207-470-8888; Greenforce@btinternet.com, [www.greenforce.org]. Recruits researchers to join conservation aid projects for a minimum of 12 weeks in Zambia (and the Amazon, Borneo, Fiji). Participation fee from £2,650.

Operation Crossroads Africa, 475 Riverside Dr., Suite 1366, New York, NY 10115-0050; 212-870-2106; oca@igc.org; [www.igc.org/oca]. Runs 7-week summer projects in rural Africa, and Bahia, Brazil, staffed by self-financing volunteers from U.S. and Canada.

Overland Adventure Tours, Overland adventure tour operators require expedition leaders aged 25-40 for at least 1 year. These include Guerba Expeditions, 40 Station Rd., Westbury, Wiltshire BA13 3JN, U.K.; info@guerba.de-mon.co.uk, [www.guerba.co.uk] and Kumuka Africa, 40 Earls Court Rd., London W8 6EJ, England; [www.kumuka.co.uk].

Paul and Delilah Roch Charitable Trust, Box 1120, Makambako, Tanzania; [www.Safari-Tanzania.com]. Volunteers needed to build computer schools in Tanzania for 3, 6 or 12 months (costs $1,000, $1,800 and $3,600).

Public Affairs Department U.S. Embassy, Madagascar English Teaching Program, 4 Lalana Dr. Razafindratandra Ambohidahy, Antananarivo, Madagascar; 011-261-20-22-202-38, fax 011-261-20-22-213-97; etptana@compro.mg, [www.usmission.mg/etp.htm]. Occasionally hires native English speakers for short-term work on local pay scale.

Regal Holidays info.sharm@emperor-divers.com or info.hurghada@emperor-divers.com. Divers employed by British-managed tour company to work at Red Sea dive resorts of Sharm el Sheikh and Hurghada, especially November-January.

S & S Human Resources Development, P.O. Box TN 1501, Teshie-Nungua Estates, Accra, Ghana; 011-233 24 37 2730; hrdev@igh-mail.com. Paid internships with organizations and institutions in Accra, Kumasi, Cape Coast, Tema, Ho and Takoradi.

SCORE (Sports Coaches' OutReach), Sports Science Institute of South Africa), Boundary Rd., Newlands, South Africa 7700 or P.O. Box 13177, Mowbray, South Africa; 011- 27-21-689-7395, fax 011-27-21-689-7486; score@iafrica.com. Program for self-funded volunteers to coach sports in deprived communities. Minimum 6 months from January or July.

SHUMAS (Strategic Humanitarian Services), P.O. Box 5047, Nkwen, Bamenda, Northwest Province, Cameroon; 237-362682. Development NGO that places volunteers aged over 21 for 3-6 months in social and environmental projects in Cameroon. Volunteers are asked to contribute £350.

Teaching for Africa, IFESH, 5040 East Shea Blvd., Suite 260, Phoenix, AZ 85254-4687; 602-443-1800, 800-835-3530, fax 602-443-1824; recep@primenet.com, [www.ifesh.org]. Arranges for teachers and college instructors to teach TESL and other subjects at schools and colleges in Ethiopia, Benin, Guinea, Malawi, Ghana, Namibia, and Nigeria. Expenses covered during 10-month program.

Traveling Seminars Abroad, 1037 Society Hill, Cherry Hill, NJ 08003; 609-424-7630. Summer and longer term programs for students and others in village in northern Ghana helping to build Habitat for Humanity homes. Estimated cost for 3-month stay is $1,200.

United Children's Fund, P.O. Box 20341, Boulder, CO 80308-3341; 303-464-0137; [www.unchildren.org]. Volunteers work in Ugandan clinics, schools, and farms for short periods or 6 months. Fees from $820 for one week to $6,750 for 6 months, plus airfare.

Visions in Action, 2710 Ontario Rd., NW, Washington, DC 20009; 202-625-7402, fax 202-625-2353; visions@igc.org, [www.visionsinaction.org]. Range of volunteer projects in Uganda, Zimbabwe, Burkina Faso, Liberia (temporarily postponed), South Africa, and Tanzania. Volunteers must raise $5,000-$6,500 and stay from 6-12 months.

Workcamps in Africa. The following organizations arrange workcamps in Africa, though applications should normally be sent to the partner organization in the U.S. (see Voluntary Service, below): **Mouvement Twiza,** A.M.T., 23 rue Echiguer Hammand, Hay Salam, B.P. 77, 15000 Khemisset, Morocco; **Tunisian Assn. of Voluntary Work,** Maison du RCD, Blvd. 9 Avril, 1938, 1002 Tunis, Tunisia. (For Morocco and Tunisia, a knowledge of French is very useful.) **Christian Welfare and Social Project Organization,** 39 Soldier St., Freetown, Sierra Leone; 011-232-22-229779. **Voluntary Development Assn.,** P.O. Box 48902, Nairobi, Kenya. **Lesotho Workcamps Assn.,** P.O. Box 6, Linare Rd., Maseru 100, Lesotho. **Swaziland Workcamps Assn.,** P.O. Box 1430, Mbabane, Swaziland. **Zimbabwe Workcamps Assn.,** P.O. Box CY 2039, Causeway, Harare, Zimbabwe. AJUPE (Mozambique), Avenida Marion Ngouabi No. 1506, C.P. 1406, Maputo, Mozambique. **Southern African Student Volunteers** (SASVO), Centre for Human Rights, Univ. of Pretoria, Pretoria 0002, South Africa. **Uganda Volunteers for Peace and Development,** P.O. Box 3312, Kampala, Uganda; 011-256-077 402201; uvpeace@yahoo.co.uk. **WWOOF-Ghana,** c/o Ebenezer Nortey-Mensah, P.O. Box 154, Trade Fair Site, La-Accra, Ghana. Places volunteers on traditional farms and bicycle workshops in Ghana). **WWOOF Togo,** B.P. 25 Agou-Gare, Togo; 011-228-471036. Places volunteers on organic farms and forest projects in Togo.

WorldTeach, Center for International Development, Harvard Univ., 79 John F. Kennedy St., Cambridge, MA 02138; 800-4-

TEACH-0 or 617-495-5527, fax 617-495-1599; [www.worldteach.org]. Recruits college graduates to teach science, English, and more in Namibia and South Africa.

YMCA Go Global Program, 71 West 23rd St., Suite 1904, New York, NY 10010; 212-727-8800, fax 212-727-8814, [www.ymcanyc.org]. Volunteer programs in Ghana, Ivory Coast, Mali, Senegal, and the Gambia, lasting 6 weeks to 6 months. Work in fields of education, agriculture, health, etc. Partner organization in Africa (Student Youth Travel Organization) arranges accommodations and backup. Program fee $400.

ANTARCTICA

Raytheon Polar Services, 61 Inverness Drive East, Suite 300, Englewood, CO 80112; 303-790-8606 or 800-688-8000; [www.rpsc.raytheon.com]. Hires 800 U.S. citizens for U.S. Antarctic Program including both general assistants and skilled staff for 4, 6, or 12 months.

ASIA

Bangladesh Workcamps Association, 289/2 Work Camps Rd., North Shahjahanpur, Dhaka 1217, Bangladesh; fax 011-88-2-956-5506/5483; [www.bwca.homepage.com]. Development workcamps lasting 7 to 10 days, October-February. Participation fee $150 plus $25 application fee.

Dakshinayan, c/o Siddharth Sanyal, A5/108, Clifton Apartments, Charmwood Village, Surajkund Rd., Faridabad 121009, India; Tel./fax 011-91-129 525 3114; dakshinayan@vsnl.com, [www.linkindia.com/ dax]. Volunteers to help with grassroots educational medical projects in tribal lands in remote areas of Bihar state. Contribution of $5 a day is expected plus $50 administrative fee.

DPCA Sikkim (Denjong Padme Cheoling Academy), c/o 53 Blenheim Crescent, London W11 2EG; Tel./fax 011-44-207 229 4772; JJulesstewart@cs.com. Volunteers assist in classrooms of this school in the restricted Indian area of Sikkim for up to 45 days.

Educate the Children, P.O. Box 414, Ithaca, NY 14851-0414; 607-272-1176; fax 607-275-0932; info@etc-nepal.org, [www.etc-nepal.org]. Provides educational opportunities for low-income women and children in Nepal.

Arranges 3-month internships; fee of $500.

Himalayan Explorers Club, P.O. Box 3665, Boulder, CO 80307; 888-420-8822; info@hec.org, [www.hec.org]. Runs Nepal Volunteer Program from September-December and February-June ($150 per month plus travel expenses). Volunteer teachers placed in Sherpa village schools while living with local families.

Insight Nepal, P.O. Box 489, Pokhara, Kaski, Nepal; insight@mos.com.np; [www.south-asia.com/insight]. Volunteer placements for one to 4 months in Nepali schools. Must be high school graduate. $400 fee for 4- to 6-week placements, $800 for longer ones.

JAFFE International Education Service, Kunnuparambil Buildings, Kurichy, Kottayam 686549, India; Tel./fax 011-481 430470. Placement agency for young foreign volunteers to teach in English-language high schools, vocational institutes, summer camps, etc. in Kerala and elsewhere in India.

JAC, (Joint Assistance Centre), G 17/3 DLF Qutab Enclave, Phase 1, Gurgaon, Haryana 122002, India; fax 011-91-124-351-308; nkjain@jac.unv.ernet.in. Community service organization near Delhi. Volunteers pay $230 for the first month and $130 for each subsequent month.

KIVA (Korean International Volunteer Association), 11th Fl., Sekwang B/D, 202 Sejong-ro, Chongro-gu, Seoul, South Korea 110-050; kiva21@hotmail.com; [www.kiva.or.kr]. Work placements throughout Korea for international volunteers for a minimum of 4 weeks. Board and lodging provided.

Missionaries of Charity, 54A A.J.C. Bose Rd., Calcutta 16, India. Runs Mother Theresa's homes for destitute people in Calcutta. Volunteers can work for short periods.

NICE (Never-Ending Workcamps Exchange), 2-4-701 Shinjuku, Shinjuku-ku, Tokyo 160-0022, Japan; nice-do@po.jah.ne.jp; [www.jah.ne.jp/~nice-do]. Applicants should contact workcamp organization in their home country (see Voluntary Service).

ROSE (Rural Organization for Social Elevation), Social Awareness Centre, Village Sonargaon, P.O. Box Kanda, Dist. Bageshwar, U.P. 263631, India. Grassroots development projects in Uttar Pradesh.

Sarvodaya,98 Rawatawatte Road, Moratuwa, Sri Lanka; 011-94-72 277375, fax 011-94-1-

646512; jdg@itmin.com. Village construction and other projects lasting 3-6 months for volunteers over 21.

The Japan Times (especially Mondays) and **Korea Times**. English-language newspapers that carry teaching advertisements; [www-japantimes.co.jp], [www.koreatimes.com].

VWOP (Voluntary Work Opportunities in Nepal), P.O. Box 4263, Kathmandu, Nepal; fax 011-977-1-416144; vwop2000@hotmail.com. Volunteers are placed in remote areas of Nepal teaching English in schools, organizing community work, and being involved in research. Placement fee of $400 plus $50 per month for homestay accommodations and food.

WWOOF Japan, c/o Glenn and Kiyoko Burns, Akebono 5-Jo, 3-chome 19-17, Teine-ku, Sapporo 006, Japan; fax 011-81-11 694 2046; burns@arabagu.com. Short-term opportunities on organic farms in Japan.

YCO (Youth Charitable Organization), 20/14 Urban Bank St, Post Office No. 3, Yellamanchili 531055, Vizag.Dt., Andhra Pradesh, India. Foreign volunteers work on soil conservation, irrigation and community development programs lasting 2-6 months. Daily charge of 320 rupees ($7.50).

AUSTRALASIA

Au Pair Australia, 6 Wilford St., Corrimal, NSW 2518, Australia; 011-61-2-42-846412, fax 011-2-42-854896. Places young women with work visas in live-in childcare positions for a minimum of 3 months.

Australian Tropical Research Foundation PMB 5, Cape Tribulation, Queensland 4873, Australia; 011-61-70-98-00-63; austrop@austrop.org.au. Volunteers over the age of 23 required for variety of tasks. Contribution of about $100 per week.

Australian Trust for Conservation Volunteers, P.O. Box 423, Ballarat, Victoria 3350, Australia; 011-61-353-331483; info@atcv.com.au, [www.actv.com.au]. Organizes short- and long-term voluntary conservation projects in Australia. Overseas volunteers participate in a 6-week package costing from AUS$840.

CALM (Conservation and Land Management), Department of Western Australia, Locked Bag 104, Bentley Delivery Centre, WA 6893, Australia; 011-61-8-9334 0251; [www.calm.wa gov.au] Volunteer program open to anyone, though accommodation not necessarily provided.

CCUSA (Camp Counselors USA), 2330 Marinship Way, Suite 250, Sausalito, CA 94965; 800-999-CAMP; outbound@camp-counselors.com, [www.campcounselors. com]. Sends American students aged 18-30 to Australia and New Zealand between June and September. Program fee is $365.

DOC (Department of Conservation), Private Bag, Nelson, New Zealand; 011-64-3-546-9355. Runs conservation projects such as kiwi monitoring in a national park. Addresses and Calendar of Volunteer opportunities listed on web site [www.doc.govt.nz/commu/involv/consvol2.htm]. Many short-term projects such as counting bats and cleaning up remote beaches.

Earthwise Living Foundation (NZ), Box 108, Thames 2815, New Zealand; US voicemail/fax 435-408-4123; [www.elfnz.com]. Volunteers placed on wilderness ecology and conservation projects. Registration fee of $200 plus $175 per week

Farm Helpers in New Zealand, 50 Bright St., Eketahuna 5480, New Zealand; Tel./fax 011-64-6-375 8955; fhinz@xtra.co.nz, [www.fhinz.co.nz]. NZ$25 membership includes booklet listing farmers looking for helpers in exchange for room and board.

Internship Programs Australia, 800-704-4880; [www.advc.com/internships]. Up to 100 interns placed in career-related field in Australia. Fees typically $5,000 for a 12-week internship.

Northern Victoria Fruitgrowers' Assn., P.O. Box 394, Shepparton, Victoria 3630, Australia; 011-61-3-5821 5844; nvfa@mcmedia.com.au. Actively recruits fruit pickers from January to March. Also **Victorian Peach and Apricot Growers' Assn.**, 30A Bank St., P.O. Box 39, Cobram, VIC 3644, Australia.

Rocky Creek Farm, Isis Hwy., M.S. 698, Biggenden, Queensland 4621, Australia; 011-61-741-271377; worsley@isisol.com.au, [www.isisol.com.au/rockycrkfarmstay]. Offers 1-week course for jackaroos and jillaroos (farm hands) for AUS$330. Those with working holiday visas can be placed on a Queensland property for an extra $110.

Stablemate Staff Agency, 1 Bullridge Rd., E. Kurrajong, NSW 2156, Australia; 011-61-2-9654-9643; STABLEMATE@bigPond.com.

Supplies staff to the horse industry. Operates exchange program with the U.S.

WWOOF-Australia, Mt. Murrindal Cooperative, Buchan, Victoria 3885, Australia; 011-61-3-5155-0218; wwoof@ozemail.com.au; [www.wwoof.com.au]. Distributes the "Auslist," with the addresses of 1,300 member farms in Australia looking for short- or long-term voluntary help. AUS$40 (which includes accident insurance) if bought outside Australia. Also publishes worldwide list of farms and volunteer work opportunities for US$20.

WWOOF-New Zealand, P.O. Box 1172, Nelson, New Zealand; Tel./fax 011-64-3-5449890; a&j@wwoof.co.nz; [www.wwoof.co.nz]. Their list of about 600 organic growers costs $20.

CENTRAL AND EASTERN EUROPE

Many opportunities, especially in English language teaching, have become available in the Baltic, Russia, and the Republics.

American Academy of Foreign Languages, Dmitreva Sat 16, Office 16, Kiev, Ukraine. Tel./fax 011-380-44-227 07 82. Also has large English institutes in Moscow (aafl@rui.ru) which employ TEFL qualified teachers.

AIEP (Association for Educational, Cultural and Work International Exchange Programs), 42 Yeznik Coghbatsi St., Apt. 22, Yerevan 375002, Armenia; 011-374-1-58 47 33, fax 011-374-1-52 92 32; aiep@arminco.co; [www.geocities.com/Athens/Academy/3522]. Sponsors camps to restore and maintain medieval buildings in Armenia and run internship program.

Baikal Institute for Environment & Natural Resources Use, Lermontov Str 104, Irkutsk 664074; 011-7-89532 430417; bienru@irk.ru. Foreign volunteers teach sports, music, English, etc. for 2-5 weeks at summer camp on Lake Baikal in Siberia. Participation fee $100.

Caledonian School, Vlatavska 24, 150 00 Prague 5, Czech Republic; Tel./fax 011-42-2-57-31-36-50; jobs@caledonianschool.com, www.caledonianschool.com. Employs 80 teachers with TEFL background to teach English in a large Prague language institute. Canadian recruitment agent: Thomas Norris, 6 Greenmount Court, Toronto, ON, M8Y 1Y1, Canada; fax 416-231-1730; norr-cal@sympati-co.ca.

Central European Teaching Program, Beloit College, 700 College St., Beloit, WI 53511; 608-363-2619; dunlopa@beloit.edu, [www.beloit.edu/~cetp]. Supplies nearly 100 English teachers to Hungary and Romania plus Poland and Lithuania. $2,000 placement fee.

CIDJ (Centres d'Information et de Documentation Jeunesse), 101 Quai Branly, 75740, Cedex 15, Paris; fax 011-33-1-40-65-02-61; [www.cidj.asso.fr]. Advisory centers for young people throughout France. Paris branch distributes leaflets *(fiches)* on work, study, etc. in France. Send 4 International Response Coupons to receive the catalog.

City University, Slovakia, Human Resources Department, 335 116th Ave. SE, Bellevue, WA 98004; 425- 637-1010; sanderson@cityu.edu, [www.city.edu]. Bratislava site: Odbojarov 10, 83232 Bratislava; Tel./fax 011-421-7-5556-7646. Trencin site: Bezrucova 64, 911 01 Trencin; Tel./fax 011-421-831-529337. Recruit 30-35 native English-speaking teachers per year (must have Master's degree and teaching experience). IEP and BSBA programs.

Czech Academic Information Agency, Dum Zahranicnich Sluzeb, Senovázné Námesti 26, 11121 Prague, Czech Republic; 011-42-2-24-22-9698; aia@dzs.cz; [www.dzs.cz/aia/lek-tori.htm]. Helps prospective English teachers find posts mainly in state schools but also in private institutes.

Ecologia Trust, The Park, Forres, Moray IV36 3TZ; 011-44 1309 690995; ecoliza@rimplc.co.uk; [www.rmplc.co.uk/ eduweb/sites.ecoliza]. Student volunteers needed for at least one month at children's home in Kaluga region of Russia. Fee is $1,000+ for up to 2 months excluding airfare.

English for Everybody, c/o ITC, Kaprova 14, 110 00 Prague 1, Czech Republic; Tel./fax 011-42-2-2481 4791; EFE@itc-training.com. EFL placement agency affiliated to US-owned TEFL training company.

English School Sunny Plus, 1-Aeroportoskaya St, Bldg. 1/3, P.O. Box 23, 125057 Moscow, Russia; Tel./fax 011-7-095-129 7303; [www.sunnyplus.ru]. Hires college-educated Americans with some teaching experience.

ESCS (English School of Communication Skills), ul. Bernarynska 15, 33-100 Tarnow, Poland; Tel./fax 011-48-14 621 37 69; personnel@escs.pl. Hires 65 EFL teachers for 4 language schools in southern Poland and summer language camps at the Polish seaside.

Galindo Skola (Sava Centar), Milentija Popovica 9, 11070 Novi Beograd, Yugoslavia; 011-381-11-311-4568; galindo@net.yu. English teachers to work with children and adolescents for at least 3 months.

INEX Czech Republic, National Centre, Senovzne nam, 24, 116 47 Prague 1; 011-420-2 241 02 527; inex@czn.cz; [www.czex.cz/inex]. Forty-five projects in Czech Republic for international volunteers in social, cultural and environmental fields.

INEX Slovakia, Prazska 11, 814 13 Bratislava; 011-421-7 524 96 249, fax: 011-421-7 524 94 707; inexsk@nextra.sk, [www.inex.sk]. Partner organization in Slovakia for workcamps.

International Exchange Center, 2 Republic Sq., LV-1010 Riga, Latvia; fax 011-371-783 0257; iec@mail.eunet.lv. Recruits English-speaking volunteers for summer projects in Latvia and Russia that may involve camp counseling, au pairing. Basic knowledge of Russian or local language required.

International House maintains a large contingent of language schools in Poland employing many certificate-qualified EFL teachers: **IH Katowice** (Ul. Sokolska 78/80, 40-128 Katowice), IH Kraków (ul. Pilsudskiego 6, Ip, 31-109 Kraków), **IH Opole** (Ul. Kosciuszki 17, 45-062 Opole), **IH Wroclaw** (Ul. Leszczynskiego 3, 50-078 Wroclaw), and **IH Bielsko-Biala** (Ul. Karsinskiego 24, 43-300 Bielsko Biala).

Language Link Russia, Novoslobodskaya ul. 5 bld. 2, 103030 Moscow; Tel./fax 011-7-095-250-8935; jobs@language.ru, [www.language.ru]. Places 400 native-English teachers in schools throughout Russia.

MOST, Breg 12, 1000 Ljubljana, Slovenia; 011-386-1-426-80-67, fax 011-386-1-251-72-08; drustvo.most@siol.net, [www.drustvo-most.si]. Sponsors 15 international workcamps in Slovenia for volunteers, mostly building renovation, ecological, agricultural or social projects.

Ormansag Foundation, Arany Janos u. 4, 7967 Dravafok, Hungary; Tel./fax 011-36-73-352 333. Unpaid gardening work in orchard, herb garden, etc. at sustainable farm. Also coordinates volunteers for neighboring farms. Free accommodations. Minimum stay 1 week.

Petro-Teach Program, c/o Prof. Wallace J.

Sherlcok, Dept. of Curriculum and Instruction, Univ. of Wisconsin, Whitewater, WI 53190; sherlocw@mail.uww.edu; [www.semlab2,sbs.sunysb.edu/Users/jbailyn.Petro.html.] Petro-Teach program in St. Petersburg places candidates in state secondary schools and private institutes. Application process begins in February and March for September 1 start date.

Project Harmony, 6 Irasville Common, Waitsfield, VT 05673; 802-496-4545, [www.projectharmony.org]. Teaching Intern Program places teachers in Russia and Ukraine (Odessa). Recent college graduates accepted.

Russia Camp Program, c/o Camp Counselors USA, 2330 Marinship Way, Suite 250, Sausalito, CA 94965; 800-999-CAMP; outbound@campcounselors.com. American counselors spend 4 or 8 weeks volunteering at Russian youth camps. Program fee of $1,600 including return airfare New York-Moscow, visa, insurance, and orientation.

Services for Open Learning, North Devon Professional Centre, Vicarage St., Barnstable, Devon EX32 7HB, U.K.; 011-44-1271-327319; [www.sol.org.uk]. Recruits graduates to teach in schools in Belarus, Croatia, Czech Republic, Hungary, Romania, and Slovakia. Interviews in Eastern Central Europe or U.K.

SPELT (Soros Professional English Language Teaching Program), Open Society Institute, 400 W. 59th St., 4th Fl., New York, NY 10019. Teaching and teacher hiring positions in Azerbaijan, Bosnia and Herzegovina, Georgia, Haiti, Kyrgyzstan, Mongolia, Russia, Tajikistan, and Uzbekistan, Yugoslavia for certified (Master's preferred), experienced professional English teachers who are ready for a Croatia challenge.

Teachers for Central and Eastern Europe, 21 V 5 Rakovski Blvd., Dimitrovgrad 6400, Bulgaria; tel/fax 011-359-391-24787; U.S. tel 707-276-4571; tfcee@usa.net; [www.tfcee. 8m,com]. Appoints 80 native speakers to teach in English language secondary schools for 1 academic year in Bulgaria, and also in Czech Republic, Hungary, Poland, and Slovakia. Details also available from InterExchange (see Worldwide Jobs).

Travel Teach St. James's Building, 79 Oxford St., Manchester M1 6FR; UK premium line: 011-44-870-789-8100; [www.travelteach.com]. Working holiday opportunities teaching

English in Moldova and Lithuania. Placement fees £445 (Moldova-minimum 2 weeks) and £495 (Lithuania-minimum 7 weeks).

Union Forum Ukraine, Lychakivska Str. P.O. 5327, Lviv 10, 79010 Ukraine; Tel./fax 011-38-0322-759488; ukrforum@ipm.lviv.ua. Invites enthusiastic individuals to participate in Voluntary International Exchange Service Program in the summer.

Willing Workers on Organic Farms Russia, Contact Orehov Vladimir Dmirievihs, Ekaterinburg, Russia; bibl@mail.ur.ru. Contact for arranging work-for-week stays on organic farms in Russia.

FRANCE

APARE/GEC, 41 cours Jean Jaurès, 84000 Avignon, France; 011-33-490-85-51-15; apare@apare-gec.org. Runs volunteer workcamps at historic sites in southern France (and in other countries). Literature printed in English.

Bombard Balloon Adventures, SRO Ground Crew, Chateau de LaBorde, 21200 Beaune, France; 011-33-3-80-26-63-30. U.S. contact fax: 240-384-7107; mike@bombardsociety.com; [www.bombardsociety.com/ jobs]. Hot-air balloon ground crew for summer season, mainly in France (winter season in Swiss Alps).

Butterfly et Papillon, 5 Av de Genève, F-74000 Annecy, France; 011-33-4-50-67-03-51; aupair.france@wanadoo.fr. All nationalities placed as au pairs in French families for 3-18 months.

Centre International d'Antibes, 28 Avenue du Chateau, 06600 Antibes; 011-33-4-92-90-71-70; cia@imcn.com. Work exchange program offered by French language school on the Cote d'Azur. Volunteers able to work in Europe do administrative or domestic work in exchange for board and lodging and/or French tuition.

Club du Vieux Manoir, 10 rue de la Cossonerie, 75001 Paris; 011-33-3-44-72-33-98. Workcamps to restore ancient monuments. Board and lodging cost FF80 per day.

Council Exchanges Paris, 1 Place de l'Odeon, Paris 75006 ,France; 011-33-1-44-41-74-69; [www.councilexchanges-fr.org]. Support office to "Work in France" participants (through Council Exchanges; see Worldwide Jobs). Program allows students to work in France for up to 3 months.

Fédération Unie des Auberges de Jeunesse, 27 rue Pajol, 75018 Paris, France; 011-33-144-89-87-27. Short-term work (catering, reception, sports, instruction, etc.) at youth hostels throughout France. Applications must be sent to individual hostels. FUAJ also organizes voluntary workcamps to renovate hostels; volunteers pay FF400 per week. Another chain of youth accommodation is **Ucrif Etapes Jeunes,** 27 rue de Turbigo, BP 6407, 75064 Paris cedex 2 001-33-1-40-26-57-64; [www.ucrif.asso.fr].

La Sabranenque Centre International, rue de la Tour de l'Oume, 30290 Saint Victor la Coste, France; 011-33-466-50-05-05. Volunteers needed to help preserve and restore monuments in France (and Italy). Inquiries to Jacqueline Simon, 217 High Park Blvd., Buffalo, NY 14226; 716-836-8698; [www.sabranenque.com].

Ministry of Culture, Sous-Direction de l'Archéologie, 4 rue d'Aboukir, 75002 Paris, France; 011-33-1-40-15-77-81; [www.culture.fr/fouilles]. Government department which deals with archaeological digs. Every May they publish a list of excavations throughout France that accept volunteers.

PGL Travel, Alton Court, Penyard Ln., Ross-on-Wye, Herefordshire HR9 5NR, England; 011-44-1989-767833. Needs outdoor activity center staff for holiday centers in France for whole season.

REMPART, 1 rue des Guillemites, 75004 Paris, France; 011-33-1-42-71-96-55; [www.rempart.com]. Needs volunteers to care for endangered monuments. Most projects charge FF40-FF50 a day, plus membership of FF220.

Star Crew, The Office, Gallerie du Port, 8 Boulevard d'Aguillon, 06600 Antibes, France; info@starcrew.com. Crewing agency for private yachts. Located in building with other crewing agencies.

The French Cultural Service, 972 5th Ave., New York, NY 10021; fax 212-439-1455/1482; new-york.culture@diplomatic.fr, [www.info-france-usa.org/culture]. English Teaching Assistantship program, SCULE, runs from October 1 to Aril 30. Must have working knowledge of French. Stipend of FF6,000 a month.

France-USA Contacts (FUSAC), P.O. Box 15, Coopers Station, New York, NY 10276; 212-777-5553; fax 212-777-5554; franceusa@aol.com; [www.fusac.com] This publication in Paris carries job ads. You can place an ad before arrival. $20 for 20 words.

American Church, 65 quai d'Orsay, Paris and the **American Cathedral**, 23 Ave George V, Paris 75008; [www.us.net/amcathedral-paris]. Both churches feature notice boards you should consult while in Paris. The latter offers volunteering opportunities in its own programs as well as career forums for job seekers.

GERMANY, SWITZERLAND, AUSTRIA

AGABUR Foundation, 9 Eastwood Rd., Storrs, CT 06268; 860-429-1279; [www.mannheim-program.necaweb.com]. Professional program that includes language training, university study, and optional paid internships in Germany.

Agroimpuls, Laurstrasse, 5201 Brugg, Switzerland; 011-41-56-462-51-44; [www.agroimpuls.ch]. Swiss Farmers' Union runs a program for trainees in agriculture and horticulture.

The American School in Switzerland (TASIS), Summer Language Programs, 6926 Montagnola-Lugano, Switzerland; 011-41-91-994-64-71; administration@tasis.ch, [www.tasis.ch]. U.S. address: 1640 Wisconsin Ave., NW, Washington, DC 20007; 202-965-5800. Work as English teachers and children's counselors at summer camp.

Arbeitskreis Denkmalpflege, Goetheplatz 9B, D-99423 Weimar, Germany; 011-49-643-502390; akdenkmalpflege@t-online.de. Volunteers restore historic buildings year round.

Bergwald Projekt (Mountain Forest Project/MFP), Rigastrasse 14, 7000 Chur; 011-41-81-252 4145; [www.bergwaldprojekt.ch]. Educational and practical workcamps in alpine forests of Switzerland, Germany and Austria. Send 12 International Response Coupons for info. Must already be in Europe to participate

CDS International, 871 United Nations Plaza, 15th Fl., New York, NY 10017-1814; 212-497-3500; info@cdsintl.org, [www.cdsintl.org]. Arranges 6-month paid internships in Germany for students or recent graduates in business, engineering, and other technical fields. Longer placements of 12-18 months also available.

Compagna, Unterer Graben 29, 8400 Winterthur, Switzerland; 011-41-52-212 5530.

Also Compagna Lausanne, Rue du Simplon 2, 1006 Lausanne; 011-41-21-616 2985; Compagna Luzern, Reckenbuhlstrasse 21, 6005 Luzern; 011-41-41 312 1173; compagna-Luzern@bluewin.ch. Au pair placements for minimum of 1 year throughout Switzerland. Registration and placement fee total SFR190.

Council Exchanges Germany, Oranienburger Str. 13-14, 10178 Berlin, Germany; 011-49-30-28 48 59-0; fax 011-49-30-28 09 61 80; InfoGermany@councilexchanges.de, [www.council.de]. Support office for "Work in Germany" participants through Council Exchanges (See Worldwide Jobs, page 71). Program allows students of German to work for up to 3 months and those who fix up a career-related job in Germany for 6 months.

English for Children, Kanalstrasse 44, P.O. Box 160, 1220 Vienna, Austria; 011-43-1-282-77-17; english.for.children@eunet.at. TEFL-trained teachers needed for residential summer camps or for academic year. Should be resident in Austria. Also: **English for Kids**, A. Baumgartnerstr. 44/A 7042, 1230 Vienna, Austria; 011-43-1-667 45 79; [www.e4kids.co.at]. EFL teachers and camp counsellors for summer language camp. Must have pre-arranged work permit.

First Choice/Skibound, Olivier House, Ski Lakes & Mountains Division, 18 Marine Parade, Brighton, East Sussex BN2 1TL, U.K.; 011-44-1273-677777. Domestic and kitchen staff needed to work winter season for tour operator which runs hotels in Alpine resorts in Austria (and also France).

GIJK Gesellschaft fur Internationale, Jugendkontakte, Baunscheidtstr. 11, 53113 Bonn, Germany; 011-49-228-95-73-00; gijk@gijk.de, [www.gijk.de] (in German). Au pair placements for people of all nationalities under the age of 24.

Gruppo Volontari, della Svizzera Italiana, C.P. 12, 6517 Arbedo, Switzerland; 011-41-79-354 0161. Conservation workcamps to help mountain communities. Particpants pay SFR15 per day to cover expenses.

Haut-Lac International Centre, 1669 Les Sciernes, Switzerland; 011-41-26-928-4200; info@haut-lac.ch, [www.haut-lac.ch]. Teachers and monitors needed for summer and winter language programs.

Hiking Sheep Guesthouse, Villa La Joux, 1854 Leysin, Switzerland; 011-41-24-494-3535; hikingsheep@leysin.net. Hostel needs good linguists for reception and general duties.

IBG, Schlosserstrasse 28, D-70180 Stuttgart, Germany; 011-49-711-649-11-28; ibg-workcamps@t-online.de. Organizes voluntary workcamps throughout Germany.

Involvement Volunteers-Deutschland, Naturbadstr. 50, 91056 Erlangen, Germany; Tel./fax 011-49-9135-8075; ivde@t-online.de. Conservation organization allied to Involvement Volunteers in Australia (see Worldwide Voluntary Service, below).

Ökista, Garnisongasse 7, 1090 Vienna, Austria; 011-43-1-401-48-220; [www.oekista.co.at]. Live-in childcare positions throughout Austria. Pocket money 700 Austrian schillings per week.

Pro Filia, 241G Rte d'Hermance, 1246 Corsier/Geneva; 011-41-22-751 02 95. Places live-in babysitters with French-speaking families for a minimum of 1 year. The office at Beckenhofstrasse 16, 8035 Zurich; 011-41-1-363-55-01; profilia@dplanet.ch deals with German-speaking Switzerland.

Swiss Travel Service, Bridge House, 55-59 High Rd., Broxbourne, Hertfordshire EN10 7DT, England. Winter and summer resort representatives needed April to end of September. Interviews held in U.K.

U.S. Military Bases throughout Germany have Civilian Personnel Offices (CPOs) that are responsible for recruiting auxiliary staff to work in bars, shops, etc., on base and as ski instructors. Heidelberg is the HQ for the U.S. Army in Europe, which creates long-term jobs for secretaries, clerks, etc. The best bet is at the **Armed Forces Recreational Centers** at Garmisch-Partenkirchen and Chiemsee, AFRC Europe, Unit 24501, APO AE 09053; 011-49-8821 750707; cpo@afrc.garmisch.army. mil, [www.afrceurope.com/empl.htm].

Vereinigung Junger Freiwilliger (VJF), Hans-Otto-Str. 7, 10407 Berlin, Germany; 011-49-30-428 506 03; office@vjf.de. Workcamps held in former East Germany. Registration fee DM220.

Village Camps S.A., 14 rue de la Morache, 1260 Nyon, Switzerland; 011-41-22-990-9405. Recruits monitors and counselors to work for the summer or winter season at children's sports camps in several Swiss resorts and Zell-am-See, Austria.

WWOOF-Austria (Willing Workers on Organic Farms), c/o Hildegard Gottlieb, Langegg 155, 8511 St Stefan ob Stainz, Austria; Tel./fax 011-43-3463 82270; wwoof/welcome@telering.at. Membership costs $25 per year and comes with list of 90 Austrian organic farms looking for work-for-keep volunteer helpers. Combined Swiss-Austrian list is $35; combined German-Swiss-Austrian list is $50.

WWOOF-Germany, Postfach 210 259, D-01263, Dresden, Germany; info@wwoof.de; [www.wwoof.de]. Volunteer openings on organic farms. Membership fee of DM30 gives access to 160 farms .

WWOOF-Switzerland, Postfach 59, 8124 Maur, Switzerland; wwoof@dataway.ch, [www.welcome.to/wwoof]. For details on working for your keep on an organic farm, send $15. Includes 45 addresses in Switzerland plus a handful elsewhere.

Young Austria Summer Camps, Ferienhofe GmbH, Alpenstrasse 108a, A-5020 Salzburg, Austria; 011-43-662-62 57 58-0; office@camps.at. Monitors and EFL teachers for summer language and sports camps near Salzburg. Application deadline end of February.

Zentralstelle für Arbeitsvermittlung, Villemombler Str. 76, 53123 Bonn, Germany 011-49-228-713-0, fax 011-49-228 713 1111. Federal employment bureau handles student applications from abroad. Applicants must speak German. Majority of jobs are in hotels and restaurants, in industry and agriculture.

ITALY

A.C.L.E. Summer and City Camps, Via Roma 54, 18038 San Remo, Italy; Tel./fax 011-39-0184-506070; info@acle.org. Need counselors and EFL teachers for multi-activity and English-language camps in northern Italy for 4, 8 or 12 weeks. Compulsory 3-day training.

Archelon, Sea Turtle Protection Society of Greece, Solomou 57, 10423 Athens, Greece; Tel./fax 011-30-1-523 1342; stps@archelon.gr, [www.archelon.gr]. Can advise volunteers on locations where they are needed over the summer to conserve and research the loggerhead turtle population.

Athanasopoulos Language Schools, 6 Einstein St., 18757 Keratsini-Piraeus, Greece; 011-30-1-43-14-921; athanasopoulos@acropolis.gr. Eight-month teaching contracts in Greece.

Athenian Nanny Agency, P.O. Box 51181, Kifissia, Athens 145 10, Greece; Tel./fax 011-30-1-808-1005; mskiniti@groovy.gr. Places nannies and experienced nurses in private families in Greece (and worldwide).

Au Pair Activities, P.O. Box 76080,17110 Nea Smyrni, Athens, Greece; Tel./fax 011-30-1-932-6016; porae@iname.com. Placement service for au pairs also offers positions in the tourist industry.

Conservation Volunteers in Greece, 15 Omirou St., 14562 Kifissia, Greece; fax 011-30-1-801-1489; cvgpeep@otenet.gr, [www.cvg-peep.org]. Projects include work in protected landscapes, conservation of traditional buildings and work in archaeological sites.

Gruppi Archeologici d'Italia, Via Degli Scipioni 30/A, 00192 Rome, Italy; 011-39-06-39 73 36 37; gruppiarch@tiscalinet.it; [www.gruppiarcheologici.org]. Regional archaeological units coordinate 2-week digs which paying volunteers can join. The web site (with an English version) gives contact details for archaeological projects throughout Italy.

Interlingue School of Languages, Via E.Q. Visconti 20, 00193 Rome, Italy; 011-39-06-323-5709; interlingue@interlingue-it.com. Native speaker English teachers needed; degree in education or TEFL background required.

L'Aquilone Service Agency, Via Giovanni Pascoli 15, 20129 Milan, Italy; 011-39-02-2952-9639; aquilone@azienda.com. Summer and year-long placements of au pairs.

LIPU (Lega Italiana Protezione Uccelli), Via Trento 49, 43100 Parma, Italy; 011-39-0521-273043; [www.lipu.it]. Long-established environmental and bird conservation association. Catalog of projects including short summary in English sent on request. Volunteer camps cost LIT250,000 per week.

Oikos Protezione Ambientale, Via Paolo Renzi 55, 00128 Rome, Italy; 011-39-06-508-0280; oilos@oikos.org. Environmental volunteers needed especially for fire prevention near Rome.

Romana Musicisti, Via La Spezia 100, 00055 Ladispoli, Rome, Italy; Tel./fax 011-39-06-9922 1766; [www.caerenet.it/romus]. Recruits Italian-speaking musicians, singers, DJs and entertainers for summer jobs around Italy. Registration fee must be paid.

Skyros, 92 Prince of Wales Rd., London NW5 3NE, U.K; 011-44-207-267-4424. Work scholars recruited to assist at Atsitsa alternative holiday center on Greek island of Skyros. Volunteers must be nurses, chefs, or experienced maintenance people. Board and lodging costs £40 per week. Workers can participate in courses offered at center from abseiling to windsurfing.

WWOOF Italia, c/o Bridget Matthews, 109 Via Casavecchia, 57022 Castagneto Carducci (LI), Italy; wwoof@oliveoil.net. Membership costs LIT20,000 to obtain list of organic farmers in Italy looking for volunteers.

English Language Schools in Italy may be found in the Italian yellow pages under *"Scuole di Lingue."*

LATIN AMERICA

American Friends Service Committee, 1501 Cherry St., Philadelphia, PA 19102; 215-241-7000/7295; afscinfo@afsc.org, [www.afsc.org]. Sends paying volunteers who speak Spanish to community projects in Mexico during the summer. Program fee about $1,000 plus travel expenses.

AmeriSpan Unlimited, P.O. Box 40007, Philadelphia, PA 19106-0007; 800) 879-6640; [www.amerispan.com/volunteer]. Runs volunteer and internship programs as well as language immersion courses in Latin America.

Amigos, 5618 Star Lane, Houston, TX 77057; 800- 231-7796, fax 713-782-9267; info@amigoslink.org. Sends about 500 volunteers aged 16-21 with knowledge of Spanish or Portuguese to Bolivia, Brazil, Costa Rica, Dominican Republic, Honduras, Mexico, Nicaragua and Paraguay. Participants pay $3,200 including return travel from U.S.

Amity Volunteer Teachers Abroad, 10671 Roselle St., Suite 101, San Diego, CA 92121-1525; 858-455-6364; mail@amity.org; [www.amity.org]. Volunteers needed to teach English in Argentina, Peru, Mexico and the Dominican Republic while living with local families. Also active in other countries.

Amizade Volunteer Vacations, 367 S. Graham St., Pittsburgh, PA 15232; 888-973-4443; volunteer@amizade.org; [www.amizade.org]. Short-term community service volunteer programs in Brazil and Bolivia (plus Montana, Navajo Nation, Australia and Nepal). Participation fees vary according to program, $1,000-$2,600.

Artemis Cloud Forest Preserve, Apdo. 937 San Pedro Montes de Oca, 2050 Costa Rica. Volunteers pay $175 per week. Tasks include trail building and tree planting. Minimum stay 1 month.

Benedict School of Languages, P.O. Box 09-01-8916, Guayaquil, Ecuador; 011-593-4-444418; benecent@telconet.net. College-educated native speakers needed for several Benedict schools in Ecuador. Minimum stay 4 months.

Bermuda Biological Station for Research, 17 Biological Ln., St. George's, GE01 Bermuda; 441-297-1880; [www.bbsr.edu]. Volunteer interns help scientists conduct research; apply 4 months in advance.

Bospas Forest Farm, c/o Casa Dobronski, Calle Guanhuiltagua N34-457 Quito, Ecuador; bospas@hotmail.com. Farm assistants with experience in gardening needed for fruit farm in subtropical valley in Northwest Ecuador. Monthly charge of $200.

Caledonia Languages Abroad, The Clockhouse, Bonnington Mill, 72 Newhaven Rd., Edinburgh EH6 5QG, U.K.; 011-44-131-621-7721; [www.caledonialanguages.co.uk]. Spanish and voluntary work programs organized in Peru and Costa Rica yer round. Community and environmental projects and teaching English, depending on skills and level of language ability.

Casa de los Amigos, Ignacio Mariscal 132, 06030 Mexico, D.F., Mexico; 011-52-5-705-0521; friends@avantel.net, [www.avantel.net/~friends]. Quaker-run service center in Mexico City with information on volunteers opportunities throughout Mexico and Central America.

Casa Guatemala, 14th Calle 10-63, Zona 1, Guatemala City; 011-502-232-5517/221-1851; casaguatemal@guate.net. Runs orphanage in the Petén region that needs volunteer medical staff, teachers, and nannies.

Casa Xelaju Guatemala, Callejon 15, Diagonal 13-02, Zonal, Quetzaltenango, Guatemala; 502-761-5955; internships@casaxelaju.com. Supervised internships in and around Quetzaltenango. Minimum stay 2 months. Must have good knowledge of Spanish. Cost of participation is $120 per week. U.S. contact: Casa Xelaju, 3034 47th Ave. S, Minneapolis, MN 55406; 888-796-CASA.

Centro Cultural Colombo Americano, Carrera 43, 51-95 Apartado Aereo 2097, Barranquilla, Colombia; 011-57-53-408084; colombo@b-quilla.cetcol.net.co. Recruits native speaker teachers. Similar centers in Cali, Bogota, Medellin, etc.

Centro Mexicano Internacional (CMI), Fray Antonio de San Miguel 173, Morelia, Michoacan, Mexico or Apartado P.O.stal 56, Morelia, Michoacan 58000; 011-52-43-12-45-96; cmi.spanish-language.com, [http://208.137.153.15/spanish]. Intern placement program with Spanish language tuition in Mexico. $370 per week. Web site lists voluntary projects in Mexico education, camp counseling, social, etc. U.S. contact: Victor Padelford, 14427 Brookhollow, Suite No. 279, San Antonio, TX 78232.

Centro Venezolano Americano (CVA), Apartado 61715 Del Este, Caracas 1060-A, Venezuela; or Avenida Jose Marti, Edif. CVA, Urb. Mercedes, Caracas 1060-A, Venezuela; 011-58-2-993-7911; infocva@cva.org.ve, [www.cva.org.ve]. Internships of at least 6 months for English teachers. In the U.S. this **Pasante Internacional** program is represented by Nancy Carapaica, 1408 NW 82nd Ave., C-525, Miami, FL 33126, fax 582-993-6812.

CIS-MAM Language School, Boulevard Universitario #4, Colonia El Roble, San Salvador, El Salvador; 011 503-226-2623; [www.cis-elsalvador.org]. Volunteer English teachers to work part-time with members of the Salvadorean opposition.

Conservation International, Eco-Escuela de Español, c/o Conservation International, 2501 M St NW, Suite 200, Washington, DC 20037; 202-973-2238; ecoescuela@conservation.org; also c/o G.A.P. Adventures, 19 Duncan St, Suite 401, Toronto M5H 3H1, Canada; [www.gap.ca/can/eco]. Students live in Guatemalan village in Peten region and help with development work while studying Spanish. Fee of $200 per week covers tuition and homestay.

Foundation for Sustainable Development, 5547 Mitcham C.t, Springfield, VA 22151; 703-764-0859; fsd@interconnection.org. Summer and longer term internships in all areas of development in Nicaragua and Bolivia (as well as South Africa and Tanzania).

Grant Foundation, 8466 N Lockwood Ridge Rd., #111, Sarasota, FL 34243; 941-355-2805; fax 941-351-0735. Work team projects use voluntary input to help at the Hopital Albert Schweizer in Haiti.

ICADS (Institute for Central American Development Studies), Apartado 3, 2070 Sabanilla, San Jose, Costa Rica; 011-506-225-0508. Also P.O. Box 025216, Miami, FL 33102-5216; [www.icadscr.com]. One-month Spanish course combined with voluntary service in Costa Rica, Nicaragua, or Belize, $1,500. Ten-week summer internships $3,400.

IMARC (Instituto Mexicano Norteamericano de Relaciones Culturales), Pres. Cardenas 840, Satillo, Coahuila 25000, Mexico; 011-52-84-14 84 22; academ@imarc.edu.mx. Experienced EFL teachers needed.

JustAct, 333 Valencia St., Suite 101, San Francisco, CA 94103; 415-431-4204; odn@igc.org. Staff research internship opportunities for U.S. students ($25 fee).

Latin Link STEP Programme, 175 Tower Bridge Rd., London SE1 2AB, UK; 011-44-207-939 9014; step.uk@latinlink.org. Self-funded team-based program for Christians. Work is on small-scale building projects in Argentina, Bolivia, Brazil, Ecuador, Mexico, and Peru. Four months in spring (March to July) or 7 weeks in summer (July and August).

Na Bolom Volunteer Program, Na Bolom Cultural Institute, Av. Vicente Guerrero No. 33, San Cristóbal de Las Casas, C.P. 29220 Chiapas, Mexico; Tel./fax 011-52-967-8-14-18; nabolom@sclc.ecosur.mx. Variety of voluntary opportunities for at least 3 or 6 months with association working to preserve indigenous culture.

Polyglot, Villavicencio 361 Of. 102, Santiago, Chile; 011-56-2-639-8078; application@polyglot.cl. Forty-50 English teachers with TEFL background hired each year.

Programa de Voluntariado Internacional, Servicio de Parques Nacionales, Apdo. 11384-1000/10104-1000, San Jose, Costa Rica; 011-506-257-0922. Spanish-speaking volunteers work in national parks for at least 45 days. Cost is $10 a day.

Pronatura Chiapas, Av. Benita Juarez 11-B, Apartado P.O.stal 219, San Cristobal de Las Casas, Chiapas, C.P. 29200 Mexico. Tel./fax 011-52-967-85000; pronaturach@planeta.apc.org. Rainforest conservation, environmental education and sustainable agriculture projects. Volunteers must be Spanish-speaking. Accommodations provided.

Tambopata Jungle Lodge, P.O. Box 454, Cusco, Peru; Tel./fax 011-51-84-245695; [www.tam-bopatalodge.com]. Takes on guides for a minimum of 6 months. They must have studied natural sciences and preferably speak Spanish.

MEDITERRANEAN

Many people find work in language schools by applying in person to schools in Madrid, Barcelona, Oporto, Thessaloniki, etc.

American Language Center Damascus, P.O. Box 20, Damascus, Syria; 011-963-11-333 7936, fax 011-963-11-331 9327. Native speaker teachers employed after local interview.

Anglo Nannies, 20 Beverly Ave., London SW20 0RL, England; 011-44-208-944-6677; info@anglonannies.gen.tr. Places mother's helpers and nannies in wealthy Istanbul households. Must be available for interview in U.K. or Istanbul.

Balkan Sunflowers, Volunteers for Social Reconstruction in the Balkans Kosovo/Macedonia/Albania), Central Office, Postfach 1219, D-14806 Belzig, Germany; 001-49-33841 30670; [www.ddh.nl/org/ balkan-sunflower]. U.S. contact: Katarzyna Wargan, 3701 16th St. NW, Suite 500, Washington, DC 20010; 202-726-3317; kate@usbsf.org. Various volunteer projects in the Balkans.

Sunsail, The Port House, Port Solent, Portsmouth, Hampshire P06 4TH, England; 011-44-1705-222325. Hires sailors, hostesses, clubhouse staff, cooks, and nannies for Greece and Turkey.

Sunworld Sailing Ltd., 120 St. Georges Rd., Brighton, E. Sussex BN2 1EA, U.K.; [www.sunworld-sailing.co.uk]. Employs instructors, maintenance staff, crew and other staff for sailing and windsurfing holidays in Spain, Greece, and Turkey.

UNIPAL (Universities Trust for Educational Exchange with Palestinians), BCM Unipal, London WC1N 3XX, U.K.; Tel./fax 011-44-207-771-7368; [www.unipal.org.uk] (written enquiries preferred). Runs a summer program of teaching in the West Bank, Gaza, and Lebanon. Volunteers teach children in refugee camps. Volunteers must be native English speakers and based in the U.K.

English-language newspapers such as the **Athens News** [http://athensnews.dolnet.gr], **Hellenic Times,** 212-986-6881, or the **Anglo-Portuguese News,** apn@mail.telepac.pt are helpful sources of tutoring or au pair positions.

MIDDLE EAST

Active English, Ataturk Bulvari 127/701, Selcan Han, Bakanliklar, 06640 Ankara, Turkey; 011-90-312-418 7973; [www.acteng.com]. Teachers for small chain of private language schools; interviews in Ankara or London.

American Univ. Language Center, 4 Zankat Tanja, Rabat, 10000 Morocco; 011-212-7-761269/766121, fax 011-212-7-767-6255; alcrabat@mtds.com. The largest of 7 ALCs in Morocco which hires EFL teachers for 1 year.

Au Pair International, 2 Desler St., Bnei Brak 51507; Tel/fax 011-972-3 619-0423, [www.aupair-international.co.il]. Placement agency for full-time nannies and housekeepers of all nationalities. Must have full health insurance and HIV test certificate.

Eliat, This prospering and expanding Red Sea resort employs many passers-through in hotels, bars, marinas, yachts, etc. Inquire at hostels or the Good Luck Bar in Israel (where the famous Peace Cafe used to be).

ELS Language Centers/Middle East, P.O. Box 3079, Abu Dhabi, U.A.E.; 011-971-2-665-1516; elsme@emirates.net.ae. Employs many EFL-trained teachers full- and part-time throughout the Middle East.

Friends of Birzeit Univ., 21 Collingham Rd., London SW5 0NU, U.K.; 011-44-207-373 8414; fobzu@arab-british.u-net.com. International summer workcamps near Ramallah in the West Bank.

Gençtur, Istiklal Cad. Zambak Sok. 15/5, 80080 Beyoglu, Istanbul, Turkey; fax 011-90-212-249 2554; workcamps.in@genctur.com. Student travel organization that arranges about 30, 2-week international workcamps and English language summer camps for which ESL teachers and monitors are needed.

GSM Youth Services Centre, Bayindir Sokak No. 45/9, 06650 Kizilay, Ankara, Turkey; 011-90-312-417-29-91. Arranges 2-week workcamps in Anatolia.

Hilma's Au Pair Intermediary, Mrs. Hilma Shmoshkovitz, P.O. Box 91, 75100 Rishon-le-Zion, Israel; 011-972-3-965-99-37; hilma@netvision.net.il. Well-established au pair and nanny agency for Israel. Also has an office in Jerusalem.

Israeli Ministry of Foreign Affairs [www.is-rael-mfa.gov.il/archdigs.html]. Lists archaeological excavations throughout Israel looking for paying volunteers. Applications are made directly to the archaeologists leading the digs.

Kent English Istanbul, Bahariye Arayicibasi Sok. No. 4, 81300 Kadikoy, Istanbul, Turkey; 011-90-216-347 2791; [www.kent-english.com]. Also in Ankara at Mithatpasa Caddesi No. 46 Kat. 3,4,5, 06420 Kizilay, Ankara, Turkey; 011-90-312-433 6010; kentenglishankara@yahoo.com. Many teachers employed; should have college diploma and TEFL certificate.

Kibbutz Program Center, Volunteer Dept., 18 Frishman St., Corner of Ben Yehuda St (No. 90), Tel Aviv 61030, Israel; 011-972-3-527-8874; kpcvol@inter.net.il. This office can place you on a kibbutz for a fee of $60, although it is better to arrive with a letter of introduction from Kibbutz Aliya Desk, 633 3rd Ave., 21st Fl., New York, NY 10017; 800-247-7852; kibbutz-dsk@aol.com, [www.kibbutz.org.il/eng] (a clearinghouse for American volunteers). Minimum stay 2 months; summer is busiest.

Malta Youth Hostels Association, 17 Triq Tal-Borg, Pawla PLA 06, Malta; 011-356-693957; myha@keyworld.net. Volunteers who spend a minimum of 21 hours a week doing hostel maintenance and administration receive free bed and breakfast for 2 weeks to 3 months.

Meira's Volunteers, 73 Ben Yehuda St., 1st Fl., Tel Aviv 63435, Israel; 011-972-3-523-7369, fax 011-972-3-524-1604. Agent for kibbutzim and moshavim for volunteers already in Israel.

Moshav Volunteer Center, 19 Leonardo da Vinci St., Tel Aviv 64733, Israel; 011-972-3-696-8335; fax 011-972-3-696 0139. Places volunteers who are already in Tel Aviv on moshavim throughout Israel.

Ottoman & Ottoman, Gaziosmanpasa Bulvari No. 9, Esen Han Kat: 5/506, 35210 Izmir, Turkey; 011-90-232-445 0599; ottomany-outh@superonline.com. Conservation camps on Turkish coasts.

Yemen-American Language Institute (YALI), P.O. Box 22347, Sana'a, Yemen; 011-967-1-416-973/4; yaliroy@y.net.ye; [www.yali.org.ye]. Educated Americans with good knowledge of American culture needed to teach, preferably for a year. Also in Sana'a, try **American School,** Box 16003; Tel./fax 011-967-1-417119; and **Modern American Language Institute** (MALI), P.O. Box 11727, Sana'a; Tel./fax 011-967-1-241561.

NETHERLANDS, BELGIUM, LUXEMBOURG

Activity International, P.O. Box 7097, 9701 JB Groningen, Netherlands; 011-31-50-3130666; aupair@noord.bart.nl, [www.activity.aupair.nl]. Au pair placements throughout Holland.

Anglo Nannies, 20 Beverley Ave., London SW20 0RL, England; 011-44-208-944-6677; info@anglonannies.gen.tr. Places mother's helpers and nannies in wealthy Istanbul households. Must be available for interview in U.K. or Istanbul.

Centre Information Jeunes (CIJ), 26 Place de la Gare, Gelerie Kons, L-1616 Luxembourg; 011-352-26 29 3-200. Run holiday job service between January and August, primarily for people with a European Union passport.

Euro Business Languages, Leuvensesteenweg 325, 1932 Zavantem, Belgium; 011-32-2-720-15-10; euro.business.languages@skynet.be. Experienced TEFL teachers needed to run business English courses.

L'Administration de L'Emploi, 10 rue Bender, 1229 Luxembourg; 011-352-478 53 00. Operates a Service Vacances for students seeking summer jobs in warehouses, restaurants, etc. Non-European students must visit the office in person.

Natuur 2000, Bervoetstraat 33, 2000 Antwerp, Belgium; fax 011-32-3-231-26-04; [http://home.planetinternet.be/~n2000[. Organizes summer conservation workcamps and study projects throughout Belgium, which cost from BF1,500.

NJBG (Nederlandse Jeugdbond voor Geschiedenis), Prins Willem Alexanderhof 5, 2595 BE Den Haag, Netherlands; fax 011-31-70-335 2536; [www.njbg.nl] (partially in English). Archaeological and building restoration camps.

Phone Languages, 65 rue des Echevins, 1050 Brussels, Belgium; 011-32-2-647-40-20; belgium@phonelanguages.com. Telephone teachers recruited for clients throughout Belgium and Luxembourg.

Stufam V.Z.W., Vierwindenlaan 7, 1780 Wemmel, Belgium; 011-32-2-460-3395; aupair.stufam@pi.be. Places au pairs in Belgium.

The Bulletin, 1038 Chaussée de Waterloo, 1110 Brussels. A weekly English-language magazine in Brussels which carries job ads. Published on Thursdays.

SCANDINAVIA

Allianssi Youth Exchanges, Olympiastadion, Etelakaarre, 00250 Helskini, Finland; 011-358-9-34824 312; [www.alli.fi/nuorisovaihto]. Coordinates workcamps in Finland; enquiries should be sent to partner organizations in the U.S.

American-Scandinavian Foundation, 58 Park Ave., New York, NY 10016; 212-879-9779; trainscan@amscan.org, [www.amscan.org]. Places summer trainees in engineering, chemistry or computer science throughout Scandinavia, mainly Finland and Sweden. Also places American students and graduates in schools and companies in Finland to teach English from August to May.

APØG, Norsk Økologisk Landbrukslag, Langeveien 18, N-5003 Bergen, Norway; fax 011-47-55 32 02 45; organic@online.no. Service for volunteers who want to work on organic farms in Norway; send $20 for list of 50+ farm addresses.

Atlantis Youth Exchange, Kirkegata 32, 0153 Oslo, Norway; 011-47-22-47 71 70; P.O.st@atlantis-u.no. Arranges summer working guest positions on farms for 2 to 6 months. Also recruits au pairs for a minimum of 6 months. Applications can be sent direct or via InterExchange in New York.

Center for International Mobility (CIMO), P.B. 343, 00531 Helsinki, Finland; 011-358-9-7747-7033; cimoinfo@cimo.fi, [www.cimo.fi]. Arranges short- and long-term traineeships with Finnish companies. Open only to those who are studying Finnish at a university.

Exis, Postbox 291, 6400 Sonderborg, Denmark; 011-45-74-42-97-49; info@exis.dk; [www.exis.dk]. Increasing number of au pair placements throughout Scandinavia, especially Denmark.

IAL/Internationella Arbetslag, Barnängsgatan 23, 116 41 Stockholm, Sweden; 011-46-8-643 08 89; fax 011-46-8-641 8188. Peace and conservation camps organized through the Swedish branch of Service Civil International.

MS/Mellemfolkeligt Samvirke, Studsgade 20, 8000 Aarhus C, Denmark. Two 4-week summer workcamps in Denmark and Greenland. Danish camp fee 885 kroner.

Stifelsen Stjarnsund, 770 71 Stjarnsund, Sweden; 011-46-225-80001; michael@stdi.w.se. Swedish community aims to encourage personal, social and spiritual development. Operates an international working guest program, 1 week to 3 months, mostly between May and September but winter visits possible.

Use It Denmark, Youth Information Copenhagen, Radhusstraede 13, 1466 Copenhagen K, Denmark; 011-45-1-33-73 06 20; useit@ui.dk. Publishes English language booklet "Working in Denmark" and provides services to job-seeking young people.

Use It Norway, Mollergata 3, 0179 Oslo, Norway; 011-47-224-15132; [www.ung-info.oslo.no/streetwise]. Services as above. Web site has some information on work.

VHH, c/o Inga Nielsen, Asenvej 35, 9881 Bindslev, Denmark. For $10 publishes a list of English-speaking organic farmers in Denmark looking for volunteers.

Vista Cultural & Educational Travel, Laekjargata 4, 101 Reykjavik, Iceland; 011-354-562 2362; vista@skima.is. Au pair agency placing foreign young people for 6 to 12 months in Icelandic households.

WWOOF-Finland, c/o Anne Konsti, Partala Information Services for Organic Agriculture, Huttulantie 1, 51900 Juva, Finland; 011-358-15-321 2380. Finnish organic farm organization. Send International Response Coupons to get list of 30 farmers looking for volunteers over the summer.

SPAIN, PORTUGAL

Acorn Adventure Ltd., 22 Worcester St., Stourbridge, West Midlands DY8 1AN, England; 011-44-1384-378827; topstaff@acornadventure.co.uk, [www.acorn-venture.com]. Activity instructors and support staff for holiday center on the Costa Brava of Spain.

Castrum Lenguas Cultures y Turismo, Ctra. de Reudas 33, 47008 Valladolid; 011-34-983-222213; [www.terra.es/personal2/castrum-spain]. Places young people with families in Castille and Leon where they exchange 3 to 4 hours of English lessons per day for room and board. They also enroll in a Spanish course.

Centros Europeos, Calle Principe 12-6ºA, 28012 Madrid, Spain; 011-34-1 532 7230. Au pair placements in Spain. Also vacancies for English teachers October-June.

Club de Relaciones Culturales, Calle Ferraz 82, 28008 Madrid, Spain; 011-34-91-5417103; rci_ic@mad.servicom.es. Places American and European au pairs and live-in language assistants in Madrid and elsewhere in Spain. Registration fee is 20,000 pesetas.

Deya Archaeological Museum and Research Centre, Deya, Mallorca, Baleares, Spain; Tel./fax 011-34-71-639001. Participants join this long-established research project and excavation for 2 weeks at a time. Room, board and tuition cost $600 for the fortnight.

Entreculturas, Rua Pereira e Sousa 76, R/C, 1300 Lisbon, Portugal; 011-351-21-387 05 09. Youth agency that arranges au pair placements.

Instituto da Português Juventude, Av. da Liberdade 194, 1259-015 Lisbon, P.O.rtugal; 011-351-21-317-9200; ipj.infor@mail.tele-pac.pt. Arranges workcamps, including archaeological digs, throughout Portugal. Applications should be sent to workcamp agency in home country.

Manga del Mar Menor Restoration and Research Project, Instituto de Ciencias Sociales y Ambientales and Amigos de la UNESCO, Paseo Marques de Corvera 33, 4BA A, Apartado de Correos 4.661 Murcia, Spain; Tel./fax 011-34-968-22-05-96; [www.ctv.es/users/murban/volunt.htm]. Volunteers stay 15 days to 3 months at this coastal wetlands center collecting data and working with the public.Two-month working stay costs 125,000 pesetas ($650).

Proyecto Ambiental Tenerife, 59 St. Martin's Ln., Covent Garden, London WC2, England; fax 011-44-207-240-5795; [www.inter-book.net/personal/delfinc]. Volunteers needed to work 2-6 weeks on whale and dolphin projects based in Tenerife, Spain. Must contribute £75 per week toward expenses.

Sunseed Trust, Apdo 9, 04270 Sorbas, Almeria, Spain; tel/fax 011-34-950-525 770; [www.sunseed.clara.net]. Invites volunteers to a remote research project on the south coast of Spain to help subsidize their stay, which costs about $150 per week.

UNITED KINGDOM AND IRELAND

Acorn Adventure Ltd., 22 Worcester St., Stourbridge, West Midlands DY8 1AN, England; 011-44-1384-378827; topstaff@acornadventure.co.uk, [www.acorn-venture.com].

Activity holiday centers in North Wales and the Lake District of England that need instructors and catering staff for full season (April-September).

Aillwee Cave Co., Ballyvaughan, Co. Clare, Ireland; 011-353-65-77036; [www.aillweecave.ie]. Cave tour guides and catering/sales staff taken on for summer season at this busy tourist attraction open March to November.

An Oige, 61 Mountjoy St., Dublin 1, Ireland; 011-353-1-830-4555. The Irish Youth Hostels Association makes use of voluntary assistant wardens in the summer months.

British Trust for Conservation Volunteers, 36 Saint Mary's St., Wallingford, Oxfordshire OX10 0EU, England; 011-44-1491-839766; [www.btcv.org.uk]. Organizes 1- or 2-week working breaks throughout Britain for environmentally concerned volunteers.

BUNAC (British Universities North America Club), P.O. Box 430, Southbury, CT 06488; 800-GO BUNAC or 203-264-0901, fax 203-264-0251; [www.bunac.org], operates the "Work in Britain" program enabling U.S. university students and recent graduates to take virtually any job in Britain for up to 6 months. BUNAC also offers work/travel programs to Australia and New Zealand for U.S. citizens aged 18-36. Participants can work for up to 4 months in Australia and for up to 12 months in New Zealand.

Caledonia Languages Abroad, The Clockhouse, Bonnington Mill, 72 Newhaven Road, Edinburgh EH6 5QG, U.K.; 011-44-131-621 7721/2; [www.caledonialanguages.co.uk]. Spanish and voluntary work programs organized in Peru and Costa Rica year round. Community and environmental projects and teaching English, depending on skills and level of language ability.

Children's Holiday Companies recruit large numbers of summer staff. **PGL Travel,** Alton Court, Penyard Ln., Ross-on-Wye, Herefordshire HR9 5NR, England; 011-44-1989-767833. Hires over 500 people as sports instructors, counselors, and general staff for activity centers throughout Britain. Other children's holiday companies include: **Prime Leisure Activity Holidays,** Ltd., 4A Chawley Ln., Cumnor Hill, Oxford OX2 9PX, England; Camp Beaumont, Linton House, 164/180 Union St., London SE1 OLH, England; **Buckswood International Summer School,**

Uckfield, Sussex TN22 3PU, England; and **Conquest Tours Ltd.,** 13 Victoria Rd., Bath BA2 3QY, England.

Community Service Volunteers Overseas Programme, 237 Pentonville Rd., London N1 9NJ, England; 011-44-207-278-6601; [www.csv.org.uk]. Places volunteers in socially worthwhile projects from 4 months to a year throughout Britain. Placement fee of £499 for overseas volunteers.

Conservation Volunteers Ireland, P.O. Box 3836, Ballsbridge, Dublin 4, or Green Griffith College, South Circular Rd., Dublin 8, Ireland; 011-353-1-454-7185. Coordinates unpaid environmental working holidays throughout Ireland. Membership is IR£15.

Council Exchanges: Work in Ireland Program, 633 3rd Ave., 20th Fl., New York, NY 10017-6706; 888-COUNCIL. Cooperates with UsitNow see below). Students can obtain 4-month work permit for a fee.

Council for British Archaeology, Bowes Morrell House, 111 Walmgate, York Y01 9WA, England; 011-44-1904-671-417; [www.britarch. ac.uk]. Publishes CBA Briefing 5 times a year with details of upcoming excavations in Britain. Membership costs £20 plus postage).

Dublin Internships, 8 Orlagh Lawn, Scholarstown Rd., Dublin 16, Ireland; Tel./fax 011-353-1-494-5277; mhrieke@eircom.net. Places American undergraduates, graduate students and graduates in professional level internships in the spring, fall, and summer across the spectrum of majors, minors, and career options. Internships are non-salaried and a fee is charged. Advisable to forward application documentation 3 months in advance.

National Trust, Residential Holidays, P.O. Box 39, Bromley, Kent BR1 3XL, England; 011-44-208-315-1111. One-week outdoor conservation camps throughout the U.K. year round. Volunteers pay £60 per week or less during winter.

Nord-Anglia International Ltd., 10 Eden Pl., Cheadle, Stockport, Cheshire SK8 1AT, England; 011-44-161-491-8477. Places more than 300 young people in English-language summer schools in Britain and Ireland as language and sports instructors. Many positions are non-residential.

TASIS England American School, Coldharbour Ln., Thorpe, Surrey KT20 8TE, England; 011-44-1932-565252;

[www.tasis.com]. EFL teaching vacancies for qualified Americans and jobs for sports monitors to work at children's summer camp.

Thistle Camps, National Trust for Scotland, 5 Charlotte Sq., Edinburgh EH2 4DU, Scotland; 011-44-131-243-9470; [www.nts.org.uk]. Similar to National Trust but in Scotland. Includes archaeological digs. Two- or 4-week projects; fee of £50-£110. Application deadline is February for overseas applicants.

Trident Transnational, Saffron Court, 14B St Cross St., London EC1N 8XA, England; 011-44-207-242-1515; info.transnational@trid-demon.co.uk. Offers unpaid work placements lasting 4 weeks to 6 months in U.K. businesses. Participants aged 18-26. Fees range from £140-£420.

UsitNow, 19 Aston Quay, Dublin 2, Ireland; 011-353-1-602-1777. Advice on job opportunities for Council Exchange participants.

Winant & Clayton Volunteers, 109 E. 50th St., New York, NY 10022; 212- 378-0271. Since 1948, has arranged for U.S. citizens to volunteer for 7 weeks during the summer in community social service agencies in Britain, followed by independent travel for 2 weeks. Application deadline is January 31.

Youth Hostels Association, National Recruitment Dept., P.O. Box 11, Matlock, Derbyshire DE4 2XA, U.K. Seasonal assistant youth hostel wardens for 240 U.K. hostels. Interviews required.

Work Abroad as an Au Pair
A Guide to Employment in Europe
By Susan Griffith

Au pairing (literally "living on equal terms") provides single women and men aged 18-27 the chance to study a language and culture while living as part of a family abroad. The demand for live-in childcare is huge. A good source of agency addresses is the web site of the International Au Pair Association [www.iapa.org], though a number of member agencies operate outgoing programs only (i.e., they send their nationals abroad, primarily to learn English).

Austria. The tradition of au pairing is well established in Austria and prospective au pairs are served by several agencies (see below), all of whom are accustomed to dealing with direct applications from foreigners. Requirements are not strenuous, and many inexperienced 18-year-olds are placed. The agencies can take a long time to reply and may need some follow-up faxes and phone calls.

The two main Vienna agencies combine forces rather than compete. They run an au pair club and provide many other services between them. Officially, au pairs from outside Europe must obtain both a work and residence permit *(Beschäftigungs-bewilligung)*. Almost no one succeeds. The majority of non-European au pairs leave the country every three months, re-registering on their return.

Belgium. Belgian agencies may charge applicants who apply directly (rather than through an agency in their own country) an administrative fee of BF1,000-BF2,000 ($22-$44). If you intend to look for a family after arrival, check the ads in *The Bulletin,* the English-language magazine for the huge expatriate community in Belgium. The current monthly pocket money for au pairs is BF10,000-BF15,000.

Non-European citizens must obtain an authorization of provisional sojourn from the Belgian Embassy in their home country before arriving in Belgium. Their contract with their host family (minimum 12 months) must be approved by the *administration communale* to get a one-year "B" work permit from the regional Office National de l'Emploi. To qualify, the applicant must show proof of having registered in a language course in Belgium.

France. Au pairing has always been a favored way for young women to learn French and, increasingly, for young men too. The pocket money for au pairs in France is currently FF1,600 per month (in Paris FF1,700 plus the *carte orange* or travel pass).

North Americans can fix up au pair placements directly with a French agency, but bear in mind that you must pay the high placement fees (typically FF1,000) in advance and that in some cases very little advance information about the family is available. Enrollment in a French language course is compulsory for non-European au pairs.

In Paris, the notice board at the **American Church** (65 Quai d'Orsay) is crammed with announcements of live-in positions. Unless you especially like small children, it might be better to look for a free room in exchange for minimal babysitting.

Germany. Non-EU citizens no older than 24 can become au pairs through a German agency. A special au pair visa must be obtained before leaving the U.S., a process that takes up to three months.

The monthly pocket money for an au pair in Germany is about DM400 plus a monthly travel pass and other benefits such as a contribution to course fees of DM200 per semester and up to DM300 for return travel at end of year. For this expect hard work that usually involves more housework than au pairs normally do.

Greece. Ads appear in the *Athens News,* usually placed by families in the wealthy suburbs of Athens. The agency **Au Pair Activities** accepts postal applications from young European and American women and also can place candidates after arrival in Athens. The **Athenian Nanny Agency** keeps detailed dossiers on vacancies, most of which tend to be for experienced nannies though there are some for au pairs. Most families ask their live-in staff to work longer hours and reward them accordingly; a full-time au pair in Athens can expect about 180,000 drachmas ($460) a month. For the limited number of summer positions available application should be made by April.

Israel. Plenty of Israeli families, especially in Tel Aviv, Jerusalem, and Haifa, are eager to employ mother's helpers, even those who lack experience but are prepared to work very long hours. Many stories circulate of exploitation and ill treatment of live-in helpers. A considerable amount of housework will be expected of mother's helpers, and plenty of evening babysitting. Au pairs should receive a day-and-a-half off per week, though these are not always consecutive. Virtually all au pairs work in Israel on tourist visas.

In return for all this hard work, wages are moderately high. Those who stay for an entire year have a chance of having their fare home paid by the family as well as a two-week paid holiday. In some cases, families will give their employee a week's holiday after six months work. The standard starting wage is the shekel equivalent of $750-$900 a month.

Ads appear constantly in papers like the *Jerusalem Post*. Note that many ads that sound attractive are placed by agencies; when you ring, they say that the advertised job has been taken but they have others on their books. You should be prepared to learn how to keep a kosher kitchen.

Italy. It is possible to apply independently through an Italian agency, but first make sure that you won't be liable to pay a hefty registration fee. There are many opportunities for au pairs during the summer holidays when most Italians who can afford au pairs migrate to the coast or the mountains and take their helpers with them. The average weekly pocket money for au pairs is 100,000 lire for working 30 hours a week or 130,000 lire for 36 hours.

Netherlands. Americans and Canadians do not have to apply for any special permits before they arrive in the Netherlands. They simply register with the immigration police *(Vreemdelingenpolitie)* within eight days of arrival in the municipality where they will be au pairing. Once the forms are in order a one-year residence permit *(Verblijfsvergunning)* will be granted.

Scandinavia. Until recently, the au pair system has not been popular in the countries of Scandinavia, probably due to the excellent state-sponsored childcare and the limited appeal for foreign young people to learn the languages. However, the concept is catching on and some of the many agencies which send Scandinavian au pairs abroad are also placing foreign young people as au pairs in Scandinvian homes, incidentally providing one of the few ways to afford an extended stay in this very expensive region.

The situation in Norway is most promising for English speakers of all nationalities, though the red tape for North Americans is still considerable. **Atlantis Youth Exchange** runs the largest program for au pairs in Norway. Applicants must be aged 18-30 and willing to stay between six months and two years. The first step is to write for an information sheet and application forms. Atlantis charges foreign au pairs a substantial registration fee of 1,000 Norwegian Kroner ($110).

For many years the Finnish Family Program accepted young people who wanted to spend the summer months helping a family with household chores and English conversation. However, this program, formerly administered by the **Centre for International Mobility** (CIMO, P.O. Box 343, 00531 Helsinki, Finland; [www.cimo.fi]), has been drastically reduced and is open only to students studying the Finnish language at university. Openings for au pairs still exist.

Interest in au pairing in Iceland is increasing, and Americans can find a family through **Au Pair Vistaskipt** in Reykjavik (the only mediating agency for au pairs licensed by the Ministry of Social Affairs). Families cover half the travel costs (if you stay six to nine months) and the full cost if you stay nine to 12 months, to a maximum of KR50,000.

Spain. The chance of arranging an au pair placement in Spain is very good. The majority of jobs are in the cities and environs of Madrid and Barcelona, though jobs do crop up in glamorous resorts like Marbella and Tenerife from time to time. Several au pair agencies in Spain are associated with language schools such as Centros Europeos Galve.

The average pocket money for au pairs at present is 7,000-8,500 pesetas a week. There are also opportunities for young people to stay with Spanish families in exchange for speaking English with the children without having any domestic or childcare duties, for example through the Vallodolid agency **Castrum**. Americans and Canadians who wish to work as au pairs should apply for a student visa before leaving home. Officially, the Embassy requires both an offer of employment from the family and a letter from the school where the au pair is enrolled (or will enroll) to study Spanish.

Switzerland. Those interested in a domestic position with a Swiss family should know the rules laid down by each Swiss canton. You must be a female between the ages of 17 (18 in Geneva) and 29 from Western Europe, North America, Australia and New Zealand, stay for a minimum of one year and a maximum of 18 months, and attend a minimum of three hours a week of language classes in Zürich, four in Geneva. Families in most places are required to pay half the language school fees of SFR360-SFR1,000 for six months.

Au pairs in Switzerland work for a maximum of 30 hours per week, plus babysitting once or twice a week. The monthly salary varies among cantons but the normal range is SF600-SF710 from which compulsory deductions are made for tax and health insurance.

Au Pair Placement Agencies

NORTH AMERICAN AGENCIES

The following North American agencies have outgoing au pair programs in Europe:

Accord Cultural Exchange, 750 La Playa, San Francisco, CA 94121; 415-386-6203. Au pair placements in France, Germany, Italy, Spain, and Austria.

Alliances Abroad, 702 West Ave., Austin, TX 78701; 888-6-ABROAD; info@alliances-abroad.com, [www.alliancesabroad.com]. Range of programs include teaching in Mexico, Africa, and the Far East; unpaid internships and volunteer work in many countries including Ireland, Germany, Jamaica, Guatemala, and Ecuador. Fees vary; samples are $1,200 for up to 5 months of teaching in Mexico, and for 2-month internship in Dublin.

Au Pair in Europe, P.O. Box 68056, Blakely Postal Outlet, Hamilton, ON L8M 3M7, Canada; 905-545-6305; aupair@princeent.com, [www.princeent.com/aupair]. Au pairs placed in 21 countries including Australia. Airfare reimbursement plan operates in Holland, Sweden, and Iceland. Administrative and referral fee $425.

InterExchange, Inc., 161 6th Ave., New York, NY 10013; 212-924-0446; info@interexchange.org, [www.interexchange.org]. Work placements in Germany, France, Scandinavia, Switzerland, Belgium, the U.K., and Eastern Europe. Also au pair placements in France, Germany, Netherlands, and Spain. Teaching English in Spain, Bulgaria, and Poland. Fees are $400-$450 for most programs.

COUNTRY-BY-COUNTRY AGENCIES

Austria

Auslands-Sozialdienst, Johannesgasse 16/1, 1010 Vienna; 011-43-1-512-7941, fax 011-43-1-513-9460. **Okista** (Austrian Committee for International Educational Exchange), Garnisongasse 7, 1090 Vienna; 011-43-1-401 48/8827; [www.oekista.co.at]. **Irmhild Spitzer,** Sparkassenplatz 1, 7th Fl., Linz; Tel./fax 011-43-732-73-78-14.

Belgium

Stufam, Vierwindenlaan 7, 1780 Wemmel; 011-32-2-460-33-95; aupair.stufam@pi.be. **Services de la Jeunesse Feminine,** 29 rue Faider, 1050 Brussels; 011-32-2-539 3514.

Denmark

Exis, P.O. Box 291, 6400 Sonderborg; 011-45-74-42-97-49, fax 011-45-74-42-97-47; info@exis.dk; [www.exis.dk].

France

Accueil Familial des Jeunes Etrangers, 23 rue de Cherche-Midi, 75006 Paris; 011-33-1-42-22-50-34; atjeparis@aol.com. Butterfly et Papillon, 5 Av. de Genève, 74000 Annecy; 011-33-4-50-46-08-33/50-67-01-33; aupair.france@wanadoo.fr. Europair Services, 13 rue Vavin, 75006 Paris; 011-33-1-43-29-80-01; europairservices@wanadoo.fr. Institut Euro Provence, 69 rue de Rome, 13001 Marseille; 011-33-4-91-33-90-60; euro.provence@infonie.fr. Soames International Services, 6 route de Marlotte, 77690 Montigny-sur-Loing; 011-33-1-64-78-37-98; soames.parisnannies@wanadoo.fr.

Germany

In Via, Ludwigstr, 36, Postfach 420, 79004 Freiburg; 011-44-761-200206.; invia@caritas.de. Has branches throughout Germany. Verein für Internationale Jugendarbeit, Goetheallee 10, 53225 Bonn; 011-49-228-69-89-52). Part of the German YWCA with 23 offices in Germany. Au Pair e.V., Staufenstrasse 17, 86899 Landsberg am Lech; 011-49-8191-941378; aupairscp@t-online,de; [www.sta-net.de/au-pair]. GIJK/Au Pair in Germany, Baunscheidtstrasse 11, 53113 Bonn; 011-49-228-95-73-00; [www.gijk.de]. Part of GIJK, a cultural exchange organization. Au Pair Network International (APNI), Augustastr. 1, 53173 Bonn; 011-49-228-956950; [www.step-in.de].

Greece

Au Pair Activities, P.O. Box 76080, 17110 Nea Smyrni, Athens; Tel/fax 011-30-1-932-6016; porae@iname.com. Athenian Nanny & Domestics Agency, P.O. Box 51181, Kifissia, 14510 Athens; Tel./fax 011-30-1-808-1005; mskiniti@groovy gr.

Finland

Allianssi Youth Exchange, Olympiastadion, Etelakaarra, 00250 Helsinki; 011-358-9-348 4244; vaihto@alli.fi.

Iceland

Au Pair Vistaskipti, Laekjargata 4, 101 Reykjavik; 011-354-556 22 352; vista@skima.is.

Israel

Hilma's Au Pair Intermediary, 5 Moholiver, P.O. Box 91, Rishon le Zion; 011-972-3-965-9937. Au Pair International, 2 Desler St., Bnei Brak 51507; 011-972-3-619-0423; [www.aupair-international.co.il].

Italy

Au Pair International, Via S. Stefano 32, 40125 Bologna; 011-39-51-267575, fax 51-236594; aupair@tin.it. L'Aquilone, Via Giovanni, Pascoli 15, 20129 Milan; 011-39-2-2952-96-39; [www.s.snf.it/aquiline]. A.R.C.E., Via Settembre 20/124, 16121 Genova 011-39-010-583020;arceita@tin.it. Aupairitaly.com, Via Demetrio Martinelli 11/d, 40133 Bologna; 011-39-051-383466; [www.aupairitaly.com].

Netherlands

Activity International, P.O. Box 7097, 9701 JB Groningen, Netherlands; 011-31-50-31-30-666, fax 011-31-50-31-31-633; [www.activity.aupair.nl]. Au Pair Discover Holland, C. Barendregtlaan 9-F, 3161 HA-Rhoon, The Netherlands; 011-31-10-50-14-652.

Norway

Atlantis, Kirkegata 32, 0153 Oslo; 011-47-22-47 71 70; post@atlantis-u.no; [www.atlantis-u.no]. 1,000 kroner registration fee for 8-12 month stay.

Portugal

Entreculturas, Rua Pereira e Sousa, 76 R/C, 1300 Lisbon; 011-351-21 387 05 09. Intercultura, Rua de Santo Antonio da Gloria 6A, 1250 Lisbon; 011-351-21-346 41 26.

Spain

Centros Europeos Galve, Calle Principe 12-6ºA, 28012 Madrid; 011-34-1-532-72-30. GIC, Pintor Sorolla, Apt. 1080, 46901 Monte Vedat-Valencia; Tel 011-34-97-03-44-818. Club de Relaciones Culturales, Calle Ferraz 82, 28008 Madrid; 011-34-91-5417103; rci_ic@mad.servicom.es. S&C Asociados, Avda. Eduardo Dato 46, 2ºB, 41005 Seville; 011-34-95-464-2447; s_c@mundivia.es.

Sweden

Scandinavian Institute, Box 3085, 200 22 Malmo; 011-46-40-93 94 40; info@scandinavianinst.com; [www.scandinavianinst.com]. Place au pairs in Sweden, Norway, Denmark and Finland.

Switzerland

Verein Compagna, Reckenbuhlstrasse 21, 6005 Lucerne; 011-41-41-312 11 73; compagna-Luzern@bluewin.ch. For the French part of Switzerland (Geneva and Lausanne), contact **Compagna Lausanne,** Rue du Simplon 2, 1006 Lausanne; 011-41-21-616-29-88, fax 011-41-21-616-29-94. **Pro Filia Geneva,** 241G Rte. D'Hermance, 1246 Corsier/Geneva; 011-41-22-751 02 95. **Heli Grandjean Placements Au Pair,** Chemin de Relion 1E, Case Postale 4, 1245 Collonge-Bellerive; Tel./fax011-41-22-752-38-23; grandjean@geneva.link.ch. **Perfect Way,** Mandacherstrasse 1, 5234 Villigen; 011-41-56-284 28 86; perfectway@pop.agri.ch.

Perspective

Crewing a Boat
The Secrets to Finding Work on a Yacht

By Robert Hein

In my more than 20 years as a yacht sailor many people have said, "I always wanted to take a voyage on a small boat; I wish I could get a job like yours." Practically all of them thought that crewing was impossible unless they had years of experience, but this is not the case. Captains routinely sign on people who have no sailing experience.

The secrets to finding a berth on an ocean-going yacht is to know where, when, and how to search. There is no shortage of opportunities. Thousands of private yachts are currently sailing on years-long extended cruises and have crew requirements that change from port to port. Some moor in foreign ports for months, hiring live-aboard maintenance or delivery crews to sail them home.

The qualities most desired in crew members are compatibility, a positive attitude, and reasonably good health. Stamina, not brute strength, is the physical requirement, so age and gender are not limiting factors. Men and women, from teens to retirees, are sailing the high seas as crew on cruising yachts.

Yachts crossing the South Pacific follow the southeast trade winds. Although they take various courses as they filter through Oceania, the great majority call at the inexpensive and friendly island nation of Fiji.

In Fiji, the best time to look for a crew position is from August through October. This is the last half of the sailing season and many yachts will stop for provisions and repairs before heading for New Zealand or Australia. Plan to arrive in Fiji in August or September and you have an excellent chance of getting a crew position. (The cost of living there is very reasonable: food and accommodations are as low as $10 a day.)

Find the captains at the Royal Suva Yacht Club near the capital and main port, Suva, or at the Tradewinds Marina a few miles out of town at the Tradewinds Hotel. Both places are easily accessible by city bus. Yacht marinas are also located at several large resorts near the town of Nadi and the International Airport and nearby

Lautoka. Yacht clubs always have bulletin boards listing want ads for crew.

Just visit yacht clubs or marinas, have a drink, and meet the yachties who gather for the "sundown hour" when they are returning from day trips or just getting off the boat for the first time that day. Introduce yourself and tell them you are looking for a crew position. Don't be discouraged if offers don't come right away; it takes a little while to build up your credibility.

Have a simple resume ready in advance. This shows that you are serious about crewing and gives the skipper a sketch of your background. Keep it simple. Just list your name, home address, and a contact person with address and phone number. Paste a passport-size photo near the top. If possible, list a few people as references. Local ones are best, but anyone who can be easily contacted by phone will do.

Next, give a brief history of your activities or occupation for the past few years. Then list your skills and hobbies. Can you cook or play a musical instrument? Seagoing cooks are always in demand and entertaining people make great shipmates. Finally, include a copy of your passport data and photo pages.

Some boats offer an airline ticket back to the port where you signed on. Some pay the crew. Others offer a free ride but the crew members pay for their own upkeep at the end of the voyage. Still others charge a few dollars a day.

The Best Web Sites

Internet Resources for Short-Term Jobs Abroad

Selected and Reviewed by William Nolting

Organizations in this section offer work permits and placements into short-term paid jobs or on-site assistance in finding them—jobs typically lasting a summer or semester, though some programs offer permits for up to 18 months. These programs are allowed to operate on the basis of official reciprocal agreements between the U.S. and foreign governments.

Web sites in this section are some of the most useful for students and graduates. They list internships, volunteer, work abroad, and study abroad programs with or without academic credit. The rating codes are as follows: ** *Essential;* * *Outstanding and of broad interest.*

(I) Informational site with directories or databases listing many programs
(P) Site for a specific work abroad program
(S) Scholarships or fellowships

* (P) AIESEC-USA [www.us.aiesec.org]. AIESEC (from the French acronym for the International Association of Students in Economic & Business Management) is an international student-run organization which offers approximately 5,000 paid internships each year in business and other fields in over 80 countries. Site has links to chapters world-wide. Note that application for AIESEC internships is possible only through campus chapters.

** (P) AIPT [www.aipt.org/programs.html] (Association for International Practical Training)Nonprofit organization offers several different programs:

• IAESTE [www.aipt.org/iaeste.html] (International Association for the Exchange of Students for Technical Experience) offers engineering and science internships in over 60 countries for students (apply by early December).

• **Student Exchanges/U.S. Reserved Offer Program** [www.aipt.org/iae_resoff.htm] provides work permits in numerous countries for nontechnical and technical fields for students who find their own internships.

• **Career Development Program** [www.aipt.org/prog_cde.html] provides work permits for up to 18 months in Austria (11 month limit), Britain (12 month limit), Finland, France, Germany, Hungary, Ireland, Japan, Malaysia, Mexico, Slovak Republic, Sweden, and Switzerland for university graduates who find their own placements.

* (I, P) **American-Scandinavian Foundation** [www.amscan.org]. The web site of this nonprofit organization includes a comprehensive directory of study, language, and work abroad programs in Scandinavian countries. ASF offers internship placements for students of technical subjects as well as English-teaching positions. ASF can also assist with short-term work permits in Scandinavian countries for those who have job offers.

** (P) **BUNAC: Work in Britain and Australia programs** [www.bunac.org]. Nonprofit organization BUNAC (British Universities North American Club) operates the Work in Britain program—with 6,000 US participants, the largest of all work abroad programs. The program provides a work permit and job search assistance. Also offers a Work in Australia program. The BUNAC Handbook has a great selection of addresses for potential internships in Britain, which can be used to arrange interviews when they arrive. For students and very recent graduates (within 1 semester of graduation) only.

* (P) **Camp Counselors USA, Outbound Program** [www.campcounselors.com/americans.html]. Nonprofit organization offers several programs for students and non-students: Work in Australia, Work in New Zealand, as well as programs which offer placements to serve as camp counselors in Russia.

* (P) **CDS International** [www.cdsintl.org]. Nonprofit organization offers several paid internship programs in Germany for students, graduates, and professionals. Web site provides program information and listings of new internship openings, plus links for information about Germany. CDS can also assist with short-term work permits in Germany for those who have job offers.

• **The Congress-Bundestag Program** [www.cdsintl.org/cbyxintro.html] consists of two months of intensive German, four months attending a technical school, and a five-month internship. All expenses paid; no application fee. Specified age of participants is 18-24. Application deadline is mid-December for the following academic year.

• **The CDS Internship Program** [www.cdsintl.org/bacintro.html] is a three or six-month program for seniors or graduates.

• **The Robert Bosch Program** [www.cdsintl.org/rbfpintro.html] offers internships for those holding graduate degrees.

** (P) **Council Work Abroad Program** [www.councilexchanges.org/work/]. The nonprofit Council Work Abroad program, one of the largest programs, offers short-term work permits and job search support for France, Germany, Ireland, Canada, Costa Rica, Australia, and New Zealand. Also offers a Teach in China program and volunteering abroad in 30 countries. For students and very recent graduates (within one semester of graduation) only.

** (P) **InterExchange** [www.interexchange.org]. Nonprofit organization offers a variety of placements for students and non-students. Apply four months in advance of desired departure date. English Teaching in Bulgaria, Costa Rica, Czech Republic, Hungary and Poland. Internships in Germany for marketing, trade and tourism, museums, and business. Intermediate German required. Agricultural work in Norway. Au Pair placements in Austria, France, Germany, Holland, Italy, Norway, Spain, and Switzerland.

** (P) **International Cooperative Education program** [www.icemenlo.com] provides paid summer internships in Switzerland, Germany, Belgium, Finland, Japan, or Singapore for students and recent graduates who have studied the appropriate language: German, French, Italian, Finnish, Dutch, Japanese, or Chinese. Apply by January.

CHAPTER 5

VOLUNTEERING ABROAD

*While volunteering means giving, it also means
receiving—friendships, knowledge of oneself, insight
into another culture, and the relationship between that
society and our own. For some it can be a
catalyst towards lifelong work for social change
at home or abroad.*

Volunteer Work Abroad

Introduction: Working to Provide for Unmet Needs

By William Nolting

Volunteering abroad is defined not so much by earnings, since volunteer programs may or may not provide some form of reimbursement, as it is by service, working to provide for unmet needs, including social (poverty, hunger, illiteracy), environmental, or educational. Traditionally, volunteering has been seen as helping others. Today, it is often seen as helping persons or groups achieve their goals as they themselves define them, building local self-reliance.

Why Volunteer?

"Before making a commitment, it is important to clarify your motives. You may be drawn to voluntary service by a desire to help impoverished people. You may be interested in learning about another culture and society. You may wish to be part of a process of positive social change. Or you may wish to gain experience which will help you find employment. Each of these motivations will direct you to distinct options for voluntary service." — *Alternatives to the Peace Corps*

Some Characteristics of Volunteer Work

● **Skills required:** These run the gamut from unskilled through professional, in areas such as teaching, business, health sciences, environment and natural resources, engineering, special education, math and sciences, and many more.

● **Time commitment:** From a few weeks to two or three years.

● **Pay or cost:** A few long-term (two or more years) volunteer programs cover all expenses plus a stipend. Many provide for room and board but not for transportation or personal expenses. Some require volunteers to cover their own expenses. Short-term programs that provide training, on-site support, and sometimes academic credit usually charge a fee, but are still generally less expensive than study programs or simply traveling.

● **Location and type of work:** You can volunteer virtually everywhere in the world. In wealthier areas such as Western Europe (or the U.S.), volunteering may be the only way for nonspecialists to work for social, educational, or environmental causes. In most countries with developing economies, volunteering is often the only work for foreigners.

● **Sponsoring organizations:** These include the U.S. government (e.g., the Peace Corps), large multigovernment organizations such as the United Nations, smaller non-governmental organizations (known as NGOs), and religious organizations. The latter may have either a social-activist or a proselytizing orientation, or both.

Funding Your Experience

The best way to find funds is to go directly to people or organizations for support. In exchange, the volunteer can provide reports from abroad or presentations upon return. Possible sources include service clubs such as Rotary or Kiwanis, religious organizations, and relatives. Other fundraising events include raffles, providing services for contributions, etc. Most organizations will assist volunteers with suggestions for raising funds.

Undergraduates should consider applying for the Council Travel Grant, sponsored by the Council on Independent Educational Exchange (Council), for use in less-developed countries. The grant pays for roundtrip transportation and a stipend. Application deadlines are October and March. Contact Council at 888-COUNCIL; ISICGrants@ciee.org, [www.ciee.org].

Selecting the Perfect Opportunity
Overseas Volunteers Receive as Much as They Give

By Christine Victorino

R eturned volunteers repeatedly say that regardless of what they contributed, they received far more in return. Volunteering allows you the incredible experience of integrating into a community different from your own, where you can make a positive contribution both to the community and to your own personal development. Volunteers say they gain a better sense of themselves, greater self-confidence, and a deeper understanding of their place in an interdependent global community. Some volunteers learn new languages, find a different career path, and even make a life-long commitment to international issues.

The longer you are able to commit, the more you will gain and the more you can contribute. For most of us, however, a short volunteer vacation is all that time permits, and first-time volunteers usually find that a short-term experience—such as a work camp, technical assignment, or reality tour—is sufficient. Longer programs offer more time to feel comfortable and to integrate into a new setting.

In selecting the part of the world in which to volunteer, a host of issues—safety concerns, medical preparations, language barriers, living situation, culture shock, etc.—will require careful consideration and research. Program staff from the sponsoring organization should be able to help you work through most of your concerns, either through printed information materials, telephone consultations, or predeparture training.

Finally, find out about the relationship between your volunteer organization and the overseas country. Organizations with well-established partnerships with the community overseas provide more productive volunteer experiences.

By volunteering abroad, individuals will face significant challenges that often cause them to question their own values and cultural assumptions. This is when tremendous learning and often profound personal transformation occurs. What better reason is there to travel?

Volunteer Placements
Coping With Potential Problems

By Susan Griffith

Many potential volunteers aspire to serve humanity or are motivated by some similarly grand ambition. Many past volunteers have discovered that the world is wider and their role smaller than they previously thought.

While most volunteers return from a project abroad buzzing with excitement and their lives enriched, others have experienced disillusionment. Either way, they have gained. The process of shedding illusions, though sometimes uncomfortable, is enlightening and ultimately positive. When starting your research for a stint abroad as a volunteer, it is important to maintain realistic expectations. Think about potential problems and how you would cope.

Begin with the Key Resources and Best Web Sites on volunteering abroad at the end of this chapter, which introduce you to the range of possibilities. Then go to the list of programs for details on the ethos and what the work involves, along with dates and costs. Ideally, your research should begin at least a year in advance of your intended departure so that applications can be lodged, sponsorship money raised, language courses and other preparatory courses attended, and so on.

When you receive a placement organization's literature, consider the tone as well as the content. For example, the glossy brochure of a U.K.-based agency that arranges short stints of volunteer English teaching reads almost like a tour operator's hard sell: "Choose your destination—colorful Ghana, exhilarating Mexico, the grandeur of Ukraine or Siberia, mystic India, lively Brazil or magical China." Sure enough, volunteers must pay from $1,350 for arrangements in the Ukraine to more than $2,000 for short placements in Ghana or Mexico, not including travel to the destination country. These contrast sharply with the cheaply produced directories sent by the main U.S. workcamps coordinators like Volunteers for Peace. For a modest contribution of $200 (plus travel costs), VFP volunteers can join anything from an environmental project in rural Italy to a community center for Aboriginal people in the center of Sydney.

To illustrate further the diversity of cost, even among projects working towards broadly similar ends, the book *Green Volunteers* (edited by Fabio Ausenda, Green Volunteers, Via Valenza, 5, 20144 Milano, Italy; greenvol@iol.it) includes many conservation organizations looking for volunteers. Of the three operating exclusively in Peru, one runs eco-safaris and charges volunteer naturalists nothing at all; another collects data on marine wildlife and charges volunteers $5 a day for food and a mattress in a shared house; and the last, which monitors the macaw population, charges $50 per day (for a minimum of four weeks). Predictably, the ones charging very little expect their volunteers to have an appropriate background or degree, previous fieldwork experience, and computer skills (in the case of the marine wildlife project). The expensive program requires nothing apart from good health.

For pre-arranged placements, much depends upon the efficiency and commitment of the representative or project coordinator on the ground. Promises of expert back-up are easier to make than to keep if the sending organization's local agent is more interested in his or her own prestige than in attending to the day-to-day problems of foreign volunteers. Few steps can be taken to guard against clashes with other individuals. The archaeologist for whom you are cleaning shards of pottery may turn out to be an egomaniacal monster. Fellow participants may not always be your cup of tea either. Voluntary projects attract a diverse range of people of all nationalities and ages, from the wealthy and pampered who complain about every little discomfort to the downright maladjusted. Assuming you fall outside both categories, you may have to call on every ounce of tolerance.

Anticipate the Unexpected

Even when good will predominates, things can go wrong. One young volunteer who arranged a stay with a small grassroots development organization in Sri Lanka felt isolated and miserable when she was billeted with a village family who knew no English. She was given very little to do apart from menial office tasks. When she asked for something more to do, she was told to visit nursery schools, but had to refuse on the grounds that her embassy had advised foreigners not to leave the main roads. Perhaps someone with a little more travel experience might not have felt so daunted by these circumstances, difficult as they were.

A more mainstream example of differing expectations comes from Israel where every year thousands of young people continue to work as volunteers on kibbutzim. In exchange for doing primarily manual work, volunteers are given free room and board, quite a bit of time off, and the chance to make a set of new international friends-all of which are sufficient rewards for most foreign volunteers. But others question the arrangement. In an era when the ideals behind the original communal societies of Israel have been replaced by a more hard-nosed business approach, some young people can't justify working for eight hours a day picking fruit or working on a factory production line for no pay.

In many cases, the longer a volunteer stays, the more useful he or she becomes, and the more interesting the jobs assigned. Of those organizations that charge volunteers by the week, some have introduced a progressively decreasing scale of charges.

In some cases, long-stay volunteers who have proved their usefulness do not have to contribute toward expenses. However, red tape sometimes gets in the way of this arrangement. Most countries of the world impose a maximum period of stay for foreigners, and it can be very difficult to renew visas in countries like Nepal and Uganda after the original tourist visa has expired. In other cases, there may be a hefty fee for visa renewals and a lot of tiresome form filling by both volunteer and sponsor.

Volunteer vacations are very different from normal vacations, though the difference in cost may be negligible. Restoring historic buildings or teaching classes is just as much work as it would be if you were still at home. Jobs are jobs wherever you do them, and there may be little chance to see the sights or sample the nightlife. Provided you are prepared for such eventualities, you will in all likelihood have a thoroughly interesting and rewarding experience.

Perspective

The Cost of Volunteering

Secrets from Behind the Nonprofit Desk

By Daniel Weiss

I am the director of Amizade, a nonprofit organization that puts together short-term volunteer programs. Many people call our office looking for volunteer possibilities that do not cost an arm and a leg.

First of all, you should know that volunteering costs money. Even when you volunteer for an organization in your community, you have expenses. For example, when you volunteer at a local animal shelter or literacy program, does the organization pay for your transportation? Your meals? Your rent? Your health insurance? Probably not. When you volunteer overseas, you cannot expect the organization to pay for these things either. When looking for a volunteer opportunity, keep in mind you will probably have to pay for your own airfare and room and board.

A variety of sources are available to help you find volunteer opportunities. The best are your library, the Internet, and *Transitions Abroad* magazine. *Alternatives to the Peace Corps, Volunteer,* and *International Exchange Directory* are good resource books that you can find at most libraries. They list a variety of organizations looking for volunteers of all types. Explain to your local librarian what you want to do, and he or she should be able to provide you with plenty of information.

Some of the best sources of volunteer information on the Internet include: Action Without Borders, [**www.idealist.org**]; Empower Web, [**www.SFtoday.com/empower. htm**]; GuideStar, [**www.guidestar.org**]; Impact Online, [**www.impactonline.org**]; NSLCC, [**www.nicsl.coled.umn.edu**]; SERVEnet, [**www.servenet.org**]; WorldWorks, [**www.vcn.bc.ca/idera/ww.htm**]; Volunteering Abroad, [**www.cie.uci. edu/~cie/iop/ voluntee.html**]; Volunteer Web, [**www.epicbc.com/volunteer**]; Volunteer Vacations, [**mel.lib.mi.us/health/health-vol-vacations.html**].

Other sources include your local church or temple. Also, talk to your local Rotary, Lions, Kiwanis, and Optimists clubs. They do a lot of international work and have connections overseas. Furthermore, many provide financial assistance to volunteers abroad. If you don't have the time to do the research yourself, organizations including the **Overseas Development Network**, 415-431-4204, and the **Catholic Network of Volunteer Service**, 800-543-5046, will help you find a volunteer placement for a nominal fee.

When applying to volunteer with an organization, be very specific about the kind of service you can provide them. Many people call me up and say, "I just want to help." This is a very pleasant sentiment, but when I ask, "What can you do?" many respond with, "I don't know, what do you need?"

Just because you want to help doesn't mean that you can. Many nonprofit organizations are underfunded, understaffed, and overworked. You must prove to the organization that you will be an asset—and not a drain—by convincing them that you understand their needs and have the skills and ability to truly help them.

It is not a wise idea to quit your job with the idea of volunteering right away. Finding a volunteer position overseas takes time. You must be persistent and patient. There is a reason why there is such a long period of time between when you apply, get accepted, and actually join the Peace Corps. Wisely, they want to ensure that your commitment to volunteering is genuine and not just a whim. It is neither fair to the people you are volunteering with nor to yourself if you are not serious about your commitment to serve.

If you have already made plans to travel, work, or study abroad, and you want to volunteer as well, I suggest bringing your resume and a generic cover letter with you. To find volunteer opportunities when in a foreign country, go to the local church or synagogue. Even though you may not be of the same faith, these institutions are often familiar with local health, education, and welfare organizations. Again, you may want to try the local Rotary, Kiwanis, and Lions clubs–international organizations with chapters all over the world.

Volunteering should be fun and rewarding. Go with an open mind and an open heart; you will return enriched with a better understanding of yourself and the world around you.

Perspective
International Monitoring
Helping with Transitions from Conflict to Peace

By Kara C. McDonald

As the international community attempts to respond to the changing nature of conflict in the post Cold War era, government and international organizations have looked to peacekeeping and monitoring missions to deliver various kinds of assistance—from traditional humanitarian aid to democracy building. While monitoring missions may be dangerous, monitors have the opportunity for meaningful involvement with a society that is making the transition from conflict to peace.

Assignments

The tasks of international monitors range from elections observation to human rights reporting to community development and civic education. The specific nature of the job depends upon the degree of stability in the country. The work may include visits to field sites to report on events, interview locals, and correspond with civilian and government counterparts. Elections often involve working with a local staff in a particular region to prepare for upcoming votes. Community and civic development could involve working as an intermediary between local groups and the international community. All assignments involve working with locals, international organizations, the military, and NGOs (nongovernmental organizations) in the field.

Skills

Depending upon the nature of the mission, you may be required to have a professional degree (law, political science, international relations). Many missions are staffed through a government seconding process to an international organization, and governments vary in the skill levels they require of their volunteers.

Because these missions arise at short notice, do not pay a salary, and offer only short-term opportunities, professionals often cannot leave their full-time work. Volunteers have included graduate students, retirees, and part-time workers with varying backgrounds. International experience isn't always necessary if you have functional experience in social work, community development, human rights, etc.

Besides job-related experience, all missions require inordinate amounts of patience and flexibility. You must be ready to deploy at a moment's notice or to wait with your bags packed for days, sometimes weeks, while bureaucrats make the necessary arrangements. You must also be willing to serve anywhere in the country of assignment. Not knowing where you will be placed requires packing lightly for all kinds of weather. Finally, monitors often travel in large groups and in clumsy operations, so mental flexibility and physical stamina are crucial.

It goes without saying that you must be in good health. Access to Western-style hospitals may be limited.

Compensation

While the U.S. government usually does not provide a salary to its volunteers, the per diem package ranges from approximately $45-$110 per day (depending on the country of assignment) and usually allows volunteers to take some cash home. The rates are meant to cover Western-style lodging and three hotel meals per day. You will most likely have a much cheaper housing arrangement. In the end, you may find that volunteering pays better than many jobs back home.

Finding a Mission

The first place to start looking for mission opportunities is the Internet. Check the web sites of the State Department and international organizations like the OSCE, OAS, and OAU (see below). Keep up with foreign affairs. When news sources start

mentioning a "possible monitoring mission," get on the phone to the regional officer at the State Department or to an officer with USAID and ask about the staffing
of the mission: Will the U.S. be sending a contingent? Who will be responsible for
hiring the volunteers?

Once you've found the personnel contact, you will most likely be asked to send a
resume. Don't be surprised if government officers are a bit curt—if the deployment
of a peacekeeping mission is underway in their region, they will be extremely busy.
Also, don't be discouraged if they don't call you back. Hiring for missions depends
upon unpredictable funding. Check weekly on the status of the hiring. Timing is
everything. The decision to begin deployment of staff may be made with as little as
24 hours notice, and a government worker won't have the time to search diligently
through a stack of 500 resumes.

Picking a Mission

Before you accept an offer to leave on an international monitoring mission, ask the
following questions: Will health insurance (including emergency evacuation) be
covered? What is the per diem rate? What kind of training will you receive? Training
will be invaluable, especially if this is your first international mission.

In areas that are conflict-ridden, tense, or politically hostile to Americans, take
appropriate precautions. Ask about the security situation in-country. Who is directly responsible for your safety (your hosting government or the international organization)? Ask about evacuation procedures. Peacekeeping missions don't need mar-
tyrs or war heroes, so don't apply if you are looking for a front-line adventure. On
the other hand, don't let tense conditions scare you off.

Long-Term Opportunities

Many civilian peacekeeping missions look for volunteers who can stay in-country
beyond the period of assignment to help with the logistics of repatriating other volunteers, wrapping up mission projects, and paving the way for a new round of
monitors. Get to know the breadth and activities of the mission while you are out
there and set up informational interviews. By being a willing and able body, you can
often find ways to extend your work with the mission.

Working with an international mission can be a most rewarding job. In fact, it will
probably change your life. You will gain practical experience, but, most importantly, you will have the chance to work alongside locals who want peace.

Useful Websites

International Organizations: the Organization for Security and Cooperation in
Europe, [www.osce.org]; the Organization of American States, [www.oas.org]; the
United Nations, [www.un.org]; United Nations Development Programme,
[www.undp.org]; UN Volunteers, [www.unv.org].

U.S. Government: the State Department, [www.state.gov]; The Peace Corps,
[www.peacecorps. gov]; USAID, [www.usaid.gov].

Volunteer Work Abroad
The Key Print Resources
Selected and Reviewed by William Nolting

Volunteering abroad is the best option for working in developing countries or for social causes anywhere. Many volunteer positions do "pay," at least room and board, and it may be possible to defer educational loans during the volunteer assignment. Typical locations include Africa, Eastern and Western Europe, Latin America, and North America (with international volunteer organizations). For summer workcamps, apply March–May. For long-term options like the Peace Corps, apply six to nine months in advance.

**Essential; *Outstanding and of broad interest.

For ordering information, if not included below, see Key Publishers, page 13.

Alternatives to the Peace Corps by Filomena Geise. 1999. 96 pp. $9.95 (including shipping) from Food First Books; foodfirst@foodfirst. org, [www.foodfirst.org]. Order from LPC Group, 1436 Randolph St., Chicago, IL 60604; 800-243-0138. Thoroughly researched guide to voluntary service, study, and alternative travel overseas and in the U.S. with organizations that "address the political and economic causes of poverty."

Archaeological Fieldwork Opportunities Handbook. Compiled by Margo Muhl Davis. 2000. 154 pp. $15 ($12 members of AIA) plus $4 s/h from Kendall/Hunt Publishing Co., Order Dept., 4050 Westmark Dr., Dubuque, IA 52002; 800-228-0810. A comprehensive list compiled by the Archaeological Institute of America of almost 300 archaeological field-schools, volunteer positions, and programs throughout the world with openings for volunteers, students, and staff. AIA also publishes *Archaeology* magazine, which lists volunteer opportunities in the Old World (Mar/Apr) and the New World (May/Jun). For membership in AIA or subscriptions, call 617-353-9361 or fax 617-353-6550.

Archaeology Abroad, 31-34 Gordon Sq., London WC1H 0PY, U.K.; archabroad@ ucl.ac.uk, [www.britarch.ac.uk/arch.abroad]. Three bulletins annually (Mar, May, and Oct). Lists worldwide projects for volunteers and professionals.

CCIVS Publications. Available from: Coordinating Committee for International Voluntary Service (CCIVS), c/o UNESCO, 1 rue Miollis, 75732 Paris, Cedex 15, France; 011-33-1-45-68-49-36, fax 011-33-42-73-05-21; ccivs@unesco.org; [www.unesco.org/ccivs]. **Running a Workcamp.** $7. A practical guide for workcamp organizers. **How to Present a Project.** $7. A guide for NGOs and individuals who want to draw up and present their projects to international organizations. **The Volunteer's Handbook.** $6. A practical guide for volunteers who wish to participate in workcamps. **Volunteering in Conflict Areas.** $9. **The Leader Trainer Handbook.** $6. **Latin America Directory.** $6. **National Service, What Are the Options?** $9. Discussion and information on civilian and youth service worldwide.

Directory of Volunteer Opportunities. Edited by Kerry L. Mahoney. 1992. 90 pp. CAN$10 (Canadian residents CAN$10.70), shipping included, in advance from Volunteer Directory, Career Resource Centre, Univ. of Waterloo, Waterloo, ON N2L 3G1, Canada; 519-888-4567 ext. 6055, fax 519-746-1309. Over 100 listings of part- and full-time volunteer opportunities in North America and overseas. Especially useful for Canadians.

*Global Work: InterAction's Guide to Volunteer, Internship and Fellowship Opportunities.** 2000. 95 pp. (oversize). $10 plus $4 shipping from Interaction, Publications Department, 1717 Massachusetts Ave. NW, Suite 801, Washington, DC 20036; 202-667-8227, fax 202-667-8236; publications@interaction.org, [www.interaction.org]. Describes opportunities in the US and abroad with over 70 major organizations working in international relief and development. Most require professional skills, though some are open to students. Indexes for location and type of work.

*Going Places: A Catalog of Domestic and International Internship, Volunteer, Travel and Career Opportunities in the Fields of Hunger, Housing, Homelessness and Grassroots Development by Joanne Woods, Yvette Bocz, and Katherine McGriffin. 1997. 49 pp (oversize). $6.25 postpaid from National Student Campaign Against Hunger and Homelessness, 11965 Venice Blvd., #409, Los Angeles, CA 90066; 800-NOHUNGR or 213-251-3690, fax 213-251-3699; nscah@aol.com, [www.nscahh.org]. Well-researched descriptions of opportunities offered by more than 100 organizations; one-third overseas. Especially useful by students.

Green Volunteers: The World Guide to Voluntary Work in Nature Conservation edited by Fabio Ausenda. 1999. Vacation Work (U.K.). $19.95 from Seven Hills. Information on conservation organizations that accept volunteers and how to apply.

*How to Serve and Learn Effectively: Students Tell Students by Howard Berry and Linda A. Chisholm. 1992. 77 pp. $8 from Partnership for Service Learning, 815 2nd Ave., Suite 315, New York, NY 10017; 212-986-0989, fax 212-986-5039; pslny@aol.com, [www.studyabroad.com/psl]. Reality-testing and exploration of motivations for students considering volunteering overseas. Not a directory of opportunities.

**The International Directory of Voluntary Work by Louise Whetter and Victoria Pybus. 2000. 319 pp. Vacation Work (U.K.). $15.95 from Peterson's. Directory of over 700 agencies offering volunteer jobs and how to apply. Most comprehensive listing of volunteer opportunities in Britain and Europe of any directory, plus worldwide listings.

**International Volunteer Programs Association (IVPA). A new professional association for international volunteer programs, IVPA sets standards for programs and lists those adhering to them on its web site in a searchable database at [wwww.volunteerinternational.org].

*International Volunteer Projects (Council). Free brochure available from Council, 205 E. 42nd St., New York, NY 10017-5706; 888-COUNCIL or 212-822-2695; IVPBrochure@ciee.org, [www.councilexchanges.org/vol]. Describes over 600 short-term summer volun-

tary service options available through Council in over 25 countries of Europe, Africa, and North America. The Council International Volunteer Projects Directory available each Apr for $12 postpaid (or free on Council's web site) describes the workcamps in depth.

*International Workcamp Directory: A Listing of Hundreds of Volunteer Projects Located in 50 Countries (SCI-IVS). Updated each Apr. $5 postpaid (or free on their web site) from SCI-International Voluntary Service, 814 NE 40th St., Seattle, WA 98105; 206-545-6585; sciinfo@sci-ivs.org, [www.sci-ivs.org]. Describes short-term volunteer options in Europe, Africa, Asia, and North America available through SCI-IVS. Their web site has links to many other volunteer organizations.

*International Workcamper (Volunteers for Peace). Free brochure available from Volunteers for Peace (VFP), International Workcamps, 1034 Tiffany Rd., Belmont, VT 05730-0202; 802-259-2759, fax 802-259-2922; vfp@vfp.org, [www.vfp.org]. The VFP International Workcamp Directory (220 pp.), available each Apr for $20 from VFP, describes over 1,800 short-term service placements in over 70 countries available through VFP for the summer and fall of the year of publication.

Just Act—Alternative Opportunities Clearinghouse. For information contact: Just Act: Youth Action for Global Justice (formerly Overseas Development Network), 333 Valencia St., #101, San Francisco, CA 94110; 415-431-4204, fax 415-431-5953; sahar@justact.org, [www.justact.org]. Inquire with Just Act about their new publication, a directory of international volunteer opportunities.

*Kibbutz Volunteer by Victoria Pybus. 2000. 223 pp. Vacation Work. $17.95 from Seven Hills. The most up-to-date and comprehensive resource on volunteering in Israel. New edition lists over 200 kibbutzim at different sites in Israel; also includes information on work on a moshav and other employment opportunities in Israel.

Making Them Like Us: Peace Corps Volunteers in the 1960s by Fritz Fischer. 1998. 256 pp. $27.95 (paper $15.95) (Smithsonian Institution Press). Based on newly available records, this book explores the dissonance between the vision of Peace Corps leaders and the realities encountered by the volunteers.

*Nepal Volunteer Handbook. 1999. $20 from Scott Dimetrosky, Himalayan Explorers Club, P.O. Box 3665, Boulder, CO 80307-3665; 303-998-0101, fax 303-998-1007; info@hec.org. Publication by nonprofit organization offers potential volunteers everything they will need to know about volunteering in Nepal, including a personal skills assessment, background on the history of foreign assistance in Nepal, tips for ensuring a worthwhile experience, and information on over 50 volunteer leads.

**The Peace Corps and More: 175 Ways to Work, Study, and Travel at Home and Abroad by Medea Benjamin and Miya Rodolfo-Sioson. 1997. 126 pp. $8.95 from Global Exchange.

Peace Corps Great Adventure 1998. 248 pp. Free from Peace Corps. Self-told true stories about life in the Peace Corps service overseas by volunteers.

**Peace Corps Information Packet. Peace Corps, 1111 20th St., NW, Rm. 8436, Washington, DC 20526; 800-424-8580; [www.peacecorps.gov]. Peace Corps seeks individuals to serve as volunteers in overseas communities in the areas of education, small business development, the environment, health, youth development, and agriculture. Tour is 27 months with $6,075 readjustment allowance upon completion of service. Must be U.S. citizen, over 18, in good health, and have education and/or experience relative to programs.

*Response: Volunteer Opportunities Directory of Catholic Network of Volunteer Service. 2000 (revised annually). 100 pp. Free (donations accepted) from CNVS, 4121 Harewood Rd. NE, Washington, DC 20017; 800-543-5046 or 202-529-1100, fax 202-526-1094; volunteer@cnvs.org. Directory also online at [www.cnvs.org]. Directory of lay mission opportunities in the U.S. and abroad.

Indexes by type of placement, location, length of placement, whether married couples or parents with dependents are accepted, age requirements, etc.

** So, You Want to Join the Peace Corps...What to Know Before You Go by Dillon Banerjee. 2000. 178 pp. $12.95 from Ten Speed Press, P.O. Box 7123, Berkeley CA 94707; 800-841-BOOK or 510-559-1600, [www.tenspeed.com]. By a former Peace Corps volunteer, this new book provides comprehensive information in a question and answer format on topics ranging from applying and training to "living like the locals," health concerns, and returning home. A must-read for anyone considering Peace Corps, and valuable for others considering volunteering abroad.

*South American Explorers Volunteer Opportunities Information Packet. 1999. 50 pp (oversize). $10 postpaid from South American Explorers, 126 Indian Creek Rd., Ithaca, NY 14850; 607-277-0488, fax 607-277-6122, explorer@samexplo.org, [www.samexplo.org]. Directory of volunteer possibilities located mainly in Ecuador, Peru, and Bolivia, some in Brazil, Chile and Costa Rica, with local and U.S.-based organizations. Divided into categories of environment, education, arts and culture, agriculture, human rights, general, working with children and working with women.

**Volunteer Vacations: Short-Term Adventures That Will Benefit You and Others by Bill McMillon. 1999. 390 pp. $16.95 from Chicago Review Press, 814 N. Franklin St., Chicago, IL 60610; 312-337-0747. Describes more than 250 organizations sponsoring projects in the U.S. and abroad. Indexed by cost, length of time, location, type of project, and season. Opportunities from 1 weekend to 6 weeks.

Volunteer Vacations
Directory of Programs
By Transitions Abroad Editors

The following listing of volunteer programs was supplied by the organizers. For the most current information check the *Transitions Abroad* web site [www.TransitionsAbroad.com], or contact the program directors. Please tell them you read about their program in this book. Organizations based in more than one country are listed under "Worldwide."

AUSTRALIA

WWOOFING (Willing Workers on Organic Farms)

Learn organic growing while living with a host family. Twelve hundred hosts in Australia or travel the world with over 600 hosts on every continent where you work in exchange for food and board.
Dates: Year round. **Cost:** AUS$45 single, AUS$50 double (add $5 for postage outside of Australia). **Contact:** WWOOF Australia, Buchan, Victoria 3885, Australia; 011-61-3-5155-0218, fax 011-61-3-5155-0342; wwoof@net-tech.com.au, [www.wwoof.com.au].

CANADA

Mingan Island Cetacean Study's Research Expeditions

Ecoresearch tours with field biologists in the Mingan Island region of the Quebec North Shore. Observation of large baleen whales, blue, fin, humpback, and minke, as well as Atlantic white-sided dolphin and harbor porpoise.
Dates: St. Lawrence Jun 15-Oct 15, Baja Feb-Mar. **Cost:** St. Lawrence CAN$1,690 or CAN$1,850 per week. Baja US$1,375 per week. **Contact:** MICS Inc., 378 bord de la mer, Longue-pointe de Mingan, PQ, GOG 1VO Canada; Tel./fax 418-949-2845; mics@globetrotter.net, [www.rorqual.com].

WWOOF-Canada (Willing Workers on Organic Farms)

In exchange for your help (4-6 hours per day, 5-5 ½ days per week) you receive accommodations, meals, and an interesting and valuable experience. Host farms/homesteads in every region of Canada, East to West, with some farm hosts also in the U.S.
Dates: Year round. Most opportunities early spring to late fall. **Cost:** $30 per person includes membership plus 2 International Postal Coupons. **Contact:** WWOOF-Canada, RR 2, S. 18, C. 9 Nelson, BC, V1L 5P5, Canada; 250-354-4417; wwoofcan@uniserve.com, [www.members.tripod.com/~wwoof].

CARIBBEAN

Historic Preservation

CVE recruits volunteers to work on historic preservation projects throughout the Caribbean. We work with local agencies: national trusts, museums, and historical societies.
Dates: One-week trips throughout year: Dominica waterwheel Aug 2000; BVI, Turks, and Caicos Nov 2000; St. Croix Moravian Cemetery Inventory Jan 2001; George Washington House, Barbardos Feb 2001. **Cost:** $500-$1,000 per week. **Contact:**CVE, Box 388, Corning, NY 14830; 607-962-7846; ahershcve@aol.com, [www.cvexp.org].

CENTRAL AMERICA ·

Nicaragua Work Trips

El Porvenir, a nonprofit dedicated to sustainable development, offers 2-week work trips to Nicaragua. Live in a small, rural community and work with local people in constructing simple water projects and other requested needs—includes recreational and educational activities. Construction skills or Spanish are not required.
Dates: Jul 29-Aug 12, 2000; Jan 6-20; Jul 14-28, 2001. **Cost:** $650 plus airfare. **Contact:** Carole Harper, El Porvenir, 2508 - 42nd St., Sacramento, CA 95817; 916-736-3663; info@elporvenir.org, [www.elporvenir.org].

CENTRAL EUROPE

Central European Teaching Program

Teach conversational English (or German, French, and other subjects) in schools in Hungary, Poland, and Romania. Live and work for a year in this rapidly changing part of the world, and immerse yourself in a new culture. Salary, housing, and health insurance are provided. Program support services. **Dates:** Sep-Jun or Jan-Jun. **Cost:** Placement fee: $1,500. **Contact:** Alex Dunlop, CETP, Beloit College, 700 College St., Beloit, WI 53511; 608-363-2619; dunlopa@beloit.edu, [www.beloit.edu/~cetp].

COSTA RICA

Costa Rican Language Academy

Costa Rican-owned and operated language school offers first-rate Spanish instruction in a warm and friendly environment. Teachers with university degrees. Small groups or private classes. Included in the programs are airport transportation, coffee and natural refreshments, excursions, Latin dance, Costa Rican cooking, music, and conversation classes to provide students with complete cultural immersion. **Dates:** Year round (start anytime). **Cost:** $155 per week or $235 per week for program with homestay. All other activities and services included at no additional cost. **Contact:** Costa Rican Language Academy, P.O. Box 336-2070, San José, Costa Rica; 011-506-221-1624 or 011-506-233-8914 or 011-233-8938, fax 011-506-233-8670. In the U.S.: 800-854-6057; crlang@sol.racsa.co.cr, [www.learn-spanish.com].

Learn Spanish While Volunteering

Assist with the training of Costa Rican public school teachers in ESL and computers. Assist local health clinic, social service agencies, and environmental projects. Enjoy learning Spanish in the morning, volunteer work in the afternoon/evening. Spanish classes of 2-4 students plus group learning activities; conversations with middle class homestay families (1 student or couple per family). Homestays and most volunteer projects are within walking distance of school in small town near the capital, San José. **Dates:** Year round, all levels. Classes begin every Monday (except Apr 17-21 and Dec 18-29), volunteer program is continuous. **Cost:** $345 per week for 23 hours of classes and group activities plus Costa Rican dance and cooking classes. Includes tuition, 3 meals per day, 7 days per week, homestay, laundry, all materials, weekly 3-hour cultural tour, and airport transportation. $25 one-time registration fee. **Contact:** Susan Shores, Registrar, Latin American Language Center, PMB 123, 7485 Rush River Dr., Suite 710, Sacramento, CA 95831-5260; 916-447-0938, fax 916-428-9542; lalc@madre.com.

Live Among the Giant Grasses

Work with tropical bamboos and learn about some of the world's fastest growing renewable resources while you live in a rural Costa Rican community. Receive a general orientation on the subject of bamboo, walk in a botanical garden, participate in the development of a small plantation and assume workshop tasks utilizing bamboos. No special skills required. **Dates:** Year-round, 1 month sessions, beginning the 1st of each month. **Cost:** $750 for 1st month, $600 additional months. Includes private sleeping space, shared bath, meals. Airfare and insurance not included. **Contact:** Patricia Erickson, Apdo. 295-7210 Guapiles, Costa Rica; fax 011-506-710-2264; brieri99@yahoo.com.

ECUADOR

Ecotrackers Network

Ecotrackers volunteers work in small towns and villages in various regions of Ecuador to help develop ecotourism, work in clinics, teach English, plant trees, work with kids, or use whatever skills they are most able to provide. Volunteer positions are customized to the needs of the volunteers and the communities. Volunteers must enroll in Spanish classes (at the institute in Quito) if they are not at an intermediate level. **Dates:** Ongoing. Volunteers commit 2 or more weeks at a time. **Cost:** $55 registration fee in Quito, $7 a day to host families in communities for room and board. If studying Spanish, students must pay for the cost of classes, and the registration fee will be waived. Volunteers are responsible for their own transportation, and housing before and after the program. Write for current class prices. **Contact:** Dr. Maximillian Moreno, ECOtrackers NETwork, Av. Amazonas y Roca, Quito, Ecuador; 011-593-2-550-208, fax 011-593-2-561-620; ecotrackers_ecuador@ hotmail.com.

EUROPE

¿?don Quijote Spanish Schools

Offers Spanish language courses in our 6 schools in Spain and 5 partner schools in Latinoamerica. Our courses (standard, intensive, business, D.E.L.E., tourism, flight attendants and refresher for teachers) are year round, from 2 weeks on. Students can combine different cities and schools. Academic credit is available.
Dates: Year round—fall, spring, winter, and summer, 2 weeks to a full year of study. Cost: Email or check web site for details. Contact: ¿?don Quijote In-Country Spanish Language Schools, calle/Placentinos n°2, Salamanca 37008, Spain; 011-34-923-268860, fax 011-34-923-268815; amusa@donquijote.org, [www.donquijote.org].

JAPAN

Teaching English in Japan

Two-year program to maximize linguistic and cultural integration of participants who work as teachers' assistants. Placements twice yearly in Apr and Aug. Most positions are in junior high schools in urban and rural areas. Bachelor's degree and willingness to learn Japanese required.
Dates: Hiring for positions every Apr and Aug. Applications accepted year round. Cost: No application fees. Contact: Institute for Education in Japan, Earlham College, 801 National Rd. West, D-202, Richmond, IN 47374; 888-685-2726, fax 765-983-1553, [www.earlham.edu/~aet].

LATIN AMERICA

Volunteer Positions

In Costa Rica, Mexico, Guatemala, Ecuador, Argentina, Peru, Bolivia. Positions in health care, education, tourism, ESL, business, law, marketing, administrative, environmental, and social work. Additional customized options available. Four weeks to 6 months. Inexpensive lodging in homestays or dorms. Some positions provide free room and board.
Dates: Year round. Flexible start dates. Cost: $350 placement and application fee. Travel insurance and pre-departure preparation included. Lodging costs depend on location. Contact: AmeriSpan Unlimited, P.O. Box 40007, Philadelphia, PA 19106; 800-879-6640, fax 215-751-1100; info@amerispan.com, [www.amerispan.com].

MEXICO

Bicultural Programs IMAC

Spanish in Guadalajara is more than a classroom. Group sizes of 1 to 5. Guadalajara offers the conveniences of a modern city. We are a few hours drive to Puerto Vallarta. Homestays with only 1 student per family. Hotel discounts available. Free Internet and email access. Excursions and extracurricular activities.
Dates: Year round. Group classes start every Monday. Individual tutoring may begin any day. Easter vacation Apr 16-30. Christmas vacation Dec 18, 2000-Jan 1, 2001. Cost: Contact organizations for details. Contact: Leticia Orozco, Instituto Mèxico Americano de Cultura, Donata Guerra 180, Guadalajara, Jalisco, 44100 Mèxico; 011-52-3-613-1080, fax 011-52-3-613-4621; spanish-imac@imac-ac.edu.mx, [www.spanish-school.com.mx].

Mar de Jade Ocean-Front Resort

Tropical ocean-front retreat center in a small fishing village on a beautiful half-mile beach north of Puerto Vallarta. Surrounded by lush jungle with the warm, clear sea at our door, enjoy swimming, hiking, horseback riding, massage, and meditation. Study Spanish in small groups. Gain insight into local culture by optional volunteer work in community projects, such as rural community clinic, our local library, or a model home garden. Mar de Jade also has meeting facilities and provides a serene and intimate setting for group events.
Dates: Year round. Cost: Twenty-one day volunteer/Spanish program May-Nov 15 $1,000 (student discount available); Nov 15-Apr $1,080. Includes room and board in a shared occupancy room and 15 hours per week of volunteer work. Vacation: May-Nov 15 room and board $50 per night; Nov 16-Apr $55 per night. Spanish $80 per week with minimum 1 week (6 nights) stay. Contact: In Mexico: Tel./fax 011-52-322-2-3524. U.S. mailing address: 9051 Siempre Viva Rd., Suite 78-344, San Diego, CA 92173-3628; info@mardejade.com, [www.mardejade.com].

NEPAL

Volunteer Nepal!

This program is designed to meet the needs of participants who desire more than typical tourist experience. It provides volunteer service opportunities for people who are genuinely interested in learning about a new and different community and culture while contributing their time and skills to benefit worthwhile community service throughout Nepal. By partaking in the program, it is hoped that participants will experience personal growth as well as open communication channels between different countries and cultures.

Dates: Feb, Apr, Aug, and Oct. Other dates can be arranged. **Cost:** $650 includes pre-service training, language instruction, homestay, trekking, rafting, jungle safari, volunteering, food and accommodations, etc. **Contact:** Rajesh Shrestha, Director, Cultural Destination Nepal, GPO Box 11535, Dillibazar, Kathmandu, Nepal; 011-977-1-426996, fax 011-977-1-428925 or 011-977-1-416417; cdnnepal@wlink.com.np, [www.volunteernepal. org.np].

PACIFIC REGION

Hawaii's Kalani Oceanside Eco-Resort

Kalani Educational Eco-Resort, the only coastal lodging facility within Hawaii's largest conservation area, offers traditional culture, healthful cuisine, wellness programs, and extraordinary natural beauty: thermal springs, a naturist dolphin beach, snorkel pools, kayaking, waterfalls, crater lake, and spectacular Volcanoes National Park. Ongoing offerings in yoga, dance, hula, mythology, and massage. Or participate in an annual week-long event: men's/women's/couples conferences, dance/music/hula festivals, yoga/meditation/transformation retreats. Applications are also being accepted for our international Volunteer Scholar program. **Dates:** Year round. **Cost:** Lodging $60-$240 per day. Camping $20-$30. $600-$1,540 per week for most programs, including meals and lodging choice. **Contact:** Richard Koob, Director, Kalani Educational Eco-Resort, RR2, Box 4500, Pahoa-Beach Rd., HI 96778-9724; 800-800-6886 or 808-965-7828, fax 808-965-0527; kalani@kalani.com, [www.kalani.com].

ROMANIA

Child Development Program

Romanian Children's Relief sponsors experienced, degreed professionals in child development (OT, Ed, MSW, etc.) fields to go to Romania and train caregivers in pediatric hospitals and orphanages. Programs are in Bucharest and Bistrita, Romania.

Dates: Vary. Minimum 2-year commitment. **Cost:** RCR pays for housing, living stipend, transportation, and health insurance. **Contact:** Eileen McHenry, Romanian Children's Relief, P.O. Box 107, Southboro, MA 01772; 508-303-6299; emmc2@ aol.com.

TAIWAN

Overseas Service Corps YMCA

BAs to PhDs placed in ESL teaching positions in community-based YMCAs in Taiwan. No Chinese language necessary. Preference given to applicants with teaching experience, either general or ESL, or degree in teaching. This conversational English program provides an opportunity for cultural exchange. Must reside in North America and be a citizen of an English-speaking country; 20 to 30 openings.

Dates: Call anytime for a brochure and application. Placement end Sep through following Sep, 1-year commitment. **Cost:** $50 application fee. Benefits include: housing, health insurance, return airfare, paid vacation, bonus, orientation, sponsorship for visa, and monthly stipend. **Contact:** Jann Sterling, Program Assistant, International Group, YMCA of the USA, 101 N. Wacker Dr., Chicago, IL 60606; 800-872-9622 ext. 167, fax 312-977-0884; sterling@ ymcausa.org, [www.ymca.net].

UNITED STATES

Masters of International and Intercultural Management

The School for International Training (SIT)—U.S.—is recognized around the world for providing students with the competencies required to teach, manage, and advocate for a just and sustainable world. An outstanding academic curriculum is integrated with field-based practice, reflection, and application and includes a period of significant professional practice. As a result, students acquire the cross-cultural, language, management, and teaching skills to be effective leaders in their fields throughout the world. SIT offers master's degrees in Teaching (ESOL, French, Spanish), Intercultural Relations, International Education, Sustainable Development, Organizational Management, and a self-design option. SIT also offers professional certificates in a variety of areas, as well as undergraduate semester abroad programs in over 45 countries.

Dates: Call for details. Cost: Call for details. Contact: Admissions, School for International Learning, P.O. Box 676, Kipling Rd., Brattleboro, VT 05302; 800-336-1616, 802-257-7751, fax 802-258-3500; info@sit.edu, [www.sit.edu].

WORLDWIDE

Cross-Cultural Solutions

Experience the vibrant, colorful culture of India, Ghana, or Peru and make a difference at the same time. This unique short-term volunteer program enables volunteers to work with local social service organizations in fields as diverse as healthcare, education, skills training, and arts/recreation. Volunteers receive continual professional support from our U.S. and India-based staff. No skills or experience required—only a desire to help and learn.
Dates: Contact organization for details. Cost: $1,950 covers in-country transportation, accommodations, board, and support. International airfare, insurance, and visa not included. Program fee is tax deductible. Contact: Cross-Cultural Solutions, 47 Potter Ave., New Rochelle, NY 10801; 800-380-4777 or 914-632-0022, fax 914-632-8494; info@crossculturalsolutions.org, [www.crossculturalsolutions.org].

Franciscan Mission Service

FMS prepares and sends Catholic women and men for extended assignments among oppressed and poor peoples of Africa, Asia, and Latin America. Volunteers are needed to work in the areas of health care, social service, education, agriculture and community organizing. Allow a different culture to expand your worldview.

Dates: Sep-Nov 2000, 2001; 3-month preparation. Contact: Joanne Blaney, Co-director, Franciscan Mission Service, P.O. Box 29034, Washington, DC 20017; 877-886-1762, fax 202-832-1778; fms5@juno.com.

Global Service Corps

Service-learning, cultural immersion in Costa Rica, Kenya, or Thailand. Live with a village family while assisting grassroots organizations on community service and development projects. Project areas: rainforest conservation, sustainable agriculture, HIV/AIDS awareness, clinical health care, women's groups, classroom teaching. Experience the challenges of developing countries from the inside out. Includes orientation, training, and excursions. University credit available.
Dates: Year round. Contact GSC office or check the web site for specific starting dates. Cost: $1,795-$1,995 for 2-4 week project trips; $595 per month for 2-6-month long-term extensions $2,815-$3,145 for summer and semester internships. Includes extensive pre-departure preparation and in-country expenses (hotel and homestay room and board, orientation, training, project expenses, transportation, excursions). Airfare not included, discount rates available. Contact: Global Service Corps., 300 Broadway, #28, San Francisco, CA 94133; 415-788-3666 ext. 128, fax 415-788-7324; gsc@earthisland. org, [www.globalservicecorps.org].

Global Volunteers

The nation's premier short-term service programs for people of all ages and backgrounds. Assist mutual international understanding through ongoing development projects throughout Africa, Asia, the Caribbean, Europe, the Pacific, North and South America. Programs of 1, 2, and 3 weeks range from natural resource preservation, light construction, and painting to teaching English, assisting with health care, and nurturing at-risk children. No special skills or foreign languages are required.
Dates: Over 150 teams year round. Cost: Tax-deductible program fees range from $450 to $2,395. Airfare not included. Contact: Global Volunteers, 375 E. Little Canada Rd., St. Paul, MN 55117; 800-487-1074, fax 651-407-5163; email@globalvolunteers.org, [www.globalvolunteers.org].

International Volunteer Projects

Council offers short-term international volunteer projects in more than 30 countries around the world. There are hundreds of projects to choose from in construction/renovation, archaeology, social service, and environmental work. For complete project listings: see [www.councilexchanges.org].
Dates: Year round. Cost: From $300-$1,200 and up. Contact: Council Exchanges, 205 E. 42nd St., New York, NY 10017-5706; 888-COUNCIL, [www.councilexchanges.org].

Internships International

Quality, nonpaying internships in London, Paris, Dublin, Dresden, Santiago, Budapest, Melbourne, Bangkok, and Glasgow. Internships in all fields, from 8 weeks to 6 months. Open to college graduates and seniors requiring an internship to graduate. **Dates:** Based on individual's needs. **Cost:** $800 program fee for all cities except Dublin ($1,000). **Contact:** Judy Tilson, Director, Internships International, 1612 Oberlin Rd., Raleigh, NC 27608; 919-832-1575, fax 919-834-7170; intintl@aol.com, [http://rtpnet.org/~intintl].

Medical Volunteer Program

CMMB recruits licensed healthcare volunteers from the U.S. and Canada, for service around the world. CMMB offers long- and short-term placements in Africa, Asia, Latin America, the Caribbean, and Near East. Our greatest need is for primary care physicians and general surgeons.
Dates: Year round. **Cost:** All volunteers receive room and board, and emergency evacuation insurance. CMMB offers in-kind support to volunteers at their site of service. Medicines and health care supplies are hand carried or sent to them. With long-term volunteers, assistance is also given for traveling, licensing, visas, and a modest stipend. **Contact:** Rosemary DeCostanzo, Catholic Medical Mission Board, 10 W. 17th St., New York, NY 10011; 800-678-5659, fax 212-242-0930; rde-constanzo@cmmb.org.

Natural History and Research Trips

Since 1969, specialists in natural history expeditions to prime wildlife habitats. Noninvasive/noncaptive wildlife field research and habitat restoration projects: dolphins, humpback and blue whales, manatees, seabirds, coral reefs, primates. No prior experience necessary. Nonprofit 501.C.3 organization.
Dates: Year round. Programs range from 5-14 days; call for current schedule. **Cost:** From $1,150. **Contact:** Oceanic Society, Ft. Mason Ctr., Bldg. E, Rm. 230, San Francisco, CA 94123-1394; 800-326-7491 or 415-441-1106, fax 415-474-3395, [www.oceanic-society.org].

QUEST

QUEST offers yearlong volunteer opportunities in the U.S., Mexico, and Haiti to women and men. Volunteers share simple living in Christian community while daily serving the poor through various agencies and schools.
Dates: Year-long: late Aug-late Aug; summer: end of Jun-early Aug. **Cost:** Volunteers must pay own costs and transportation to site. **Contact:** Jenny Audrecht, Program Coordinator, 3706 Rhode Island Ave., Mt. Rainier, MD 20712; 301-277-2514, fax 301-277-8656; questrjm@erols.com.

SCI International Voluntary Service

Volunteers needed in Europe, Asia, Africa, and Australia. We also cover Armenia, Azerbaijan, Belarus, Georgia, Hungary, Slovakia, Slovenia, Ukraine, Russia as well as in Bulgaria, Croatia, Kosovo, Macedonia, and Romania.
Dates: Two-week summer international group workcamps or in 3-12 months year round volunteering with a small stipend. Room and food provided. Participants responsible for $125 fee and airfare. **Cost:** $125 per program. **Contact:** SCI International Voluntary Service, 814 NE 40th St., Seattle, WA; 206-545-6585, fax 206-545-6585; sci-info@sci-ivs.org, [www.sci-ivs.org].

Service Learning Programs

The International Partnership for Service-Learning, founded in 1982, is an incorporated not-for-profit organization serving colleges, universities, service agencies, and related organizations around the world by fostering programs that link community service and academic study. Countries include: Czech Republic, Ecuador, England, France, Jamaica, Israel, India, Mexico, Philippines, and Scotland. Students gain hands-on experience in an international community service agency. We also offer a Master's degree in International Service.
Dates: Summer, semester, year, or intersession. **Cost:** Vary. **Contact:** The International Partnership for Service-Learning, 815 2nd Ave., Suite 315, New York, NY 10017; 212-986-0989, fax 212-986-5039; pslny@aol.com, [www.studyabroad.com].

Teaching and Projects Abroad

With Teaching and Projects Abroad you can enjoy adventurous foreign travel with a chance to do a worthwhile job. You can teach conversational English or gain experience in medicine, veterinary medicine, conservation, journalism, or business.
Dates: Programs available throughout the year. **Cost:** From $1,280, includes all accommodations, food, placement insurance, and local support. **Contact:** Teaching and Projects Abroad, Gerrard House, Rustington, W. Sussex BN16 1AW, U.K.; 011-44-1903-859911, fax 011-44-1903-785779; info@teaching-abroad.co.uk, [www.teaching-abroad.co.uk].

Volunteer Opportunities

ACDI/VOCA is a nonprofit international

development organization providing technical expertise in 33 countries worldwide, with over 700 volunteer opportunities each year. ACDI/VOCA manages long- and short-term economic development programs that focus on: business development, cooperative development, rural finance, agricultural extension, and food security.
Dates: Year round. **Cost:** None. **Contact:** ACDI/VOCA, Attn: Recruitment, 50 F St., N.W., Suite 1100, Washington, DC 20001; 800-929-8622, fax 202-626-8726; volunteer@acdivoca.org, [www.acdivoca.org].

Volunteers for Peace

Short-term voluntary service opportunities around the world. Live and work with volunteers from several countries doing community service work. We offer now over 1,800 programs in 70 countries.
Dates: Year round. **Cost:** $200 per program. **Contact:** VFP, 1034 Tiffany Rd., Belmont, VT 05730; 802-259-2759, fax 802-259-2922; vfp@vfp.org, [www.vfp.org].

WorldTeach in Developing Countries

WorldTeach is a nonprofit, nongovernmental organization which provides opportunities for individuals to make a meaningful contribution to international education by living and working as volunteer teachers in developing countries.
Dates: Year round. **Cost:** $3,990-$5,990. Includes international airfare, health insurance, extensive training, and in-country support. **Contact:**

WorldTeach, Center for International Development, Harvard Univ., 79 John F. Kennedy St., Cambridge, MA 02138; 800-4-TEACH-0 or 617-495-5527, fax 617-495-1599; info@worldteach.org, [www. worldteach.org].

Worldwide Volunteers and Services

WWVS is a personalized placement service that locates challenging volunteer positions to meet your special interests and skills. Opportunities are global, of long or short duration (including summers). Placements usually provide free room and board.
Dates: Year round. **Cost:** Vary. **Contact:** Director, WWVS, P.O. Box 3242, West End, NJ 07740; 732-571-3215; worldvol@aol.com, [http://welcome.to/volunteer-services].

Youth International

An experiential education program focusing on international travel and intercultural exchange, adventure, community service, and homestays. Teams of 12, aged 18-25, travel together for 1 semester to Southeast Asia and India/Nepal, or East Africa and the Middle East. Assist refugees, hike the Himalayas, live with and help an African tribe, scuba dive, and much more.
Dates: Fall semester: early Sep-mid-Dec (15 weeks); spring: late Jan-late May (18 weeks). **Cost:** Fall 2000: $6,500 (Asia), $7,000 (Africa); spring 2001: $7,500 (Asia), $8,000 (Africa). **Contact:** Brad Gillings, Youth International, 1121 Downing St., #2, Denver, CO 80218; 303-839-5877, fax 303-839-5887; director@ youthinternatonal.org, [www.youthinternational. org].

Transitions Abroad magazine *is a primary source of practical travel information for travelers who want to experience the thrills and lifelong rewards of immersion travel. For 24 years* Transitions Abroad *has helped independent-minded readers plan trips and discover new and more direct ways to see the world. To that end we publish comprehensive guides, directories, books and an acclaimed web site* [www.TransitionsAbroad.com]. *Please see page 187 for more information.*

Volunteer Work Abroad
The Best Web Sites

Selected and Reviewed by William Nolting

Volunteering may be the best option for working in less-developed countries, or to work for social causes anywhere. And volunteering does not necessarily mean unpaid work—see the Peace Corps, for example. Duration of volunteer abroad programs may range from two weeks to two years or more. ** *Essential;* * *Outstanding and of broad interest.*
(I) Informational site with directories or databases listing many programs
(P) Site for a specific work abroad program
(S) Scholarships or fellowships

(I) Directory on International Voluntary Service [www.astro.virginia.edu/~rd7a/ more-links.html]. Site provides extensive links to volunteer organizations worldwide; mirrors site by the Association of Voluntary Service Organizations (based in Belgium).

** (I) Idealist [www.idealist.org]. This site's claim of tens of thousands of nonprofit organizations "under one roof" says it all. Excellent search provisions give useful results using "internship" or "volunteer." Also has lists of volunteer, internship, and job opportunities. Search possible by country, type of work, and many other variables. The "browse by country" section lists organizations according to their work focus. Note, however, that not every volunteer abroad program is listed here, so you'll still want to check hard-copy volunteer directories such as The Peace Corps and More. Site includes organizations worldwide, not only U.S.-based ones.

** (P) Peace Corps [www.peacecorps.gov]. One of the largest work-abroad programs for U.S. citizens. It provides some of the best-paid opportunities in over 90 countries in less-wealthy regions such as Africa, Latin America, South and Southeast Asia, and even Eastern Europe and the former USSR. Program is funded by the U.S. government, while projects are determined by the host countries. Volunteers receive all expenses paid, training, health insurance, and a "resettlement allowance" of over $5,000 after completing the two-year assignment. Even if you're not interested in the Peace Corps, this web site has lots of information about international work and careers—see **Peace Corps Career TRACK** [www.peacecorps.gov/rpcv/ careertrack].

* (I) PCORPS-L (a listserv discussion group). Discussions by former and prospective Peace Corps volunteers of interest to anyone interested in studying or working in developing countries. This group is unofficial. To join (free) send an email message with the subject: "PCORPS-L yourfirstnameyourlastname" to: listserv@cmuvm.csv.cmich.edu.

** (I, P) Quaker Information Center [www.afsc.org/qic/oportnty.htm] by Peggy Morscheck. This very comprehensive web site includes links to hundreds of organizations sponsoring overseas volunteer, internship and study programs with a focus on social justice, relief, and development.

* (I) Response [www.cnvs.org/vo-rdir.htm], a comprehensive directory to Catholic and other Christian overseas volunteer organizations (most focus on areas such as social justice, relief and development), is online and searchable.

** (I) University of Minnesota ISTC [www.istc.umn.edu]. This site has several searchable databases. Each one produces lots of listings by using the term "volunteer." Searches possible by country and many other variables.

** (P, I) Volunteers for Peace [www.vfp.org]. VFP offers over 1,000 low-cost, short-term (a few weeks) volunteer abroad programs. The VFP site also has extensive links to other international volunteer organizations.

Volunteer Abroad

A World Of Opportunities Is Yours!

Join us as an international volunteer today.

For 6-months or 1-year community development projects
contact Visions In Action at 1-202-625-7403 or
www.visionsinaction.org

For English teaching or summer teaching internships
contact WorldTeach
at 1-800-4-TEACH-0 or www.worldteach.org

For 2-week to 6-month volunteer programs
contact Cross-Cultural Solutions
at 1-800-380-4777 or www.crossculturalsolutions.org

For 3-month programs
contact Global Routes at 1-510-848-4800 or www.globalroutes.org

CHAPTER 6

TEACHING ENGLISH
ABROAD

The bulk of overseas teaching opportunities are for English teachers, as the world rushes to acquire the new lingua franca of international commerce, diplomacy, and higher education. Your "credential" is simply being a native speaker of the English language. That may be all you need to obtain a job and a work permit in areas such as Asia and Eastern Europe.

Teaching Jobs Abroad: Overview
English Teaching Jobs Are the Most Accessible Jobs Abroad for Those Without Special Training or Skills

By William Nolting and Anthony Hand

In addition to native fluency in English, many programs are now requesting experience in Teaching English as a Foreign (or Second) Language, known by the acronyms TEFL, EFL, TESL, ESL, or even TESOL (Teaching English to Speakers of Other Languages). Formal credentials in TEFL can be gained in a one-month course. This could open doors in extremely competitive areas like Western Europe. Those with a master's in TEFL, available through a one-year program at many universities, can teach virtually anywhere.

Qualified teachers have still another range of options. Yet, other teaching possibilities, some of which we list here, exist for those with knowledge of special fields such as business, health, math or science (through the Peace Corps and Teachers for Africa) or for graduate students (through the Civic Education Project).

Earnings can be good in wealthy countries like Japan, South Korea, and Taiwan. In China, Eastern Europe, Russia, and the Newly Independent States, pay may be high by local standards but not sufficient for savings. Africa and Latin America are primarily served by volunteer organizations. Western Europe presents dim prospects for Americans, even those with formal credentials, because British and Irish teachers do not need work permits as members of the European Union.

In general, if your main motivation in teaching is to make a lot of money, you will likely be disappointed. In some cases the experience may even cost you more than you earn, but this is usually still far less than the cost of study or travel abroad. (Student loans can often be deferred during volunteer work; inquire through your loan and program sponsors.)

Before You Begin

Before you begin your search, determine what you hope to gain from your overseas experience. Are your goals to experience a different culture? Gain language proficiency? Try out teaching as a career? How important is money--do you hope to make a lot of money, is it okay to break even, or can you spend more than you might make for the sake of the cross-cultural experience?

The answers to your money questions may limit your choices. The highest number of well-paying teaching jobs are in Asia.

Next, try to narrow down your geographic preferences to a few countries or regions. Do you hope to tie your experience to career objectives? How does this affect the money issue?

About a year before you begin teaching abroad, think about getting TEFL experience or a certificate. You will be glad you did the first time you face a class thousands of miles from home. Opportunities are available as a literacy volunteer or through local ESL programs for international students or refugees offered by colleges, schools, and religious organizations almost everywhere.

Finding a Job

One way to find an overseas teaching position is to apply through a U.S.-based organization. These usually arrange placement and provide for logistical matters, such as housing and a work permit.

The second strategy is to write directly to overseas schools. Chances of success are limited without going to that country for an interview.

The third strategy is to go to the country where you want to work and apply in person. The major downside to this is cost: airfare, housing (possibly paying several months' rent up front), and the need to travel to a third country to get a work permit once you land a job. The total up-front investment required by this last approach could easily be $2,000-$3,000 or more–something to keep in mind when evaluating program fees.

We generally recommend applying through U.S.-based organizations rather than seeking a job on-site because of the uncertainty and expense of the latter two strategies. Most U.S.-based teaching placement organizations are small nonprofits, some staffed by volunteers. All (except for private language schools) view their primary mission as cultural exchange, not as placement agencies for well-paid overseas jobs.

Choosing a Placement Program

Programs vary widely in the fees, services, and assistance they offer. When choosing a program, inquire about: fees, salary, job placement, work permit, health insurance, housing, teacher training and materials, whether there is an orientation, and level of on-site support. It is better to be clear about these basics before you apply than to turn up and find you do not have a legal work permit.

Fees. What exactly do they include?

Placement. Find out who you will be teaching (elementary, high school, university students, or adults?) and where (a state school, private school, or for-profit language institute?).

Salary. How much and how often will you be paid? Compare your salary with the local cost of living.

Health insurance may not be provided by program fees, or you may be covered by socialized medicine available only in-country. Get an International Teachers' ID Card for $20 from CIEE (800-GET-AN-ID) which includes a minimal health insurance policy and which gives access to student-rate airfares. Consider special comprehensive coverage for educators provided by such organizations as John Hancock (800-767-0169), Hinchcliff International (607-257-0100), Seabury and Smith (800-331-3047), or Wallach and Company (800-237-6615). Costs begin at approximately $50 per month.

Materials and training. If they don't provide materials, what do they recommend to bring with you? Even if some training is provided, would it still be useful to get experience teaching or tutoring in the U.S.?

For comprehensive listings of worldwide placement organizations, see the article "Teaching Without Certification" on Univ. of Michigan web site [www.umich.edu/%7Eicenter/overseas/work/teach_no_cert2.html].

Preparing to Teach
Pick the Training Course That Best Suits You

By Erika Weidner

For college-educated native English speakers looking to finance extended travel abroad, teaching English as a foreign language (TEFL) is often the first thing that comes to mind. The question is, how does one prepare?

Most TEFL training courses prepare you to teach English to non-native speakers using a method commonly called European-direct. The variations in courses are worth investigating to find the course that best suits you.

But before you start researching the different TEFL schools you should determine if you need one at all. First, decide what part of the world you wish to work in, the length of time you wish to work there, and how important it is that you work legally.

If you want to work for only six months to a year it may be smarter to put your money toward living expenses—especially if you are going someplace where the dollar is relatively strong and there is ample opportunity for private tutoring without a certificate. However, if your intention is to work in a private school, you should be aware that most reputable schools require previous training.

If you are determined to teach in Western Europe you should also be aware that you will face stiff competition from legal EU residents who possess an RSA/Cambridge certificate. You may want to arm yourself with the same credential, although this course is considerably more costly than a noncertificate course. RSA/Cambridge courses are monitored by exams from Cambridge and thus their standards are uniform throughout the world. This is not to say that other courses cannot offer you a jump start for teaching English and give you the same fundamental training based on the same methodology.

If you are only interested in teaching in Asia you may not need a certification course: most recruiters who place teachers in Japan and Korea have their own training sessions. In fact, for those seeking structure and direction in teaching, Japan and Korea may be good choices. But the better your credentials, the greater your opportunities.

Certification Courses

Certification courses differ in that some are 100-hour crash courses offered through specialized schools like New World Teachers and St Giles, while others are offered through universities in degree programs.

Intensive part-time classes are excellent for working students. Such courses give you the tools to effectively interact with a class full of non-native speakers using the European-direct method of teaching. Rather than spending a lot of time studying linguistics, you learn how to teach on a day-to-day basis. Learning to teach through teaching is highly effective and also fun.

University-based courses, on the other hand, may be taught in a more traditional way. You study linguistics and history of language, but that may not prepare you to teach a classroom full of teenaged Argentines or a group of Hungarian business-people. Compare the syllabus of university-based courses with that of an intensive program to determine which will give you the appropriate practical tools for teaching. Short courses offered in major metropolitan areas with large immigrant communities may offer you the best chance to teach actual classes of non-English speakers while being critiqued by trainers, an invaluable experience.

Another consideration is your long-term goal. If you plan to travel from country to country for a few years, a certificate with strong emphasis on practical skills is essential. If you are considering a career in ESL, a university-based degree program may be more appropriate.

Schools break down the 100 hours of training differently. Some may spend five hours on practice teaching; others may spend none. In some schools the education trainers hold masters degrees. In other schools the trainers have no more qualifications than you would have after a few years of teaching. If the level and field of education of your trainer is a concern, you may want to ask. You may also want to inquire how long the school has been in business and if it is licensed by the state in which it operates.

What About Placement?

One of the most important factors to consider when choosing a course is placement assistance. Be aware that schools do not place you in jobs (unless you are going through a volunteer organization). When a school says they have job placement assistance, it simply means that they have materials available for you to do your own research—binders filled with feedback from previous students and bulletin boards with available job openings at language schools around the world. The school provides you with guidance and resources, but you are on your own when it comes to an actual job search.

Carefully check out the school's placement services before enrolling. Some may offer Internet access at no extra charge. Some send you lists of schools with job openings (for a small fee) once you have graduated.

Ask specific questions when comparing schools. Find out the total cost including books, tests, etc. Some schools that offer RSA/Cambridge certification may charge extra for the exam. Other courses offer discounts of up to $300 if you sign up with a friend.

The cost of living in the city in which the course takes place is also an important consideration. So is housing. Some courses may have dorm-like housing–essential in cities like San Francisco where the competition for rentals is fierce and the cost comparable to New York.

Teaching ESL Training Courses

For a directory of training courses, by country, leading to the RSA/Cambridge Certificate (CTEFLA) see Susan Griffith's Teaching English Abroad (Peterson's Guides) and the "Key Resources" on page 13.

For a guide to academic courses in the U.S. (but not short courses) see the Directory of Professional Preparation Programs in TESOL in the U.S. available from TESOL, Inc., 1600 Cameron St., Suite 300, Alexandria, VA 22314-2751; 703-836-0774, fax 703-836-7864; place@tesol.edu, [www.tesol.edu].

For a current directory of TESOL training and placement programs, both academic and short-term, see the end of this chapter, the January/February issue of *Transitions Abroad* magazine and [www.TransitionsAbroad.com].

Work in Europe
Teaching English Offers the Most Opportunities

By Susan Griffith

Whatever transatlantic trade agreements now exist or might exist in the future, one thing is sure: there will be no free exchange of labor between North America and Europe. As the ties between European nations strengthen, particularly among the 15 members of the European Union, the employment opportunities for non-Europeans decline. Yet thousands of Americans live and work in Europe at this moment. Many of them have arrived in the past year and have found a niche, comfortable or otherwise.

The business of teaching English absorbs a considerable percentage of these temporary European residents. North Americans with a professional background in language teaching (e.g., a degree in applied linguistics and some relevant experience) might find an employer willing to sponsor them for a work visa. This is more plausible in some countries than others—easier in Portugal than Italy, for example. The alternatives are to work for an employer who is not bothered about officialdom (this often implies a similarly casual approach to pay and working conditions) or to work on an informal or freelance basis. In European cities of any size the pool of native speaker teachers on the spot is so large that language school proprietors almost always have a choice of hopeful applicants to interview. In most cases a speculative application and resume sent from the U.S. will not meet with a favorable response.

Freelancing

It is always difficult to start teaching without contacts and a good working knowledge of the language. When you do get started, it may be difficult to earn a stable income because of the frequency with which pupils cancel. It is unrealistic for a newly arrived freelancer to expect to earn enough to live on in the first six months or so.

Getting clients for private lessons is a marketing exercise, and all the avenues that seem appropriate to your circumstances have to be explored. Here are some ways you can market yourself:

● Put a notice up in schools and universities, supermarkets or corner shops, and run an advertisement in the local paper if you have the use of a telephone.

● Send neat notices to local public schools, announcing your willingness to ensure the children's linguistic future.

● Compile a list of addresses of professionals (lawyers, architects, etc.) who may need English for their work and have the resources to pay for it. Then contact them.

● Call on export businesses, distribution companies, perhaps even travel agencies.

These methods should put you in touch with a few hopeful language learners. If you are good at what you do, word will spread and more paying pupils will come your way, though the process can be slow.

Working solo has disadvantages. Everyone, from lazy Greek teenagers to stressed Barcelona businessmen, cancels or postpones one-on-one lessons with irritating frequency. Since your clients are paying for your flexibility, you can't afford to take too tough a line. Unless your place is suitable for teaching, you will have to spend time traveling to your clients.

If you are more interested in integrating with the local culture than making money, exchanging conversation for board and lodging may be an appealing possibility. This can be arranged by answering (or placing) small ads in appropriate places. The American Church in Paris notice board is famous for this.

Language Schools

When you arrive in a likely place your initial steps might include some of the following: copy a list of schools from the yellow pages in the telephone office; read the classified columns of the local papers; check notice boards in likely locations such as universities, TEFL training centers, English language bookshops (where you should also notice which EFL materials are stocked), or hostels and bars frequented by teachers.

After putting together a list of potential employers, get a detailed map and guide to the public transport network so you can locate the schools. Phone the schools and try to arrange a meeting with the director or academic director of studies. Even if an initial chat does not result in a job offer, you may learn something about the local TEFL scene that will help you at the next interview, especially if you ask lots of questions.

France: French Majors Encouraged to Apply

Advanced TEFL qualifications seem to be less in demand in France than business qualifications and experience or even just "commercial flair." Anyone who has a BA and is comfortable in a business setting has a chance of finding teaching work, particularly if they have a working knowledge of French. The French Cultural Service (972 5th Ave., New York, NY 10021; fax 212-439-1455; [www.info-france-usa.org/culture]) runs an English Teaching Assistantship program called SCULE. A working knowledge of French is required so French majors are encouraged to apply. The assistants in France receive a stipend of about FF6,000 a month for the duration of the program (October 1-April 30).

Work permits must be obtained before leaving home, which is simply impracticable unless you have spent time in France and developed a working relationship with a co-operative employer. (Note that the Paris TEFL training organization, WICE, at 20 boulevard du Montparnasse [www.wice.org], runs occasional information evenings for Americans on how to get working papers.) Students at a French university are allowed to teach 10 hours a week. The U.S. Information Service of the American Embassy runs an English Teachers' Resource and Information Center at 2 rue de Constantine, 75001 Paris (011-33-1-4-12-22-22) though it cannot give individual help or deal with resumes.

At a more casual level, language exchanges for room and board are commonplace in Paris; these are usually arranged through advertisements or word of mouth. You can also offer English lessons privately in people's homes for FF100 a session.

Expatriate grapevines can be found all over Paris and are very helpful for finding teaching work and accommodations. The one in the foyer of the CIDJ at 101 Quai Branly (Métro Bir-Hakeim) is good for occasional student-type jobs, but sometimes there are ads for a *soutien scolaire en Anglais* (English tutor). It is worth arriving early to check for new notices (the hours are Monday-Friday 9:30 a.m. to 6 p.m. and Saturday mornings).

Other meccas for job-hunters include the American Church at 65 Quai d'Orsay (Métro Invalides) and the American Cathedral in Paris (23 av. George V; [www.us.net.amcathedral-paris]). Both have notice boards crammed with employment opportunities, courses and housing listings. The Cathedral even offers career forums for job-seekers.

Highly qualified TEFL teachers from the U.S. might approach some of the important Paris companies such as Le Comptoir des Langues, 63 Re la Boetie, 75008 Paris; 011-33-1-45-61-53-53) and Transfer, 15 rue de Berri, 75008 Paris; 011-33-1-56-69-33-40; dmachat@transfer.fr who between them employ over 100 teachers on a short- or long-term basis.

Most expat meeting places in Paris distribute the free bilingual newsletter *France-*

USA Contacts [www.fusac.com] that comes out every other Wednesday. Its classified ads are best followed up on the day the paper appears. It is also a good place to put your own "Work wanted" ad, which will cost $20 for 20 words. You can do this ahead of time by contacting FUSAC in the U.S. at P.O. Box 115, Coopers Station, New York, NY 10276 (212-777-5553, fax 212-777-5554).

An interesting development in the TEFL world is teaching by telephone, which is becoming more and more popular among language learners both for its convenience and for the anonymity. For many people, making mistakes over the phone is less embarrassing than face to face. Apparently this method of teaching is great fun for teachers since the anonymity prompts people to spill out all their secrets. It is not necessary to be able to speak French. The standard rate of pay for telephone teaching is FF45-FF50 plus telephone expenses for half an hour.

Germany: Business and IT Experience Can Help

Although Germany is a Eurocentric country, it is generally more tolerant of U.S. nationals working in certain sectors than its neighbors are, and that includes English teaching. The Padaggogischer Austauschdienst (Nassestr. 8, Postfach 22 40, 53012 Bonn; 011-49-228-0228 501-0; [www.kmk.org/pad/ home.htm]) distributes information on the teaching assistant program in Germany, which is also available through the Institute of International Education, 809 United Nations Plaza, New York, NY 10017-3580.

People with a strong business or IT background and a knowledge of Germany might find their applications acceptable to language training companies like Artes Sprachen & Bildung, Paul-List-Str. 8, Leipzig; Tel./fax 011-49-341-211-12 82; artes@planet-interkom.de. Deutschland GmbH employs up to 20 native speakers at its Language Center at Petersstrasse 39-41, 04109 Leipzig; 011-341-211-48 17. Both the Inlingua and Linguarama groups have an extensive network of schools and frequently post vacancies on their web sites [www.inlingua.com] and [www.linguarama.com]. For example, the Inlingua school in Munich employs about 30 native speaker teachers for whom the minimum requirement is a university degree; inlingua, Sendlinger-Tor-Platz 6, 80336 Munich; 011-49-89-231-15-30; [www.inlingua.de/muenchen]. The central contact address for Lingarama Spracheninstitut Deutschland is Rindermarkt 16, 80331 Munich; 011-49-89-260 7040 where again the emphasis is on teaching business English.

Obviously speakers of American English will have a better chance of finding teaching hours at an institute which caters to that market, like the Germany American Institute in Tubingen, Karlstrasse 3, 72072 Tubingen; 011-49-7071 34071; [www.dai-tuebingen.de].

Adult education courses are offered throughout Germany at about 1,000 *Volkhochschulen*. English teachers must apply to the individual centers whose addresss are listed on the central web site [www.vhs.de].

Greece: Permits Required, Difficult to Obtain

Fewer Americans teach in Greece since stiff penalties for breaking the rules were brought in. Work permits are required, and the Ministry of Education delays and often refuses to grant them. Americans of Greek extraction might consider claiming citizenship (while bearing in mind that this might make them liable to compulsory national service). A prospective teacher must obtain a letter of hire from the employer sent to an address outside Greece. The teacher then takes the letter to the nearest Greek consulate and applies for a work visa, a procedure that takes at least two months. Yet a number of schools, especially small ones in remote locations, may be prepared to tackle the bureaucratic procedures. Decisions are often based more on whether or not you hit it off with the interviewer than on your qualifications and experience.

The best times to look are early September, or possibly again at the beginning of January. Finding work in the summer in Athens is impossible.

Advertising in *The Athens News,* the *Greek Weekly News,* or in local Greek papers seems to pay fewer dividends in Greece than in France. It is normally necessary to knock on the doors of *frontisteria*, the private language crammers attended by the vast majority of secondary school students outside school hours. By asking enough questions (try the local English language bookshop) you can find individual school addresses. The current hourly wage is about 1,650 drachmas (net). It should be possible to supplement the meager wage with private tutoring at a rate of about DR3,000 to DR5,000 an hour.

Spain: Market for English Teachers May Have Peaked

Recent years have seen unprecedented economic growth in Spain as business and industry forged ahead in the wake of European economic unification. Few job interviews would have omitted the question, "Can you speak English?" It seems now the market has peaked and the boom in English is over.

Work permit applications must be lodged in the applicant's country of residence and collected there as well, sometimes months later. Although teachers from outside the EU are occasionally hired on the spot by "storefront" schools and paid cash, the wage will normally be below the going rate. The area of the market that continues to grow is the teaching of children, starting with the pre-school age group. A knowledge of Spanish is virtually essential if you are going to teach young children (with whom the total immersion method is not really suitable).

The probable scenario for the new arrival is that he or she will elicit mild interest from one or two schools and will be told to contact the school again at the beginning of term when a few hours of teaching may be offered. Spanish students sign up for English classes during September and into early October; consequently, the academies do not know how many classes they will offer and how many teachers they will need until quite late. It can become a war of nerves; if you can afford to stay you have an increasingly good chance of becoming established.

Jobseekers in Madrid mainly rely on the Yellow Pages and the Madrid Blue Pages (a directory organized by street address). It is possible to pick out language schools in neglected neighborhoods this way, i.e., near where you are staying. It is also worth checking advertisements in the press, like *La Vanguardia* in Barcelona (especially the Sunday edition) and *El Pais* in Madrid. Alternatively, of course, you can simply wander the streets looking for schools. The density is so high that you are bound to come across them. Wherever you are looking for work, you can consult the Yellow Pages online at [www.paginas-amarillas.es].

An independent TEFL training organization whose courses are patronized mainly by people from the U.S. is the International Career Center (ICC) in Barcelona ([www.teflbarcelona.com] or in the U.S. 888-256-2519). Their monthly courses include on-going job assistance (not necessarily in Spain) and advice on obtaining work permits in Europe.

Because schools run the whole gamut from prestigious to cowboy, every method of jobhunting works at some level. The big chains like Berlitz are probably a good bet for the novice teacher because of the stability of hours they can offer. Anyone hired by Berlitz receives a free week-long training course in the Berlitz Method. Similarly the Wall Street Institutes with 140 academies in Spain (Rambla de Catalunya 2-4, 08007 Barcelona; [www.wsi.es]) are always looking for teachers whom they train in their own method. Another major chain is Opening Schools also headquartered in Barcelona; 011-34-93-241 8900.

For voluntary work as an English assistant on summer camps, try Relaciones Culturales, a youth exchange organization at Calle Ferraz 82, 28008 Madrid; 011-34-91-541-7103, fax 011-34-91-559-1181, which places native speakers with Spanish families who want to practice English in exchange providing for room and board. Another agency involved in this sort of live-in placement is Castrum, Ctra. Ruedas 33, 47008 Valladolid; 011-34-983-222213; their fee is 25,000 pesetas.

Portugal: Demand for Teachers Mostly in North

Unlike in Spain, some schools in Portugal claim to be willing to hire non-European nationals. According to official sources, once an American finds a teaching job in Portugal he or she can apply for the appropriate permits locally. After arrival, take the contract of employment to the local aliens office (Serviço de Estrangeiros e Fronteiras—in Lisbon the SEF is at Avenida António Augusto Aguiar 20; 011-351-21-315-9681) or to the local police. The permit obtained here is sent off together with the contract of employment to the Ministry of Labor. The final stage is to take a letter of good conduct provided by the teacher's own embassy to the police for the work and resident permit.

Outside the cities, where there have traditionally been large expatriate communities, schools cannot depend on English speakers just showing up and so must recruit well in advance of the academic year. The demand for English teachers is mostly in the north. Apart from in the main cities of Lisbon and Oporto, jobs crop up in historic provincial centers such as Coimbra and Braga and in small seaside towns like Aveiro and Póvoa do Varzim. The small group Royal School of Languages (Av. Lourenco Peixinho 92-2°, Andar and Rua Jose Rabumba 2, 3800 Aveiro) employs about 30 teachers with TEFL certificates in their eight schools in small towns. These can be a welcome destination for teachers burned out from teaching in big cities or first-time teachers who want to avoid the rat race.

Italy: Work Permits Difficult to Obtain

Red tape is most daunting in Italy, and work permits are virtually impossible for non-EU citizens to obtain. There is a pronounced bias towards hiring Britons as indicated by the names of the main language school chains (the British Schools Group, British Colleges, British Institutes, Oxford Schools). Yet there are also those willing to hire qualified Americans, such as the Interlingue School of Languages in Rome (Via E. Q. Visconti 20, 00193 Rome; 011-39-06-321 5740).

Yet enrollment in English language schools continues to increase at a dramatic rate among ordinary Italians, and there will always be schools that choose not to comply with the very strict labor regulations. Milan is considered a promising destination, even for the unqualified and for non-Europeans. Yet it is not just the sophisticated urbanites of Rome, Florence, and Milan who long to learn English. Small towns in Sicily and Sardinia, in the Dolomites, and along the Adriatic all have more than their fair share of private language schools and institutes.

Italy has a complete range of language schools, as the heading *Scuole di Lingue* in any Yellow Pages will confirm; the *Paginas Gialle* can be consulted on [www.paginasgiale.it]. At the elite end of the market, there is a handful of schools (34 at present) which belong to AISLI, the Associazione Italiana Scuole di Lingua Inglese, located at Via Campanella 16, 41100 Modena; [www.eaquals.org/aisli/ aisli.htm]. Strict regulations exclude all but ultra-respectable schools.

Another possibility is to set up as a freelance tutor, though a knowledge of Italian is even more an asset here than is knowing the local language elsewhere in Europe. You can post notices in supermarkets, tobacconists, and primary and secondary schools. It may be worth advertising in a local paper. The starting wage for qualified private tutors is LIT14,000 and rises to LIT45,000 an hour in Rome.

Perspective

Teach English in Spain?

It's Possible, But Only if You Have *Ganas*

By Kate Doyle

For several years it's been illegal for language academies and companies in Spain to hire non-EU residents; however, many still hire North Americans and Australians without proper papers. While finding a job is about four times as difficult for an American as it is for a Brit, it is entirely possible if you have *ganas* (gumption) and the energy and savings for a possibly long job search. If you must teach in Spain, here are some suggestions:

Research your destination. Think about the city size that you'll be most comfortable with and the surrounding areas you'd like to visit. In general it's better to start off in a city where the number of schools and companies gives you better odds. Keep in mind that the cost of living is generally lower in southern Spain and highest in Madrid and Barcelona.

Enroll in a teacher-training course in your desination city. This is particularly important if you've never taught before. One-month intensive courses, offered by several large organizations, are rigorous and notoriously difficult. But having a certificate makes getting work easier, and, more importantly, it gives you some know-how in the classroom. Having English as your mothertongue and a great personality does not necessarily make you a good beginning English teacher.

While the course will keep you incredibly busy, you will inevitably become friends with other students in the school. Business contacts develop quickly this way. Bulletin board postings in the language schools are vital, too. It's unlikely that you'll have much time to fax or hit the pavement till your course is over, but with minimum effort you could have a list of leads to explore upon finishing.

Another good option or complement to a teacher-training course is a short Spanish class—especially if you have never studied it. You will need Spanish for everything you do here when you're not teaching English, and it's another good way to meet people in and around a school. Through either course you can do a family homestay or share an apartment with young Spaniards. Both options can lead to English-teaching job leads.

Save money. Academies only offer jobs onsite, so you'll have to job search here. While the peseta-dollar exchange rate is favorable for Americans, you should still aim to have several thousand dollars at your disposal to cover a basic U.S. health-care plan while you are away, a teacher training course, and living expenses while you find a job and an apartment. Everyone here, regardless of profession, is paid once a month, so you'll want to have the first of couple months of rent before you start working. And, of course, you won't get rich teaching English anywhere, so it's nice to have some dollars for occasional luxuries.

The job hunt. Prepare a special seeking-an-English-teaching-job resume. Most training courses will advise you on the contents and the accepted European style. Academies receive hordes of resumes; the more succinct and clear yours is, the more you will stand out. Visiting schools in person is best. Be prepared for automatic rejection if you don't have proper papers, but pay attention to how emphatically the schools say no. In the mad rush of early October, many administrators change their tune. The same holds for employment agencies that place English teachers in companies. If you appear at the right time, they make exceptions.

Working illegally has few disadvantages. It means you don't sign a contract, and in theory the stability factor is lower. But it also means you don't pay taxes. In some cases you will be paid in cash, while some schools and agencies will give you a monthly pay-to-bearer check cashable at a designated bank.

When to go. The end of September is the best time to look for work, since hires are made at the last minute possible. August and September, then, are the months to arrive and get settled here so that you're ready to teach when most schools begin in October.

Language schools offer few classes during the summer, and companies offer none. And, of course, cities slow to a crawl in August, the traditional month of vacations. All this makes it nearly impossible to find work without proper papers.

So yes, a bit of a *lio* (trouble) awaits you if your American heart is set on teaching on the Iberian penninsula (or in other EU countries for that matter), but Americans without credentials can teach in Spain—if they come with enough time and money and inform themselves upon arriving.

On Being Legal

The tourist time limit throughout the EU is three months. To stay longer, technically you must have either a work/residency visa or a student visa.

To obtain a work visa, find a school, employment agency, or company that is willing to petition the Spanish government for your residency/working papers. The employer must prove that a Spanish native cannot do the job adequately. With a huge number of Brits, Scots, and Irish looking for work, very few schools are willing to do this. It takes up to 12 months to complete the process, in which time you must fly to the U.S. to obtain and sign documents.

A student visa, which must be obtained before leaving the U.S., allows you stay a minumum of six months. You must apply in person at a Spanish consulate. You will need a passport valid for a minimum of six months, four recent passport photos, original letter from a school or university saying you are a full-time paid-up student, a letter typed on doctor's stationery saying that you are in good health, and one of the following: $350 in traveler's checks per month of stay in Spain, a bank account in a Spanish bank with a minimum balance of $350 per month of stay in Spain, a letter from a study abroad program assuming full financial responsibility for tuition, room, and board for the length of stay in Spain and proof of having received financial aid covering expenses for tuition, room, board and personal expenses ($350 per month).

For more visa information, visit [www.spainconsul-ny.org].

The Eastern Mediterranean
English Teachers in Demand

By Susan Griffith

Turkey: Middle Class Eager to Learn

The increasingly prosperous Turkish middle classes are more eager than ever to learn English. Dozens of private secondary schools (*lises*) and a few universities use English as the language of instruction, and many secondary schools hire native speaking teachers. Among the main indigenous language teaching organizations (see addresses below) are English Fast (employs about 100 native speakers), Kent English, and The English Centre—all with branches in Istanbul, Ankara, and Izmir. Although Istanbul is not the capital, it is the commercial, financial, and cultural center of Turkey, so this is where most of the EFL teaching goes on. For less competition, consider Ankara and other inland cities.

A TEFL qualification may not be a prerequisite, but a university degree and a commitment to stay for a year usually are. Private language schools will expect you to work the usual unsocial hours and may chop and change your timetable at short notice, while *lises* offer daytime working hours plus (sometimes onerous) extracurricular duties such as marking tests, attending school ceremonies, etc.

Wages and working conditions often leave much to be desired. Teachers complain that the accommodations supplied by employers may be worse than mediocre and far from the workplace. Teachers have had difficulty collecting promised wages on time. Rampant inflation can cause a salary that seems reasonable at the beginning of the year worth far less at the end of nine months.

Egypt: Prosperous Residents Employ Private Tutors

Institutions like the American Univ. in Cairo and the International Language Institute have very exacting standards. At the other end of the spectrum there are plenty of commercial language institutes, often located in the back streets of Cairo, which are less fussy about the backgrounds of their teaching staff.

In prosperous residential areas like Heliopolis, Mardi, and Zamalek anyone who can cultivate contacts may be able to set up private lessons. If you have no acquaintances among affluent Cairenes you will have to advertise with notices written in Arabic and English or in the expatriate press. A simpler way to advertise your availability might be to place an ad in the expatriate monthly *Cairo Today* or try the notice board at the Community Services Administration (Road 21, Maadi, Cairo; [www.csa-egypt.com]) where expats sign up for adult education courses.

Partly because inflation is very high in Egypt, expenses are low. This is also true for the TEFL training course offered by the American University in Cairo and the International Language Institute in Heliopolis, Cairo.

Most teachers enter Egypt on a tourist visa (which you can purchase at the airport), then ask their school to obtain a work permit for them from the Ministry of the Interior. Work permits are not processed abroad.

Morocco: English Gaining Prominence

Although Morocco is a Francophone country, English is gaining prominence in both academic and business circles. Ten American Language Centers in all the main cities (see below) employ a number of native speakers—mostly those who are already residents and want to work for only a few hours a day.

The Moroccan Ministry of Labor stipulates that all foreign teachers have a university degree to qualify for a work permit. Permits are obtained after arrival. Although knowing French is not a formal requirement, it is a great asset for anyone planning to spend time in Morocco. The hourly rate of pay is between $8 and $12. Net salaries for contract teachers are usually about 8,000 dirhams per month.

Eastern Mediterranean Language Schools

Turkey

Native English, Ataturk Bulvari 127/701, Selcan Hanbakanliklar, 06640 Ankara; 011-90-312-418-7973; [www.acteng.com].

Antik English, Bakirkoy, Istanbul; 011-90-212-570-4847; Taksim, Istanbul 011-90-212-293 5600; antiktaksim@hotmail.com.

Best English, Bayinder Sokak No. 53, Kizilay, Ankara; 011-90-312-417-1819; [www.besteng-lish.com.tr].

Dilko English, Hatboyu Caddesi No. 16, 34720 Bakirkoy, Istanbul; 011-90-212-570-1270; dilko@superonline.com. Sixty teachers for 4 centers in Istanbul.

The English Centre, Rumeli Caddesi 92/4, Zeki Bey Apt., Osmanbey, Istanbul; 011-90-212-247-0983; [www.englishcentre.com]. Also in Ankara and Izmir.

English Fast, Zuhuratbba Cad. 42, Bakirkoy, Istanbul; fax 011-90-212-561-3231. Three branch schools in Istanbul and 1 each in Ankara and Izmir.

English Time, Istanbul; englishtime@superon-line.com or teachers@englishtime.com. Recruits native speaker teachers year round. Salary equivalent to $650 a month.

Istanbul Language Centre, Yakut Sok. No. 10, Bakirkoy, Istanbul; 011-90-212-82 84-94;

ilm@ilm.com.tr. Forty teachers in 4 branches.

Kent English, Mithatpasa Caddesi No. 46 Kat. 3,4,5, 06420 Kivilay, Ankara; 011-90-312-433 6010; kentenglishankara@yahoo.com; [www.kent-english.com]. Thirty teachers in Ankara plus more in Izmir and Istanbul (Bahariye Arayicibasi Sok. No. 4, 81300 Kadikoy, Istanbul; 011-90-216-347 2791; kent@veezy.com.

Egypt

American Univ. in Cairo, Division of Public Service, English Language Program, Room 108, Falaki St., Cairo; 011-20-2-354-2961 9/354 6870; in the U.S., 420 5th Ave., 3rd Fl., New York, NY 10018-2729; 212-730-8800.

ELS Language Centres/Middle East (ELSME), P.O. Box 3079, Abu Dhabi, United Arab Emirates.; 011-971-2-651516; Elseme@emirates.net.ae. MA in TESOL preferred.

International Language Institute, 2 Mohamed Bayoumi St., off Merghany St., Heliopolis, Cairo. Offers RSA/Cambridge Certificate course seven times a year.

Amideast American Cultural Center, English Teaching Program, 3 El Pharana St., Alexandria; Tel. 011-20-3-483-1922, fax 011-20-3-483-9644; [www.amideast.org].

Morocco

American Language Center, rue des Nations-Unies, Cite Suisse, Agadir; 011-212-8-821589.

American Language Center, 1 Place de la Fraternite, Casablanca 2000; alc.casa@casanet.net.ma.

American Language Center, Rue de Sebta, Complexe Mont Joli, 2nd Fl., Appt/ 15, Mohammedia; 011-212-3-32 68 70.

American Language Center, 4 Zankat Tanj, Rabat 10000; 011- 212-7-761269/766121, fax 011-212-7-767255; alcrabat@mtds.com. Has 25 full-time and 20 part-time teachers.

Business and Professional English Centre, 74 rue Jean Jaurès, Casablanca; 011-212-2-470279, fax 011-212-2-296861. Several qualified teachers needed to teach professionals and executives.

EF English First, rue du Marche, Residence Benomar, Maaris, Casablanca; 011-212-2-255-174.

New Destinations
ESL Teaching Jobs in Central and Eastern Europe
By Susan Griffith

The dramatic changes which took place in the former Communist bloc 10 years ago mean that over the past decade native speakers of English have flooded the major population centers, taking advantage of the unprecedented demand for Western input. Americans, Britons, and other foreigners have been hired by companies, boards of education, tourism authorities, and governments from Kraków to Kiev. Thousands of joint ventures have been launched and academic alliances forged between East and West, almost all of them underpinned by the English language.

The stable Central European states of Hungary, Poland, the Czech Republic, and Slovakia have largely found their democratic feet. The situation for prospective English teachers has settled down so that now it is almost essential to have some ESL training and/or experience, or at the very least friends and contacts *in situ,* in order to get a full-time job as an English instructor in Prague or Budapest. Vacancies tend to be in the less appealing industrial cities and provincial towns.

Demand for native speakers of English—with or without qualifications—is still increasing in the less developed parts of Eastern and Central Europe, especially in the Baltic states and other former satellite republics of Russia. In many of these regions, economic hardship prevails, which means that relatively few paid opportunities exist for expatriate teachers. Although ordinary people are very keen to learn English, they cannot afford to pay for a course of English lessons. These countries are desperate to develop economic links with the West; yet their economies are not strong enough to attract commercial language schools from the U.S. and Britain.

In other former Eastern bloc nations huge strides have been made in turning around the state-controlled economies and there will be a great demand for native EFL teachers for many years. And though these may not be the best-paid EFL jobs, Eastern Europe offers historic and beautiful cities, gregarious and open-minded people, and a unique chance to experience life in the "other Europe."

A number of independent placement organizations and commercial companies in the U.S. and U.K. send teachers to Eastern and Central Europe. Such programs (some are listed below) are designed primarily for individuals in search of a cultural experience who don't mind financing themselves.

Anyone with a relevant resume should contact the well-established schools in East European cities. To find the smaller schools on the spot, check the English language press, look for notices in English language bookshops or at universities, try to meet teachers in their favorite watering holes, or ask the U.S. Embassy if it can offer any advice.

Russia and the Newly Independent States: A TEFL Boom

Because of the political and economic crisis in Russia, many private schools have closed or, at best, reduced their teaching staffs. But the mainstream academic institutes and international language chains continue to recruit teachers abroad. Anyone with contacts anywhere in the (not so) Newly Independent States, or who is prepared to go there to make contacts, should be able to arrange a teaching niche on an individual basis, always assuming money is no object.

The development of the oil industry in the Caspian Sea has resulted in an unexpected economic boom (and therefore a TEFL boom) in the former Soviet republics of Kazakhstan, Azerbaijan, Uzbekistan, and Turkmenistan. The U.S. investment in infrastructure may gradually result in a switch from Russian to American English as the language of commerce.

In the mid-1990s, the **Soros Foundation** moved into the region, recruiting a number of ELT professionals to introduce modern methodology in English teaching to local schools. Since the Central Asian republics became independent, the old Soviet order has quickly evaporated. For example, Almaty, the capital of Kazakhstan—the ninth largest country in the world—is now a relatively cosmopolitan city with international hotels and private language schools. Yet it is still impossible to enter the country without an official invitation from a sponsor.

Petro-Teach has nothing to do with the petroleum industry. This teaching internship program based in St. Petersburg places teachers and students of Russian in the state education system for a year. Fee-paying participants must be college graduates and apply in February or March for a September starting date. Accommodations are with Russian families. Information is available from Prof. Wallace Sherlock, Dept.

of Curriculum and Instruction, Univ. of Wisconsin, Whitewater, WI 53190; 414-472-1831; sherlocw@mail.uww.edu, [http://semlab2.sbs.sunysb.edu/Users/jbailyn/Petro.html].

The Teacher Internship Program run by Project Harmony (6 Irasville Common, Waitsfield, VT 05673; 802-496-4545, fax 802-496-4548; [www.project-harmony.org]) arranges for recent college graduates and experienced teachers to work in host schools and institutions in Russia and Odessa in the Ukraine for six months or a year. The placement fee of $2,250 includes airfares from the U.S. but not health insurance.

Baltic States: Looking Toward the West

Arguably the most westernized of the old Russian states, Lithuania, Latvia, and Estonia are looking toward a future as part of Western Europe. Estonia seems to be the most progressive while Latvia has changed the least and at present can offer very few paid TEFL possibilities. However, there are some volunteer opportunities.

The International Exchange Center (2 Republic Sq., 1010 Riga, Latvia; 011-371-2-327476; iec@mail.eunet.lv) invites volunteers to work as counselors in summer camps for children in Latvia (and also Russia), though these are not primarily English language summer camps. There is a registration fee of $100. By all accounts the living conditions at these camps are extremely spartan.

Lithuania, on the other hand, desperately needs English teachers, especially in Kaunas, the second largest city. The Ministry of Education and Science will try to place anyone with a degree by calling schools to arrange interviews. The pay (as little as $20 per week) can be supplemented with private tutoring. Accommodations with a family follow easily. No background in teaching is required, but a week's preparatory course on teaching in Vilnius is offered. Contact the Teacher Training Office, Ministry of Education and Science, Volano Gatve 2/7, 2691 Vilnius, Lithuania; 011-370-2-622483, fax 011-370-2-612077.

The American Partnership for Lithuanian Education (APPLE), P.O. Box 617, Durham, CT 06422; 203-347-7095, fax 203-347-5837, may be able to assist prospective teachers looking for opportunities in the state education system.

Ukraine: Serious Shortage of Teachers

Ukraine has a serious shortage of English teachers, among other things. In addition to the placement organizations already mentioned which send volunteers to the Ukraine, several emigré organizations in the U.S. recruit volunteers, warning that teachers must be prepared to accept a modest standard of living.

The Ukrainian National Association (2200 Route 10, P.O. Box 280, Parsippany, NJ 07054; Tel./fax 973-292-9800) sends volunteer teachers to many Ukrainian cities during the summer.

Czech and Slovak Republics: Opportunities in Small Towns

A decade after the Velvet Revolution of 1989, Western-backed language schools have been joined by many private schools run by locals in both the Czech and Slovak republics. While there seems to be an equal demand for English in both republics, the majority of TEFL teachers tend to gravitate to the Czech Republic, partly because there are more established language schools in Prague than Bratislava.

It remains very difficult to obtain either employment or accommodations in the Czech capital because of the competition from other foreigners. Some of the smaller Czech towns, including the Moravian capital Brno, offer teachers more opportunities.

Qualified EFL teachers are being recruited to teach in primary and secondary schools, usually on a one-year contract with low-cost or free accommodations and a salary of at least 6,000 crowns (about $200) net per month. The centralized contact is the **Academic Information Agency (AIA)** in Prague, part of the Ministry of Education. The AIA simply acts as a go-between, circulating resumes and applications to state schools, which then contact applicants directly.

The English language *Prague Post* [www.praguepost.cz] carries extensive classified advertisements including some job vacancies. In Bratislava, check the *Slovak Spectator* published every other Thursday.

Academic Information Agency, Dum Zahranicnich sluzeb MSMT, Senovázné nám. 26, 111 21 Prague 1, Czech Republic; 011-420-2-24-22-96-98; [www.dzs.cz/aia/lektori.htm].

Akademie J. A. Komenskeho, Trziste 20, Mala Strana, 118 43 Prague 1, Czech Republic; 011-4290205753 1476; akademie@login.cz. Many posts available as English lecturers in 5-0 adult education centers and schools throughout the Czech Republic.

Akcent International House Prague, Bítovská 3, 14000 Prague 4, Czech Republic; 011-420-2-6126 16 38; brian@akcent.cz. Positions for qualified teachers in and outside Prague.

Anglictina Expres, Korunni 2, 12000, Prague 2, Czech Republic; Tel./fax 011-420-2-2251 3040. Employs up to 20 teachers.

Caledonian School, Vltavska 24, 150 00 Prague 5, Czech Republic; jobs@caledonianschool.com. Employs 80 teachers with TEFL background to teach English in Prague and in Nova Jicin to professionals working for American companies. North American Director of Professional Recruitment may be contacted at 6 Greenmount Ct., Toronto, ON M8Y 1Y1, Canada; 416-231-9546, fax 416-231-1730; norrcal@sympatico.ca.

Akademia Vzdelavania, Gorkého 10, 815 17 Bratislava, Slovak Republic; 011-421-7-531-0042; hriscova@aveducation.sk. Has many adult education centers around Slovakia and hires most of its teachers through its U.K.-based affiliate, Language Link (address above).

Poland: More Jobs Than Other Central European Countries

Prospects for English teachers in Poland remain more promising than in the rest of Central Europe. Even the major cities like Warsaw, Wroclaw, Kraków, Poznan, and Gdansk are hopeful destinations for the job-seeking teacher, though the job hunt is predictably easier in the lesser-known cities and towns. As in the Czech and Slovak Republics, possibilities exist in both state and private schools. Any number of school directors are delighted to interview native English speakers who present themselves in a professional manner. But it must be borne in mind that although the reverence for native speakers of English still runs high, the EFL public in Poland has slowly become more selective. Interested teachers should not expect to be snapped up by every high-quality school to which they apply unless they have at least a TEFL certificate and some sort of teaching experience.

Contacting private schools ahead of time may produce some interest, though it is much easier to find a job on the spot. Would-be teachers should dutifully do the rounds of the Dyrektors.

The current average wage in the private sector is the zloty equivalent of $10 an hour. The standard deduction is 21 percent for taxes and contributions. As long as there's subsidized or affordable housing, this is enough for teachers working at least 20 hours a week, though most foreigners supplement this income with tutoring.

Albion Language Services,Noakowskiego 26/26, 00-668 Warsaw, Poland; Tel./fax 011-48-22-628 89 92; languages@albion.com.pl. Teachers receive assistance with accommodations and visas. Local interviews essential.

Cambridge School of English, ul. Konwiktorska 7, 00 216 Warsaw, Poland; 011-48-22-635 24 66. Employs 35 qualified TEFL teachers for academic year.

English School of Communication Skills, ul. Bernardynska 15, 13 100 Tarnow, Poland; Tel./fax 011-48-14-621 37 69. Private language schools that employ teachers, also runs summer language camps.

English Unlimited, ul. Podmlynska 10, 80-885 Poland; Tel./fax 011-48-58-301-3373; kamila@eu.com.pl. A large English language school with seven centers around Gdansk, Sopot, and Gdynia.

JDJ College, ul. Bninska 26, Poznan, Poland; 011-48-61-827-71-24; jdj@ikp.atm.com.pl. About 40 experienced teachers for various schools. Employers has flats available in some towns.

Target Professional English Consultants, ul. Polna 50, 7th Fl., 00-644 Warsaw, Poland; fax 011-48-22-870 35 57; info@target.it.pl. Large language provider employing 50 teachers.

Worldwide School, Berezynska str. 27, apt 1, Warsaw, Poland; 011-48-22-617 34 79; urbanasiewicz@post.pl. Operates an adult and children's language school and provides in-company English courses.

Hungary: Opportunities Are Mostly in Provinces

Partly because the Hungarian language is so difficult to master and partly because of the success of the program to retrain teachers who taught Russian in the bad old days, many schools prefer native Hungarians as English teachers. Despite this, a demand for qualified native speakers still exists, especially in the business market. For example the **Atalanta Business and Language School in Budapest** (Visegradi u. 9, 1132 Budapest; Tel./fax 011-36-1-339 8913; market.atalanta@qwertynet.hu) employs 60 native speakers of all nationalities.

The invasion by foreigners of Budapest was never as overwhelming as it was (and is) in Prague, but Budapest still has a glut of teachers. Opportunities are mostly in the provinces. Even in the more remote parts of the country, formal academic qualifications are important.

Central Europe: English Schools and Placement Organizations

Bridges for Education, 94 Lamarck Dr., Buffalo, NY 14226; 716-839-0180, fax 716-839-9493; [www.bridges4edu.org]. Sends groups of teachers and unskilled teaching assistants to summer language camps in Eastern Europe.

Central European Teaching Program, Beloit College, 700 College St., Beloit, WI 53511; 608-363-2619, fax 608-363-2449; [www.beloit.edu/~cetp]. About 90 placements in state schools in Hungary, Romania, Poland, and Lithuania. The program offers "cultural immersion through teaching" and is open to anyone with a university degree, some experience of TEFL, a strong interest in the region, and $2,000 for the placement fee.

EF (English First) Education, Human Resources, 1 Education St., Cambridge, MA 02141; 617-619-1955; Careers@ef.com. European office: Teacher Recruitment Centre, EF House, 1-3 Farman St., Hove, East Sussex BN3 1AL; 011-44-1273 747308; kate.guy@ef.com or e1recruitment@ef.com. Expanding group of schools worldwide with vacancies for TEFL-trained teachers in Russia (mainly Moscow), Lithuania, Poland, Azerbaijan, Kazakhstan, and Slovenia.

English for Everybody (ITC) (International TEFL Certificate), Kaprova 14, 110 00 Prague 1; 011-420-2-2481 4791; EFE@itc-training.com (Subject: EFE). Agency matches clients with suitable posts in the Czech Republic and elsewhere in Eastern Europe. Candidates must have a university degree and either a TEFL certificate or relevant experience. Assistance fee $450.

International House, 106 Piccadilly, London W1V 7NL, U.K.; 011-44-207-518 6970, fax 011-44-207-518 6971; hr@ihlondon.co.uk, [www.ihlondon.com]. One of the first language teaching organizations in Eastern Europe, IH continues to be one of the most active and has expanded into the Central Asian Republics. Open only to teachers with a Cambridge CELTA certificate or equivalent.

i-to-i, 1 Cottage Rd., Headingley, Leeds LS6 4DD, U.K.; 011-44-113-217-9800, fax 011-44-113-217-9801; travel@i-to-i.com, [www.i-to-i.com]. TEFL training company places graduates in short-term voluntary teaching posts in Russia (St. Petersburg), Georgia and Uzbekistan for a fee (e.g. $1,970 for Russia and $1,795 for Uzbekistan including pre-service TEFL course but excluding airfares).

Language Link, 21 Harrington Rd., London SW7 3EU, U.K.; 011-44-207-225-1065; languagelink@compuserve.com. Mainly active in Russia and Slovakia but also has positions in their network of schools in other parts of East and Central Europe.

Peace Corps, Rm. 803E, 1111 20th St., NW, Washington, DC 20526; 800-424-8580. Electronic application forms are available online at [www.peacecorps.gov/volunteer/education/assignments.html]. Formal TEFL training is not required though volunteers must have at least 3 months experience of 1-to-1 ESL tutoring or classroom teaching.

Saxoncourt & English Worldwide Recruitment, 124 New Bond St., London W1Y 9AE; 011-44-207-491 1911; recruit@saxoncourt.com. Frequently advertise to fill teacher vacancies in Moscow, Siberia, Poland, and many other countries.

Services for Open Learning, North Devon Professional Centre, Vicarage St., Barnstable, Devon EX32 7HB, U.K.; 011-44-1271-327319, fax 011-44-1271-376650; sol@enterprise.net. U.K. charity recruits graduates to teach in state schools in Belarus, Croatia, Czech Republic, Hungary, Romania, and Slovakia for local salaries and accommodations.

Soros Professional English Language Teaching (SPELT) Program, Open Society Institute, 400 W. 59th St., 4th Fl., New York, NY 10018; 212-548-0136; spelt@sorosny.org. Instructors placed in universities and teacher colleges in most Russian republics from Azerbaijan to Kyrgyzstan. An MA in Linguistics or TESOL is required in most cases.

Teachers for Central and Eastern Europe (TFCEE), 21 V 5 Rackovski Blvd., Dimitrovgrad 6400, Bulgaria; Tel./fax 011-359-391-24787, or in the U.S.: 707-276-4571; tfcee@usa.net. Eighty teachers for English language secondary schools in Bulgaria, Czech Republic, Hungary, Poland, and Slovakia. Placements can also be made via InterExchange (see above).

Teaching Abroad, Gerrard House, Rustington, W. Sussex BN16 1AW, U.K.; 011-44-1903-859911, fax 011-44-1903-785779; [www.teaching-abroad.co.uk]. Self-funding volunteers are placed in schools in Moscow, St. Petersburg, Siberia, and the Ukraine as well as many other countries worldwide. No TEFL background required. Sample cost of package is £800 for Ukraine including placement and homestay but not travel. Volunteers should be prepared to be self-reliant during their stay. Flexible starting dates.

Travellers, 7 Mulberry Close, Ferring, West Sussex BN12 5HY, U.K.; 011-44-1903 502595; teach@travellersworldwide.com. Paying volunteers teach conversational English in Russia

(Moscow, St. Petersburg and Siberia) and the Ukraine (Kiev and Crimea). Placements last from two weeks; sample price is £775 for up to three months in the Ukraine and £895 for Russia, excluding travel.

Travel Teach, St. James's Building, 79 Oxford St., Manchester M1 6FR; 011-44-870-789 8100; [www.travelteach.com]. Working holiday opportunities teaching conversational English in Lithuania and Moldova. Fees of £445 Moldova/£495 Lithuania include airfare from the U.K.

Perspective

An American at Home in Russia
Teach and Live Alongside Russian Families

By Charity Ryabinkin

Walking down the frosty streets of Vladimir, one is hard pressed to find any signs of Western culture. All around are symbols of old Russia: the glorious Golden Gates, the imposing Uspenskii Sobor, the babushkas selling potatoes at the markets. In contrast to Moscow and St. Petersburg, it is nearly impossible to find a billboard written in English. Vladimir is, in almost every respect, hardcore Russian.

Or so it would seem. Ask any cab driver in town what "Letne-perevozinskaya, house 3" means and he'll say, "That's the address of the American Home." Talk to the English-speaking students at the Pedagogical Univ. and many of them will tell you they study at the American Home. In short, the American Home has become something of a legend in this sleepy winter wonderland. With approximately 250 students taking classes every semester, the interaction between Russians and Americans has reached new heights.

The American Home exists not only to provide its students with high-quality English instruction but also to spice up the study of English with American colloquial speech, cultural information, and humor. Students are encouraged to do everything they can to effectively communicate with each other in class and out.

Most of the locals have never left Russia. Some of them have not made it as far as Moscow. But here, only a trolley bus ride away from their homes, is a bastion of American culture. Six native speakers. Dozens of films. Hundreds of books and magazines. America the beautiful, right in Vladimir's backyard. A substantial number of the students are eager to study in American universities and are grateful for the information and assistance the American Home staff is able to provide. Equally satisfied are the teachers who work at the American Home every year. It is an incredibly exciting time to be in Russia, a country constantly in transition.

Teaching at the American Home allows one to observe these changes firsthand.

TEFL
INTERNATIONAL

TEACHING ENGLISH AS A FOREIGN LANGUAGE

my life
my adventure

Two weeks into the course I signed a contract with a Thai university.
TEFL International even placed my girlfriend who had a certificate from another school.
- Lionel McCauley

I will be retiring in a few years and wanted a career change.
Teaching gives me the opportunity to see the world while still being productive.
-Bob Bradshaw

- 4-week TESOL Certificate Course available in Thailand, China and Brazil

- Advanced Credential (Diploma)

- Job guarantee and lifetime job placement

Cost for the Thailand course is $1500 which includes tuition and accomodations on the beach in Ban Phe.

Contact us: e-mail: info@teflintl.com

phone: 66 38 652-280

www.teflintl.com

The Russian economic crisis, while certainly not pleasant, made working here particularly interesting. The fact that people haven't received a paycheck or pension in months, yet somehow manage to survive, clearly demonstrates the extraordinary nature of Russian life.

In addition to the cultural, social, economic, and historical education that one can receive in Vladimir, the chance to greatly improve one's Russian is another major benefit. Teachers work alongside a Russian staff and live with Russian host families. This informal language training is complemented by three hours a week of lessons with private tutors. It is impossible to walk away from this experience without a noticeable improvement in one's language ability.

All in all, the American Home provides a program that benefits both the students and the teachers, a situation difficult to find these days in Russia. Teachers receive a stipend, room and board with a Russian family, one-on-one Russian lessons, and a well-equipped working environment. More importantly, they leave with an experience they will never forget.

Contact: Dr. Ronald Pope, President, Serendipity: Russian Consulting and Development, Ltd.; 309-454-2364; ruskii_ dom@msn.com, [www.serendipity-russia.com].

Perspective

Work in Prague
Despite EU Regulations Jobs Are Still Plentiful

By Mishelle Shepard

Teaching jobs are still plentiful in Prague and throughout the Czech Republic in high schools, private language centers, and, more rarely, universities. Qualified native-speaking language teachers are difficult to find. The demand for teachers will become more intense now that a new Czech residency law has taken effect. Applicants for residency permits (or long-term visas) now must apply through a Czech embassy or consulate *outside* Czech territory.

In the past, the easiest way to find a job in Prague has been simply to come and hit the pavement. The new regulations, passed to bring Czech law into line with EU legislation, will make things much more complicated for long-term visitors. Expect the processing to take much longer than the usual two to three months for both the combined work and residency permits. According to sources at the U.S. Embassy in Prague, the strict new visa regulations may be lightened a bit in 2001. The new law has caused considerable criticism and officials seem ready to negotiate on at least the types of documentation needed to receive the long-term visa. Stay tuned to the embassy web site for new information.

However, a prospective expat shouldn't be discouraged. Native English speakers are still in high demand in Prague, and not just in the education sector. The best jobs outside of teaching usually require some knowledge of Czech, but, despite

Czech's reputed difficulty, it can be learned. The majority of good teaching jobs require at least a bachelor's degree and either teaching experience or a TEFL certificate. Wages range from 150 to 300 crowns (about $4.30 to $8.60) per hour.

A good place for non-Czech speakers to start the job hunt is *The Prague Post* [www.praguepost.cz]. Both *The Prague Post* and *The Prague Business Journal* [www.pbj.cz] publish an annual "Book of Lists," which can be a very helpful resource in locating real estate agencies for the dreaded apartment hunt (in Prague decent and affordable housing can be more difficult to find than work) as well as schools, personnel services, and government and trade organizations.

An individual earning a median local income can expect to pay half his or her salary in living expenses. In- and out-of-country travel by bus is still very reasonable, and, thanks to Prague's central European location, many off-the-beaten path destinations are fairly close by.

Despite the increase in costs and complications, Prague is still a great place to live. It's beautiful, exciting, still affordable, and becoming more cosmopolitan every day. For more detailed information and an explanation of the required documents and how to get them, check the following web sites: [www.czech.cz/ Washington] and [www.praguepost.cz/touristinfo].

Work in Asia
Where and How to Find ESL Jobs
By Susan Griffith

Despite the rumors, a native's knowledge of the English language is not an automatic passport to employment *anywhere* abroad. It can, however, be put to profitable use in many Asian countries. In Korea, Taiwan, Japan, Thailand and, increasingly, China a high proportion of the population are eager for tuition from English speakers. A university degree in any subject is the only prerequisite, though in some cases just a degree of enthusiasm will suffice.

Most foreign teachers work as employees of privately-run language institutes whose owners are often much more interested in maximizing profits than in maintaining high educational standards. Working as a self-employed private tutor is more lucrative than teaching at an institute but normally requires considerable experience of the market and suitable premises from which to work.

Teachers must be prepared to face a range of problems and disappointments-from the high cost of housing in Japan to ingrained racist attitudes in many quarters-and a resistance to innovation. However, with tact and perseverance it is possible to overcome some of the obstacles encountered by new arrivals.

Persuading shy or under-confident students to speak in class will be a challenge in many Asian contexts. Like teachers the world over, those who can make their classes fun and can encourage students to use the English they already know, however limited, get the best results and find the job more rewarding.

China: An Explosions of Private Language Schools

The Chinese nation is huge and hungry for the English language. For two decades now there has been a flow of native speakers from the West to teach at schools and academic institutions around the country. But the past two years have seen a remarkable explosion in the number of private language institutes and companies, something that would have been unthinkable just a few years ago. The emerging middle class aspires to send their children for private tuition just as in the capitalist countries of Taiwan, Korea, and Japan. So a great many opportunities are opening up and are being advertised abroad.

The eagerness to import English teachers continues unabated in provincial academic institutes. Many middle schools and normal schools (teacher training colleges) have trouble filling teaching posts and turn to foreign recruitment organizations like the Council for International Educational Exchange which place about 100 U.S. nationals in their Teach in China Program, 633 3rd Ave., 20th Fl., New York, NY 10017; 888-268-6245; [www.councilexchanges.org/work/ticfacts.htm]. Application deadlines fall on May 1 for a late August departure and early November for departures in mid-February. The Chinese Education Association for International Exchange (CEAIE), 37 Damucang Hutong, Beijing 100816; 011-86-10-664 16582, fax 011-86-10-664 16156; [www.ceaie.org] carries out most recruitment for institutes of high education. CAEIA co-operates with Chinese embassies in the west.

Requirements for teaching posts in China are not always stringent: a university degree is often sufficient and teaching experience counts for more than formal training. In many cases teachers receive free airfare, a local salary, and perks. Wages are best in the big cities (Beijing, Guangzhou, and Shanghai) where there are scores of English schools. But many teachers feel that the drawbacks of Chinese city life are so great that they prefer to work in the provinces for less money. The western provinces like Yunnan are more pleasant and less money-mad than the east coast cities. Once you get a job make sure the school sorts out the various permits for which you are eligible, particularly a teacher's card that permits half-price rail travel. Ask for help in obtaining a temporary residence so you can avoid the tedious and expensive necessity of renewing your visa.

Indonesia: Foreign Teachers Receive 10 Times Local Wage

The world's fifth most populous nation, Indonesia, has been rapidly recovering from the political and economic instability that rocked the country at the end of the 1990s. The major language schools survived the crisis and continue to be staffed by foreign teachers. Big companies and rich individuals support about a dozen large schools that can afford to hire trained foreign teachers and pay them about 10 times the local wage. Unlike in Thailand and Korea, beginners lacking the appropriate background or training will have to confine their job search to the locally-run backstreet schools. Most contracts start in July or October.

The best teaching prospects in Indonesia are for those who have completed some TESL training and are willing to sign a 12- or 18-month contract. Most jobs are in Jakarta, though there are also schools in Surabaya, Bandung, Yogayakarta, and Solo (among others). Jobs are occasionally advertised in the *Jakarta Post* or *Indonesian*

Observer. Schools are willing to hire teachers with either a British or North American accent.

Visas are an issue whatever the nationality. Work permit regulations are rigidly adhered to in Indonesia, and all the established schools will apply for a visa permit on your behalf. You must submit your CV, teaching certificate, and other documents to the Indonesian Ministry of Education, the Cabinet Secretariat, and the Immigration/Manpower Developments. English teachers must have English as their first language and be nationals of the U.S., Canada, Britain, Australia, or New Zealand. With more informal teaching positions it is necessary to leave the country every two months (normally a day trip to Singapore).

Salaries have declined sharply since the Asian economic crisis but still permit a comfortable lifestyle. Most schools pay between five and eight million rupiahs (net) per month ($575-$900).

Japan: The Financial Rewards Can Be Considerable

For decades, North Americans have been tempted to spend a year or two working in the land of the rising yen. The demand for language tuition remains strong, although recession in the late 1990s resulted in the closure of some major companies when fewer Japanese people were willing to pay for expensive English lessons. Consequently, competition for teaching jobs has become more acute. Be prepared to spend a sizable sum of money while conducting the job hunt because of the high cost of living in Japanese cities. But many people persevere because of their commitment to an extended stay in Japan and also because of the potential earnings. Once established, the financial rewards can be considerable.

Japanese people of all ages eagerly sign up for lessons, especially evening classes, held in schools, town halls, and offices. "Conversation lounges" or "voice rooms" are popular among young adults who simply want to converse or socialize with a native speaker. These can have a relaxed and pleasant atmosphere, though they do not pay well and are probably unsatisfactory for serious English teachers.

The most common means of recruitment is by advertising in English language newspapers, especially the *Japan Times* on Mondays and, to a lesser extent, *Kansai Time Out* magazine [www.japanfile.com]. Also check the jobs-in-Japan web site [www.ohayosensi.com].

To shine over the competition, you must be prepared when you present yourself to a potential employer. Dress as impeccably and conservatively as possible. Take along (preferably in a smart briefcase) any education certificates you have earned and a well-produced resume that does not err on the side of modesty. Be prepared at the interview to be tested or to be asked to give a demonstration lesson.

Anyone arriving in Tokyo to conduct a speculative job hunt should go straight to one of the dozens of "gaijin houses," cheap (relatively) long-stay hostels for foreigners, listed in guidebooks or the glossy monthly *The Tokyo Journal*. Popular gaijin houses will be full of new or nearly new arrivals chasing teaching jobs. Because rents in Tokyo are virtually prohibitive, some foreign teachers stay in gaijin houses throughout their stay.

Most Americans enter Japan on a 90-day tourist visa and then begin the job hunt. The best times are late March and August. The key to obtaining a work visa is to have a sponsoring full-time employer in Japan. If you are hired by a school or company able to offer a full timetable, your employer must take your documents to the Immigration Office for processing within six weeks. Technically, you are not supposed to work until this process is complete, but most schools seem to get you working immediately. Once your visa is confirmed, you must leave the country and apply to a Japanese embassy abroad for your tourist visa to be changed. You can do this in 48 hours in Seoul. The government of Japan will not give work permits to anyone without a university degree.

A third visa option is a "cultural visa." To qualify, you must be able to prove that you are studying something Japanese like flower arranging, Shiatsu massage, martial arts, or the Japanese language.

If you want to arrange a teaching job in advance, the best bet is the government's JET (Japan Exchange and Teaching) Program. Each year, about 6,000 foreign language assistants from 34 countries receive one-year renewable contracts to work in private and state junior and senior high schools. Anyone with a university degree who is under 35 is eligible to apply. The program is fairly competitive, partly because of the generous salary of 3,600,000 yen (about $33,500) in addition to a free return air ticket on completing a contract. Americans, who make up more than half of the total of JET participants, should contact their nearest Japanese consulate or the embassy in Washington (2520 Massachusetts Ave., NW, Washington, DC 20008; 800-INFO-JET or 202-238-6772, fax 202-265-9484; eojjet@erols.com; [www.jet.org] or [www.mofa.go.jp]).

A number of large private organizations recruit abroad. Most pay about 250,000 yen ($2,250 per month). A few of the major chains to look out for are GEOS, Nova, and ECC (for these and others see below).

Korea: Competition for Jobs Less Acute Than in Japan

Competition for jobs is less acute in Korea than in Japan, partly because earnings are lower and conditions generally less favorable. Language institutes advertise for teachers in the English language press, principally the *Korean Times* and *Korean Herald*. The bias in favor of American accents helps in the job search. There is a wealth of information on the internet and a search for "teaching English in Korea" produces contact details for a number of North American recruiting agents such as Ko-Am Academy Consulting Inc, 14080-D Sullyfield Circle, Chantilly, VA 20151; apply@koam.org, [www.koam.org] and Goal Asia, 49 McCaul St., Toronto, Ontario, Canada M5T 2W7; 416-820-5042; apply@goalasia.com, [www.goalasia.com]. The latter works with language institutes in Thailand and Taiwan as well as Korea. Another recruiting agent in Canada is Russell Recruiting (3080 West 42nd Ave., Vancouver, BC, Canada V6N 3H2; 604-267-3648; jimkrussell@hotmail.com) which arranges one-year contracts for people with university diplomas. Those with additional ESL qualifications or experience can earn higher salaries. A typical package available through recruiters in exchange for signing a contract to teach a minimum of 120 hours a month is return airfare, free accommodations, paid holidays, medical insurance, and a bonus on completion of the contract.

Job prospects are best at *hogwons* (language schools) in the Chongro district of Seoul, in Pusan, and in the smaller cities. The minimum qualifications are fluency in English, a bachelor's degree, and a positive attitude. Berlitz Korea hires dozens of teachers at its franchise schools, while Ding Ding Dang Children's English also hires 50 native speaker teachers for 18 schools throughout Korea. The U.S.-based chain of English language schools, ELSI, has a major operation in Korea, including five institutes in different cities and affiliated ECC Language Institutes in Seoul and throughout the country.

The English in Korea Program (EPIK) is a scheme run by the Ministry of Education to place nearly 2,000 native speakers in schools and education offices. The monthly salary is between 1.6 and 2 million won plus accommodations, roundtrip airfare, medical insurance, and visa sponsorship. Contact the nearest Korean Consulate, check the web site, or contact the office in Korea 011- 82-431-233-4516/7; epik@cc.knue.ac.kr.

Some neophyte teachers who arrange their jobs while still in North America wish they had waited until arrival in Seoul before committing themselves to a school. Often better wages and working conditions can be negotiated in person. Twelve-month contracts normally include a sizable bonus, so it is in the teacher's interest to complete the contract. For new arrivals who have not prearranged a job, a good place to pick up information is from the Internet; Dave's ESL Cafe has a link to the "Gray Page," specifically about Korean employers. The U.S. embassy in Seoul issues a free information booklet, "Teaching English in Korea: Opportunities and Pitfalls" (American Services Branch, 82 Sejong Rd., Chongro-ku, Seoul) which is posted on the Internet [http://travel.state.gov/english_in_Korea.html].

Private tutoring normally requires traveling to the clients, though in Seoul this is less stressful than in Japan since the subway stops are announced in English. Most people who have taught in Korea report that the students are friendly and eager to learn but the hogwan owners are difficult to trust. Lessons are not generally strenuous since the emphasis is on conversation rather than grammar.

Taiwan: Only Requirements Are College Degree and a Pulse

It has been said that the only requirements for being hired as an English teacher in Taiwan are a college degree and a pulse. Despite changes in immigration legislation which have made it more difficult for foreigners to undertake casual teaching work, the demand for college-educated native speaking teachers who are prepared to stay for at least one year is huge. Many of the hundreds of private language institutes (called *buhsibans*) and also some state secondary schools are keen to sponsor foreign teachers for the necessary visas.

The requirements for a work permit/residence visa include a copy of your university diploma, health certificates issued in Taiwan (including an HIV test and chest X-ray), and a letter from a Chinese guarantor. After the application has been submitted it is necessary to finance a trip to collect the visa outside Taiwan (usually Hong Kong). The whole process takes between four and six weeks.

The American accent is invariably preferred, especially in the capital Taipei. Yet not everyone wants to stay in Taipei where the air pollution is second only to that of Mexico City, the traffic congestion is appalling, and the rents are high. Jobs are plentiful in the other cities of Taiwan such as Kaohsiung, Taichung, and Tainan. The majority of schools pay about NT$500 ($16) per hour, though higher wages are possible. Fees for private tuition are considerably higher.

To see which schools are hiring, check ads in the daily *South China Post* and notice boards at travelers' hostels and the Mandarin Training Center of Taiwan Normal Univ. on Hoping East Rd. North American graduates can fix up a one-year job ahead of time with the Overseas Service Corps of the YMCA (see below). You might also make useful expat contacts in Taipei at the Community Services Center, 25 Ln., 290 Chung Shan Rd., North Rd., Sec. 6, Tien Mu (011-886-2-2833-7444). One web site worth investigating if you want to teach English while studying Mandarin is [www.eslhouseonline.com].

Thailand: Teaching Jobs Are Virtually Guaranteed

While Bangkok absorbs an enormous number of English teachers, both trained and otherwise, there is also demand in the other cities such as Hat Yai, Chiang Mai in the north, and Songkhla in the south, where there is less competition for work. Not much teacher recruitment takes place outside Thailand. Even Thai universities and teachers' colleges, as well as private business colleges, all of which have EFL departments, depend on finding native-speaking teachers locally.

In short, anyone who is determined to teach in Thailand and prepared to go there to look for work is virtually guaranteed to find opportunities. Finding language schools to approach is not a problem. Most new arrivals in Bangkok start with the English language yellow pages. Job vacancy notices appear in the English language press: the *Bangkok Post* and the *Nation*. Popular hostels often have bulletin boards with job notices and other information for foreigners. The best place to start the actual job hunting is around Siam Square and the Victory Monument where language schools and institutes abound. Check the teaching in Thailand web site [www.ajarn.com] for inside information on potential employers.

First impressions are important throughout Asia. Dress smartly for interviews. A professional-looking resume and references help. University graduates *(ajarn)* are highly respected in Thailand and are expected to look respectable. At your interviews, be prepared to undergo a grammar test. As usual, it may be necessary to start with part-time and occasional work with several employers, aiming to build up 20- to- 30 hours in the same area to minimize traveling in the appalling traffic conditions of Bangkok (smog masks are cheap and a wise investment).

The busiest season for English schools is mid-March to mid-May during the school holidays, when many secondary school and university students take extra tuition in English. This coincides with the hot season. The next best time to look for work in private schools is October. The worst time is January and February.

Working as a self-employed private tutor pays better than working for a commercial school, but tutoring jobs are hard to set up until you have been settled in one place for a while and found out how to tap into the local elite community. Placing an ad for private pupils in English language papers often works. Possible venues for would-be teachers include hotels where a native speaker is needed to organize conversation classes for staff.

The vast majority of EFL teachers in Thailand do not have a work visa, and this seems to cause no serious problems. At present, foreigners mostly teach on a tourist visa or (preferably) a non-immigrant visa. So far a crackdown, threatened by the authorities, has not happened. Universities and established language schools may be willing to apply for a work permit on behalf of teachers who have proved themselves successful in the classroom and who are willing to sign a one-year contract. To be eligible for a work permit you must have a minimum of a BA and, in most cases, a relevant teaching certificate. However, most teachers simply cross the border into Malaysia every three months where a new visa can quickly and easily be obtained from the Thai consulate.

In a country where teaching jobs are so easy to come by, there has to be a catch— low wages. The basic hourly rate in Bangkok is only about 250-300 baht (less than $6), with a few schools paying less and some promising considerably more, especially if travel to outside locations is required. Rates outside Bangkok are lower.

By the same token, living expenses are also low. Out of an average monthly salary of 25,000 baht ($600) teachers can expect to pay 3,000 baht ($70) in rent, even in Bangkok. Tasty food can be had from street stalls for a few baht, and more substantial and exciting meals exploiting the area's marvelous fresh fish and fruit cost about $2. There is no reason why even part-time teachers should not be able to afford to travel around the country, including to the islands, where life is slow and the beaches are wonderful.

South Asia: Jobs Scarce Because of Poverty

In contrast to Thailand and Indonesia, other countries between Pakistan and the Philippines are generally not easy to find work in as an English teacher. Poverty is the main reason for the small market for expatriate teachers. Singapore, Malaysia, and Brunei, which are relatively wealthy, mainly turn to Britain for teachers.

However, those foreigners prepared to finance themselves and volunteer their time can find eager students simply by asking around in Sri Lanka, India, and (especially) Nepal. Vietnam, Cambodia, Laos and even the pariah state of Myanmar are developing a range of commercial institutes devoted to English language teaching. In Vietnam, the daily paper *Nguoi Vet* publishes its Thursday edition in English, so check for ads (or consider placing your own). **World Universities Service of Canada** (WUSC), Recruitment Section, 1404 Scott St., Box 3000, Ottawa, ON J8P 6H8, Canada (613-798-7477; recruit@wusc.ca) recruits Canadian ESL teachers for a range of countries, especially Vietnam.

Private language schools are opening in the Laotian capital of Vientiane. Two established English teaching centers are **Vientiane Univ. College**, P.O. Box 4144; (011-856-21-414-873/414052; [www.geocities.com/vientianecollege]), which employs 25 teachers on sessional and one-year contracts, and the **Lao American Language Center**, 152 Sisangvone Rd., Saysettha, Ban Nazay, P.O. Box 327, Vientiane (011-856-21-414-321), whose American owner runs an internship program for U.S. university students to spend time teaching.

Visas can be a problem since countries understandably want to control the number of long-stay foreigners. For example, with very few exceptions the Nepali government does not allow foreigners to stay for more than three months in any 12. One possibility in India is to become a volunteer teacher with **Jaffe International Education Service** (Kunnuparambil Buildings, Kurcihy, Kottayam 686549, India; Tel./fax 011-91-481-430470), which tries to place young volunteers in English medium high schools and training institutes for short periods.

Nepal is a more promising destination than India for short-term English teachers willing to work for low wages.

Insight Nepal (P.O. Box 489, Pokhara, Kaski; insight@mos.com.np) has a Placement for Volunteer Service Work program in which a few volunteers are allocated to primary and secondary schools in different areas of the country for between three and four months to teach English, science, and sport. Starting dates are in February, April, and August. The registration fee of $800 covers pre-orientation and a one-week trekking excursion; the host village provides food and accommodations. Another alternative for volunteers wishing to teach in Nepal is to apply to the **New International Friendship Club Nepal** (P.O. Box 11276, Maharajgunj, Kathmandu; 011-977-1-427-406; fcn@ccsl.com.np). **The Himalayan Explorers Club** (P.O. Box 3665 Boulder, CO 80307; info@hec.org) sends teaching volunteers to mountain villages. The program costs $150 per month excluding airfare.

English Schools in Asia

China

Amity Foundation, 71 Hn Kou Rd., Nanjing, Jiangsu 21008; 001-86-25-332-4607; afn71@public1.ptt.js.cn, [www.,amityfoundation.org]. From 60-80 native speaker teachers each year.

Beijing New Bridge Foreign Language School, Chao Yang Uq Yong An Nan Li, Beijing 100022; fax 011-86-10-6568 5135; [www.newbridgeschool.com]. Private language school employing native speaker teachers.

China English Language Training Services, 2D Zhao Feng Building 9, Ln. 396, Chang Line Rd., Shanghai 200042; fax 011-86-21-62623 5692. Recruits North Americans with an interest in China.

Colorado China Council, 4556 Apple Way, Boulder, CO 80301; 303-443-1108; alice@asia-council.org. From 20-35 American graduates are placed in institutes throughout China and Mongolia.

IEF Education Foundation, U.S. office fax 626-965-1675; mwurmlinger@ief-usa.org. University students and graduates teach junior high and high school aged students in many Chinese cities.

New China Education Foundation, San José Chapter, 1587 Montalban Dr., San José, CA 95120; 408-268-0418; 1-year program for university graduates.

Ready to Learn, Administrative Office, 1st Fl., 4 W Ng Sing Lane, Yau Ma Tei, Kowloon, Hong Kong; 011-852-2388-1318;

[www.rtl.com.hk]. Employs 30 native speakers with college degrees.

Western Washington Univ., China Teaching Program, Old Main 530A, Bellingham, WA 98225-9047; 360-650-3753, fax 360-650-2847; ctp@cc.wwu.edu. Applicants must have a university degree.

WorldTeach, Center for International Development, Harvard Univ., 79 John F. Kennedy St., Cambridge MA 02138; 800-4-TEACH-O; [www.worldteach.org]. Summer teaching program at a language camps for Chinese high school students and 6-month opportunities in Yantai. Participation fee approximately $4,000.

Indonesia

EF English First—Menteng, Jl. Timor No. 25, Menteng, Jakarta 10350; 011-62-21 3148815. Varying number of native English-speaking teachers for this and other EF schools in Indonesia. Application can be made through EF office in Boston.

English Education Center (EEC), Jalan Let. Jend. S. Parman 68, Slipi, Jakarta 11410; 011-62-21 532 3176/532 0044; eec@vision.net.id, [www.indodirect.com/eec]. Thirty teachers for 3 schools in Jakarta.

Executive English Programs (EEP), Jalan Lombok No 43, Bandung 40115; 011-62-22-7208254; eepbdg@bdg.centrin.co.id.

International Language Centre, Jl. Samanhudi No 22, Medan 20151; 011-62-61-451 5766; ilc@mdn.centrin.net.id. New school opened April 2000 and recruiting native speaker teachers.

International Language Programs (ILP), Jalan Jawa 34, Surabaya 60281, Jawa Timor; 011-62-31-502 3333; tjahjani@rad.net.id, [www.ilp-surabaya.com]. 25 native speaker teachers.

School for International Training (SIT), Jalan Sunda 3, Menteng, Jakarta Pusat 10350; 011-62-21-390 6920/337240/336238. Twenty teachers for this branch plus two in Jakarta and one in Surabaya.

Japan

AEON International USA, 1960 East Grand Ave., #550, El Segundo, CA 90245; 310-14-515, fax (310) 414-1616; aeonla@aeonet.com, [www.aeonet.com]. Recruits throughout the U.S. for 200+ branches in Japan. Other North American recruiting offices: 203 North LaSalle St., #2100, Chicago, IL 60601; 312-251-0900, fax 312-251-0901; aeonchi@aeonet.com. 230 Park Ave., #1000, New York, NY 10169; 212-808-3080, fax 212-599-0340; aeonnyc@aeonet.com. 145 King St., #1000, Toronto, Ontario, Canada M5H 1J8; 416-364-8500, fax 416-364-7561; aeontor@aeonet.com. Adler Recruiting Service, 242-301 Maude Rd., Port Moody, BC, Canada V3H 5B1; 604-461-5131, fax 604-461-5133; aeoncanada@attcanada.net.

English Multimedia Systems, Yokohama YMCA, 1-7 Tokiwa-Cho, Naka-Ku, Yokohama 231-8348; 011-81 45 662 3721, fax 011-81 45 664 4018; ymjohn@yokohama-ymca.or.jp. Two hundred full-time and part-time positions for graduates with TESOL training.

GEOS Language Corporation, Simpson Tower, Suite 2424, 401 Bay St., Toronto, ON M5H 2Y4, Canada; 416-777-0109, fax 416-777-0110; geos@istar.ca; [www.geoscareer.com]. Recruits 1,800 graduates to teach at 450 schools.

Interac Co Ltd, Fujibo Bldg. 2F, 2-10-28 Fujimi, Chiyoda-ku, Tokyo 102; 011-81 3 3234 7857, fax 011-81 3 3234 6055; recruit@interac.co.jp, [www.interac.co.jp/recruit]. Nine branches recruit most of their 280 teachers locally.

Interact Nova Group, 2 Oliver St., Suite 7, Boston, MA 02110; 617-542-5027 or 601 California St., Suite 702, San Francisco, CA 94108; 415-788-3737; [www.nova-group.com]. Has 390 schools throughout Japan; teachers recruited throughout the year.

ECC Foreign Language Institute, 15th Fl., San Yamate Building, 7-11-10 Nishi-Shinjuku, Shinjuklu-ku, Tokyo 160-0023; 011-81-3-5330 1585; [www.ecc.co.jp]. Offices in Osaka and Nagoya also. Over 300 teachers recruited in Japan only.

Prometheum School of Languages, 415-543-2992; psl@teflpro.com, [www.teflpro.com]. Paid internships for graduates with TEFL Certificate in Japanese universities.

Korea

Berlitz Korea, Sungwood Academy Building 2F, 1316-17 Seocho-Dong, Seocho-Gu, Seoul 137-074; 011-82-2-3481-5324; pamela.hughes@berlitz.com.sg.

Ding Ding Dang Children's English, 1275-3 Bummel-dong Soosung-gy, Taegu 706-100; 011-82-53-782 5200; dings@thrunet.com.

English Friends, 733 Bang Hak 3 Dong, Do Bong Ku, Seoul; 011-82-2-3491 1431; 2003 @hotmail.com, [www.tefa.net]. Up to 30 teachers hired by email.

English in Korea Program (EPIK), The Center for In-Service Education, Korea National University of Education, Chongwon, Chungbuk, 363-791, Korea; 011-82-431-233-4516/4517, fax 011-82-431-233-6679; epik@cc.knue.ac.kr. North American applicants for teaching posts in schools and education offices through the Ministry of Education should contact their nearest Korean Consulate for information.

Nelson Foreign Language Institute, North American Office, 95 Hess St., South, #610, Hamilton, ON, Canada L8P 3N4, Canada; canlink@bigwave.ca. Sixty branches in Korea hiring about 20 new teachers a month.

Oregon Language Institute, Beomo 4-dong 206-6, Suseoung-ku, Taegu; 011-82-53-741 2511. Native speakers hired year-round for 5 institutes in Korea.

YBM/ECC. Largest network of children's schools in Korea; fax 011-82-2-553 2354 Att: Nathan Underwood; ybmecc@yahoo.com.

YBM Education Inc. Foreign Teacher Recruitment Manager, Trecruting Office, 55-1 Chongno 2 Ga, chongno Gu, 3rd Fl., Seoul 110-122; 011-82-2-2264 7472, fax 011-82-2-2264-9011, 82-2-2269 0275; teach@ymbsisa.co.kr, [www.ybmsisa.com/els/ info/rec-1.asp]. Can leave voicemail or fax in North America: 509-463-5118. Recruits hundreds of teachers for 11 language schools throughout the country (phone numbers and email addresses on web site).

Taiwan

ELS Taiwan, 6 Fl, No. 9 Ln 90, Sung Chiang Rd., Taipei; 011-886-2-2581 8511; [www.elstaiwan.com]. From 200-300 teachers in 3 main cities.

Epact Educational Services, apply@teachtaiwan.com, [www.teachtaiwan.com]. Recruits recent graduates for minimum of a year.

Hess Educational Organization, 235 Chung Shan Rd., Chung Ho City, Sec. 2, No. 419, Chung Ho City, Taipei County; 011-886-2-3234-6188; hesswork@hess.com.tw, [www.hess.com.tw]. Specializes in teaching children. Over 250 teachers for 100 schools and 40 kindergartens.

Noble American Children's School, No. 850 Ta-Ya Rd, Sec. 1, Shiayi 600; 011-886-5-275 9951; shereed@telusplanet.net. Teachers for young children's English classes.

Overseas Service Corps, YMCA, 101 N. Wacker Dr., Chicago, IL 60606; 800-872-9622 ext. 343. Twenty-five English teachers needed for minimum of a year in Taiwan.

Shane English School, 5F, 41 Roosevelt Rd., Sec. 2, Taipei; 011-886-2-2351 7755; sest@ms12.hinet.net. Over 50 qualified or experienced TEFL teachers.

Thailand

American University Language Centre, 179 Rajadamri Rd., Bangkok 10330; 011-66-2-252-8170. Employs about 90 teachers at main branch and about 100 at other branches in 11 provinces, mainly at universities. Applicants should have a BA and be able to commit themselves to a six-week stint. Also try Chiang Mai branch: 73 Rajadamnern Rd., Amphur Muang, Chiang Mai 50200; 011-66-53-211973.

British American, Ladprao Soi 58-60, Bangkok; 011-66-2-539 4866/9; british_american2000@hotmail.com. About 100 teachers for five schools.

Bell Associate Language Centres, 204/1 Ranong 1 Road, Samsen, Dusit, Bangkok 10300; (011) 66-2-668 2124; gbradd@loxinfo.co.th. Over 60 teachers, preferably with qualifications.

ECC (Thailand), 430/17-24 Chula Soi 64, Siam Sq., Bangkok 10330; 011-66-2-253-3312; eccthai@comnet3.ksc.net.th or jobs@ecc.ac.th. Around 500 native speakers teaching at 60 branches (40 in Bangkok).

Nava Language Schools, 34 Payolyothin 7, Phayathai, Bangkok 10400; (011)-66-2-617-1391; navaoperations@nls.ac.th. TESOL training and experience not required.

Siam Computer and Language Institute, 471/19 Ratcha Withi Rd., Victory Monument, Ket Ratcha Tevi, Bangkok 10400; 011-66-2-247-2345 ext. 370-373. Over 70 branches in Bangkok and the provinces.

TCD Co. Ltd., 399/7 Soi Thongloh 21, Subhumvit Soi 55, Bangkok 10110; Tel./fax 011-66-2-391 5670; johnstcd@hotmail.com. Hires 45 teachers for long-established school owned by expat.

Teaching in China
Do-It-Yourself Steps to Finding a Job

By Daniel Walfish

If you want to join the growing number of Westerners teaching English in mainland China, all you really need is a college degree and native fluency in English. Training in ESL is useful and you might feel at a loss without it, but a certificate is not necessary to convince a Chinese university or private language school to hire you as a teacher of English.

If you're not eligible for a university exchange program and you're unwilling to pay the fee for an independent sending organization, you can go on your own. But apply early: While some positions are open as late as July or August, try to make contact by March. (Occasionally, positions are open for the second semester, too, which begins in February.) Here's what to do:

1. Learn about China and the experience of teaching English in China. Indispensable for these purposes is *Living in China* (Rebecca Weiner, Margaret Murphy, and Albert LiChina Books & Periodicals, 415-282-2994, $19.95). The book provides incredibly useful advice on many aspects of living and teaching in China, and also contains a virtually complete directory of Chinese schools of higher education.

2. Decide on a list of universities to apply to. Use the directory in *Living in China* or the sidebar to this article (located on the *Transitions Abroad* web site [www.TransitionsAbroad.com]).

3. Contact someone at the school responsible for hiring foreign teachers. No other individual, no matter how important or friendly they seem, is likely to have the authority to hire. So who is the right person? Individual academic departments—usually foreign languages or English—hire their own foreign teachers, so the right person is usually the chair or vice-chair of that department. The foreign affairs office is often useless for getting job offers. However, larger universities might have other departments (e.g., "Public English") which need teachers, and you won't find out about them unless you ask someone.

One way to get in touch with the right person is to be in China while you're looking. Bring application materials with you. But keep in mind that if you do line up a job as a student or tourist you will probably have to leave the country or go to Hong Kong to get your visa changed.

International dialing from the U.S. can be cheap. For example, from a residential phone you can use the company PT-1 [www.pt-1.com] by dialing 101-6868 and the phone number. The cost for China is 39 cents per minute. Your phone bill might get quite large, but it's still cheaper than paying thousands of dollars to a sending organization. Most of the people you reach by phone will know English. If the right person isn't in, say you're calling from abroad and you need the right person's home number. But don't call after 9:30 p.m. China time (12 hours ahead of Eastern Standard Time).

4. Send a resume. Highlight any teaching or tutoring experience. You may also want to include references and a letter of explanation. Keep in mind that anyone reading these materials is likely to have very good English reading ability but may not understand Western resume jargon.

5. If you are ultimately offered a position you like, you may want to try a little negotiating. But you're unlikely to be successful if the school has a standard contract. In public universities, compensation for inexperienced foreign teachers is never very much. Expect to get housing, anywhere from RMB1,400 to RMB2,200 ($169-$266) a month, and sometimes a one-way ticket home as well.

Chinese universities rarely require foreigners to teach more than 14 or 15 hours of English classes each week. If the department wants you to do more, ask if some lessons can be converted to optional office hours. Also, if you're teaching any writing or "content" courses, you should have significantly fewer classroom hours.

6. When you consider a job offer, ask for the names of foreigners who are currently teaching or have recently taught at that school so you can get the real scoop on the university and its treatment of foreigners.

Other Teaching Jobs: A master's degree or a doctorate may qualify you to work as a "Foreign Expert" in a university and to teach more advanced courses for much more pay than a "Foreign Teacher" receives.

Private language schools and companies also recruit foreigners. These organizations pay better but are not really service experiences. One possibility is the New Bridge language school in Beijing [www. newbridgeschool.com]. **Dave's ESL Café** [www.eslcafe.com] is a great starting point to search for private school openings. **China's State Bureau of Foreign Experts** (Friendship Hotel, 3 Bai Shi Qiao Rd., Beijing 100873; 011-86-10-6849-9753; sbfe@chinaonline.com.cn.net) has been known to match applicants with jobs in universities and state-owned companies.

Perspective

Teaching in The Big Mango
Bangkok is Strange—Until You Get Used to It

By Brian Thornton

Bangkok is a very strange place. American guidebooks use words like chaotic, wild, manic, and out of control. Tourists, when asked to describe their first impression invariably say, "Intimidating."

When my girlfriend and I arrived to begin a year's contract teaching English it was more than intimidating. We were speechless on the 30-minute journey from the airport, but not the taxi driver who talked incessant taxi-English all the way. It was easy for him, I thought. He didn't have a sick feeling in his stomach and a "Whose idea was this anyway?" thought in his head.

In two days we had to begin teaching. The first classes were a disorganized, nerve-racking mess. If you are untrained, as we were, you must learn as you go and accept that you're going to make countless mistakes along the way. In Thailand, knowing English is the quickest way to get a job or a promotion, and since every wealthy family wants its children to attend a university abroad, the children must know enough English to pass the entrance exams. I've been offered marriage, received expensive gifts. One 9-year-old kid even told me: "Do my homework or I'll call the police and tell them you kill people."

As months pass, you get used to things. The traffic becomes less of a hassle. The food is less of a mystery. You feel a real sense of achievement just to be living in such an unusual place. But you can't maintain that initial level of excitement or constant surprise anywhere, even in Bangkok. You no longer notice an elephant passing, and the street children whose plight first appalled you become invisible.

Teachers who have been living here for a few years nod knowingly as they listen to your complaints about the daily grind. "It's the 6-month blues," they explain. It's at this time that a lot of teachers quit and go home, leaving a rushed note pinned to their locker. It's just culture shock, and it does pass.

My solution was to take more holidays and get to know the famous islands of Thailand. It worked. They are magnificent. They give you a chance to relax, read good books, and get some perspective on how lucky you are to have such impressive places in your backyard. Before you know it you're back to practicing your bad Thai in the local restaurant and marveling at the craziness of the city.

I've come to the end of my contract now. A couple of days ago I was sitting in the staff room when the head teacher came to introduce me to a new teacher. I realized he was to be my replacement and that I was expected to show him around. He stood there wearing a shirt and tie, soaked with sweat. He had that wide-eyed excitement that I must have had when I first came. I asked about his flight and what he thought of Thailand so far.

"It's great, mad, y'know."

After the tour of the school we stood outside looking at the busy street. I wondered if I should recite my litany of mistakes so he might learn from them or impart some useful advice. But I didn't. There was no point. He wasn't listening. He was staring in slack-jawed amazement as a kid who couldn't be more than 14 got out of a BMW and walked past us talking on a cell phone.

Ticket to Latin America
Infinite Possibilities for English Speakers

By Susan Griffith

From specialized language training for the business communities of Buenos Aires and Brasilia to informal conversation exchanges with Mexican fishermen and Venezuelan waiters, the English language can provide a link between north and south, between visitors and residents. The vast continent of Latin America holds an almost infinite range of possibilities for anyone who wishes to share a knowledge of his or her native English.

Seldom will you find the glut of teachers you find elsewhere in the world, possibly because South America is perceived as a place of poverty and crime, danger and corruption, dictators and drug barons. But behind the sensationalist images is a wondrous and diverse collection of countries and a staggering variety of people and landscapes. From the sophisticated urbanites of Santiago to the street children of Lima, South America is home to millions of charming and generous people eager to meet travelers and improve their knowledge of the gringos' native tongue. The stampede to learn English seems unstoppable; company employees are often told by their bosses to learn English or risk demotion. Consequently, the demand for English language instruction continues to increase in all the institutions engaged in promoting English, from elite cultural centers supported by foreign governments to agencies which supply private tutors to businessmen.

The greatest demand for English in the big cities comes from big business, and because of the strong commercial links between the two American continents the demand tends to be for American English. The whole continent is culturally and economically oriented towards the U.S. and there is often a preference for the American accent and for American teaching materials and course books—which explains why so many language institutes are called Lincoln and Jefferson.

Among the most important providers of the English language are American binational centers and cultural centers. Scores of these centers—there are more than 20 in Brazil alone—are engaged in the teaching of English. Addresses, including email addresses, can be found on the web at [http://e.usia.gov/education/engteaching/eal-elp1.htm]. While some institutes want a commitment from teachers to stay for two years, others are happy to take a native speaker on for two or three months. While some want teachers with a BA/MA in TESL from a U.S. university, others require only a good command of English and a tidy appearance.

Career TEFL teachers should contact LAURELS, the Latin American Union of Registered English Language Schools, which currently has over 70 members in Brazil and a number of others in Uruguay: International House Goiania, Rua 4, 80 Setor Oeste, Goiania 74110-140, GO, Brazil (011-55-62-224-0478, fax 011-55-62-223-1846; [www.edunet.com/laurels]).

Several South American nations have a number of American or British-style bilingual schools and *colegios.* Although they are normally looking to hire state-accredited teachers, some do consider EFL teachers. In fact a number take on students and university graduates looking for brief periods of work experience. For example, the **Centro Venezolano Americano** (addresses below) takes interns for a minimum of six months to teach English to children or teenagers in Caracas.

Voluntary and international exchange organizations involved in arranging English tutoring include **WorldTeach,** with programs in Costa Rica and Ecuador, and **Alliances Abroad,** which arranges for fee-paying volunteers to teach in several Latin American countries. An increasing number of language schools offer Spanish tuition to fee-paying foreigners in the mornings and arrange a community volunteering program in the afternoons which often involves teaching English to locals (for example, **Latin American Language Center** and **CIS-MAM**).

TEFL training colleges in the U.S., like Transworld Teachers and New World Teachers, often have close ties with Latin American language schools and send large numbers of their graduates to posts in South America.

Even the poorest of Latin American nations offer possibilities to EFL teachers, provided you are prepared to accept a low wage. In contrast to the standard hourly wage of $10-$20 in Europeanized cities like Buenos Aires and Santiago, the wages paid by language schools in La Paz and Quito are equivalent to about $2.

Picking up Casual Work

Many aspiring teachers find that the response to sending their resumes to addresses abroad is disappointing. It's best to present yourself to language schools in person (although having sent a "warm-up" resume can do your cause no harm).

If you are looking for casual teaching work after arrival, it is a matter of asking around and knocking on doors. Check ads in the English language press such as Mexico City's *The News*, the *Buenos Aires Herald*, or the *Caracas Daily Journal*. English language book stores are another possible source of teaching leads; for example, the English Book Center in Guayaquil (Ecuador), El Ateneo in Buenos Aires, and Books and Bits in Santiago.

Many foreign teachers are simultaneously learning Spanish, so a good place to link up with people in the know is to visit the local **Instituto de Lengua Espanola para Extranjeros** or equivalent. Ask in expatriate bars and restaurants, check out any address claiming to be an English school. In larger cities try deciphering the telephone directory for schools or agencies. In Lima or Quito visit the clubhouses of **South America Explorers,** which keep lists of language institutes and are staffed by expats who are happy to share information with members.

No Special Qualifications Required

The majority of ordinary privately-owned language institutes are not looking for advanced qualifications. If you have a good education, are carrying references and diplomas, and are prepared to stay for an academic year, it should be possible to arrange a contract with a well-established language institute. Many institutes offer their own compulsory pre-job training (to be taken at the teacher's own expense) which provides a useful orientation for new arrivals. Provided you are willing to work for local teaching wages, you should be able to create your own job.

As everywhere, local applicants often break into the world of language teaching gradually by teaching a few classes a week. Noncontractual work is almost always offered on an unofficial part-time basis. So if you are trying to earn a living you will have to patch together enough hours from various sources. Finding the work is simply a matter of asking around and knocking on enough doors. For those who speak no Spanish, the first hurdle is to communicate your request to the secretaries at language schools. Try to memorize a polite request in Spanish (or Portuguese in Brazil) for them to pass your CV and letter to the school director.

The academic year begins in February or early March and lasts until November or December. In the southernmost nations of Chile and Argentina, January and February are very slack months for language schools; further north, in Bolivia for example, the summer holiday are December through January. The best time to arrive to look for work is a few weeks before the end of the summer holidays. But many institutes run 8- to 12-week courses year round and will be interested in acquiring the services of a native speaker whatever the time of year.

In-company teaching usually takes place early in the morning; middle-ranking staff tend to be scheduled before the official working day begins; while directors and higher-ranking executives take their classes at a more civilized mid-morning hour. People learning English outside their workplaces usually sign up for evening lessons. Most teachers enjoy the variety of off-site teaching; classroom teaching tends to be more textbook-based.

Work visas are invariably a problem for long-stay teachers, though some countries make it easier (like Ecuador) than others (Brazil). It is standard for work visas to be available only to teachers on long-term contracts after many documents have been gathered—including notarized and officially translated copies of teaching qualifications-not to mention a hefty fee. This means that a high percentage of teachers are forced to work on tourist visas. These must be kept up-to-date by applying for an extension from the immigration department or by crossing into and back from a neighboring country.

Not only will a stint of teaching benefit eager language learners throughout Latin America, it will give foreign teachers the chance to experience the Latin zest for life. Students throughout the region are almost always communicative, lively, and full of enthusiasm (unless there is a conflict with a big soccer game or local fiesta). Be prepared to share your knowledge of your culture with pupils who are curious and well informed.

Teaching Contacts in Latin America

Argentina
ABS International, Buenos Aires; [www.educa.com.ar/abs]. Qualified teachers for business clients.

CAIT (Capacitacion en Interpretacion y Traducciones), Maipu 863, 3rd Fl. C, 1006 Buenos Aires, Argentina; 011-54-11-4311-8544/4314-2583; cait@ciudad.com.ar. Thirty freelance teachers for in-company language training, must be available for local interview.

Bolivia
Centro Boliviano Americano (CBA), Parque Iturralde Zenon 121, Casilla 12024, La Paz; 011-591-2-431779; cbalp@datacom-bo.net. The binational centers in Bolivia are the largest English language provider in Bolivia with 4 locations in La Paz plus schools in Sucre, Santa Cruz de la Sierra, and other cities.

Anglo-American Cultural Center, P.O. Box 54, Oruro; 011-591-52 50901. Pan American English Center, Avenida 16 de Julio 1490, Edificio Avenida 7 piso, Casilla 5244, La Paz; Tel./fax 011-591-2-340796. Reputable language school with new branch in Cochabamba; 011-591-42-97027.

Brazil
Britannia Schools, Central Department, Av. Borges de Medeiros 67, Leblon, Rio de Janeiro (RJ); Tel./fax 011-55-21-511 0143; sdmace@britannia.com.br, [www.britannia.com.br]. Employ 20 native speaker teachers for schools in Rio de Janeiro and Porto Alegre. Despite name, North American teachers are hired.

IICA Brazil, Instituto de Intercambios e Cultura Americana, Huiutaba, Minas Gerais; 011-55-34-269 6099. Runs a trainee teacher scheme lasting 6 to 18 months for candidates

(aged 21-32) with a BA. Homestays are provided and a monthly salary of $600 is paid.

Lex English Language Services, Rua Humberto 1, No. 318, Vila Mariana. Sao Paulo, 04018-030 SP; 011-55-11-5084 4613; [www.lexenglish.com.br]. Looking especially for lawyers or law students to teach legal English.

M & M Consultaria Linguistica—Internlanguages, Av. Presidente Vargas 446 grupo 1407 Centro, Rio de Janeiro (RJ); Tel./fax 011-55-21-224 9413; intlang@domain.com.br, [www.domain. com.br/clientes/inlang]. Eighteen American and British TEFL teachers employed as freelancers to work with business executives.

New Start Comunicacoes Ltda., Av. Rio Branco 181/702, Centro, 20040-007 Rio de Janeiro, RJ; 011-55-21-240 5807; newstart@prolink.com.br, [www.newstart.com.br]. TEFL certificate required and preferably professional experience in a non-teaching area.

Chile
Typically these schools may offer a newcomer a full timetable only after a probationary three months. American job-seekers, especially those with a TEFL background, should approach one of the Institutos Chileno Norteamericano which are located in Arica, Curico, and Valparaiso as well as the capital.

Berlitz, Av Pedro de Valdivia 2005, Providencia, Santiago; 011-56-2-204 8076.

Fischer English Institute, Cirujano Guzman 49, Providencia, Santiago; 011-56-2-235-6667. Teaches both on and off-site. Offers plenty of structure in planning lessons.

Linguatec, Av. Los Leones 439, Providencia, Santiago; 011-56-2-233 4356; [www.linguatec.cl]. Large branch of U.S.-based teaching organization which considers itself main rival to Berlitz. Compulsory 1-week training course for all accepted teachers is unpaid but guarantees the offer of some hours of work on completion.

Polyglot, Villavicencio 361 Of. 102, Santiago; 011-56-2-639 8078; application@polyglot.cl, [www.polyglot.cl]. 40-50 teachers a year.

Sam Marsalli, Av. Los Leones 1095, Providencia, Santiago; 011-56-2-231-0652; marsalli@intelchile.net. Hires only North Americans after 2-week training course to be based in one of 3 institutes in Santiago.

Tronwell, Apoquindo 4499, 3er Piso, Las Condes, Santiago; 011-56-2-246 1040; [www.tronwell.com]. From 40-50 teachers.

Wall Street Institute, Av. Apoquindo 3502, las Condes, Santiago or 11 de Septiembre 1982, piso 2, Providencia, Santiago; 011-52-3-335 62 56; wsichile@netline.cl.

Colombia

Colombia is even more strongly oriented toward the U.S. than other countries in South America; an extensive network of Colombian-American Cultural Centers include the following which teach English:

Centro Cultural Colombo Bogota, Avenida 19 No. 3-05, Santafé de Bogota; 011-57-1-334 7641, fax 011-57-1-282 3372; colombo@colomsat.net.co.

Centro Cultural Colombo Barranquillo, Carrera 43, No. 51-95, Apartado Aereo 2097, Barranquilla; 011-57-5-340 8084, fax 011-57-5-340 8549; colombo@b-quilla.cetcol.net.co.

Centro Cultural Colombo Cali, Calle 13 Norte 8-45, A.A. 4525, Cali; 011-57-2-668 1922; cencolam@cali.cetcol.net.co.

Centro Cultural Colombo Medellin, Cra. 45 No. 53-24, A.A. 8734, Medellin; 011-57-4-513 4444, fax 011-57-4-513 2666; bncmde@medellin.cetcol.net.co).

Other prominent schools include:

EF English First, Calle 76, No. 9-66, Santafé de Bogota; Diana.Pinilla@ef.com. Also Carrera 38, No. 10A-40, Medellin; 011-57-4-311 3969/347 8055.

Praxis, Calle 79, No. 39-30, Medellin; 011-57-4-250 0515, fax 011-57-4-250 8239. Two

schools which hire native speakers for three months and pay 410,000 pesos a month (just enough to live on).

For a list of schools in Medellin (a mountain city considered by official sources to be potentially dangerous because of its association with drug barons) see [www.ontonet.be/~karel7/cworklistschools.html].

Ecuador

The market for English, particularly American English, continues to thrive despite grave economic difficulties in the country. The devaluation of the currency means that almost no school can pay more than the equivalent of $3 an hour. Dozens of language academies and institutes can be found in Quito, the second city Guayaquil, and in the picturesque city and cultural center of Cuenca in the southern Sierra.

Benedict Schools of Languages, P.O. Box 09-01-8916, Guayaquil; 011-593-5-444 4418; fax 011-593-5-444 1642; benecent@telconet.net. Fifteen teachers in various branches plus 10 more for Quito branch at Edmundo Chiriboga N47-133 y Jorge Paez, Quito; Tel./fax 011-593-2-432729; benedict@accessinter.net. College degree needed.

CEDEI (Centro de Estudios Interamericanos), Casilla 597, Cuenca; 011-593-7-839003; English@cedei.org, [www.cedei.org]. Eigheen university-educated native speakers to teach for at least 6 months.

Inlingua, Arroyo del Rio y Manuel Maria Sanchez 320, Quito; 011-593-2-243 788; [www.inlingua.com]. Thirty native speakers. Preference given to those with Inlingua experience.

Key Language Services, Alpallana 581 y Whymper, Quito (Casilla 17-079770); fax 011-593-2-220956); kls@hoy.net.

El Salvador

CIS (Centro de Intercambio y Solidaridad) MAM Language School, Colonia El Roble, Boulevard Universitario, Casa No. 4, Colonia El Roble, San Salvador, El Salvador; Tel./fax 011-503-226-2623; cis@netcomsa.com. Volunteer teachers to give evening English lessons to members of the Salvadorean opposition. Training provided, and also Spanish classes and a political-cultural program.

Guatemala

Modern American English School, Calle de los Nazarenos 16, Antigua; 011-502-932-3306; fax 011-502-932-0217. Experienced teachers can be interviewed by telephone. From 30-50 quetzales per hour. Board and lodging provided.

Mexico

One of the most important language training organizations with 22 franchise schools is **Wall Street Institutes,** *Presidente Masaryk #49, Mezzanine, 11570 Mexico D.F.; 011-52-5-545 23 53; wsimarcillac@infosel.net.mx. A number of other key organizations are members of the Union Nacional de Escuelas de Idiomas; links to the web sites of the member schools may be found on [www.unei.org]. Among the most important member language schools are:*

Berlitz Mexico, Ejército Nacional 530 29 Piso, Col. Polanco, 11550 Mexico D.F.; 011- 52-50-71-20.

IMARC (Instituto Mexicano Norte Americano de Relaciones Culturales), Pres. Cardenas 840, Satillo, Coahuila 25000; 011-52-84-14 84 22, fax 011-52-84-12 06 53; academ@imarc.edu.mx, [www.imarc.edu.mx]. Interviews can be carried out at TESOL conferences in U.S.

Harmon Hall, Puebla No. 319. Col. Roma, 06700 Mexico; 011-52-11-60 60; [www.harmonhall.com.mx]. Has numerous branches around Mexico City and elsewhere.

Anglo American, Campos Eliseos No. 111, Col. Polanco 11560 Mexico D.F.; 011-52-54 15 66; [www.angloamericasno.com.mx].

Glen Internacional instituto Superior de Idiomas, Viena No. 71-301 Col. Del Carmen, Coyoacan 04100 Mexico D.F.; 011-52-56 59 37 74; [www.colucion.com/glen].

English First Mexico, Londres 188, Col.Juarez, 06600, D.F. Mexico; 011-52-5-514 3333; fax 011-52-5-514 1362; sharon.reed@ef.com, [www.ef.com] and [www.englishtown.com]. A number of teachers for 12 schools in Mexico City. Visa, return flight, paid holiday, bonus, ongoing teacher training, and medical insurance provided as well as salary of 7,000-9,500 pesos per month.

If you have a specific destination in mind, you might wish to purchase the relevant back issue of the Teach English in Mexico Newsletter *for*

$3; see their catalog on [www.employnow.com/2000back.htm].

Many universities, institutes of higher education and bilingual schools hire teachers.

American School of Veracruz, Progresso 52 Jardinas de Mocambo, Boca del Rio, Veracruz 94298; 011-52-29-21 97 78. Package includes immigration clearance, shared accommodation (females only), contribution to airfare and approximately $650 per month.

English Unlimited, Valentin Gama #800, Colonia Jardin, San Luis Potosi, SLP 78270; Tel./fax 011-52-4-833 1277; [www.englishunlimited.com]. No special qualifications.

Centro Mexicano Internacional (CMI), Apartado Postal 56, Morelia, Michoacan 58000; [http://208.137.153.15/Spanish]. Range of voluntary internships including some as English teachers.

Peru

Berlitz HQ, Av Santa Cruz 236, San Isidro, Lima 00; 011-51-1-440 8077.

Foster & Foster Private Institute for English, Miguel Dasso 139-301 San Isidro, Lima (Tel. 011-51-1-949 1902, fax 011-51-1-442 7520).

William Shakespeare Instituto de Ingles, Apartado Postal 18-0310, Lima (Tel. 011-51-1-968 0107/884 6607).

U.S. and U.K. (Placement)

Alliances Abroad, 702 West Ave., Austin, TX 78701; 888-622-7623; info@alliancesabroad.com, [www.alliancesabroad.com]. A program combines teaching English with learning Spanish in Mexico, Ecuador, and Costa Rica. Teaching program also available in Brazil. Volunteers get a monthly stipend or free board and lodging with host family. Sample placement fee is $1,200 for up to five months in Mexico which includes 80 hours of Spanish instruction.

AmeriSpan Unlimited, P.O. Box 40007, Philadelphia, PA 19106; 800-879-6640, fax 215-751-1100; [www.amerispan.com]). This Spanish language and travel organization offers unpaid volunteer placements in Argentina, Bolivia, Costa Rica, Ecuador, Guatemala, Mexico, and Peru. One-month language program followed by 1- to 6-month placements. Application and placement fee is $350 including travel insurance. Lodging with local family provided.

Amity Volunteer Teachers Abroad (AVTA), 10671 Roselle St., Suite 101, San Diego, CA 92121-1525; 858-455-6364; mail@amity.org. Sends volunteers to teach in Argentina, Mexico (Guadalajara), Dominican Republic, and Peru. Volunteers must be over 21, in their final year or two of a degree course or a graduate, have a working knowledge of Spanish, and be able to stay for nine months. Homestay accommodations and a small allowance ($15-$25 a week) are provided.

Association of American Schools in South America (AASSA), 14750 NW 77th Ct., Suite 210, Miami Lakes, FL 33016; 305-821-0345, fax 305-821-4244; info@aassa.com. Coordinates teacher recruitment for 32 international schools in 11 South American countries. Candidates who attend a recruiting fair in November must be state-certified teachers and pay a placement fee of $300 if hired (which is usually reimbursed by employer).

i-to-i, 1 Cottage Rd., Headingley, Leeds LS6 4DD, UK; 011-44-113-217-9800, fax 011-44-113-217-9801; [www.i-to-i.com]. TEFL teacher training and travel organization which accepts North American participants for 3-month voluntary teaching placements in Bolivia and Costa Rica. Fee approximately $1,900 excluding airfare.

Latin American Language Center, PMB 122, 7485 Rush River Dr., Suite 710, Sacramento, CA 95831-5260; 916-447-0938; lalc@madre.com. Program in Costa Rica combines Spanish age language classes and ESL volunteer teaching in public schools. Participation fee $355 per week.

South America Explorers, 126 Indian Creek Rd., Ithaca, NY 14850; 607-277-6122; explorer@samexplo.org, [www.samexplo.org]. Annual membership costs $40. Allows access to SAE clubhouses with useful notice boards and contacts. SAE is working on a Volunteer Resource Database to which members can gain access.

Office of English Language Programs, U.S. State Department, SA 44, Room 304, 301 4th St., SW, Washington, DC 20547; 202-619-5892; [http://exchanges.state.gov/education.engteaching]. Formerly known as the U.S. Information Agency and now part of the State Department, this office runs a network of overseas field offices based in U.S. embassies, many of which have English teaching programs employing native speakers of American English. To find a list of binational centers offering English instruction look at [http://e-usia.gov/education/ engteaching/eal-elp1.htm].

WorldTeach, Center for International Development, Harvard Univ., 79 John F. Kennedy St., Cambridge, MA 02138; 617-495-5527; info@worldteach.org, [www.worldteach.org]. Nonprofit organization which places several hundred graduates as volunteer teachers of EFL or ESL in many countries including Costa Rica and Ecuador for one year, and Mexico and Honduras for six months. The inclusive cost is about $5,000.

Venezuela

Oil wealth abounds in the business community and many corporations hire in-company language trainers through Caracas-based agencies.

Centro Venezolano Americano, Av. Asé Marti, Edf. CVA, Urbanizacion Las Mercedes, Caracas 1060-A; or: Apartado 61715 Del Este, Caracas 1060-A; 011-58-2-993 7911, fax 011-58-2-993 6812; [www.cva.org.ve]). Combined work/study internships open only to U.S. citizens. Details in U.S. available from CVA, Pasante International Program, Attn. Nancy Carapaica, 1408 NW 82nd Ave., C-525, Miami, FL 33126; 582- 993-6812.

Centro Venezolano Americano del Zulia, Calle 63, No. 3E-60, Apartado 419, Maracaibo; 011-58-61-911436/911880; cevaz@cantv.net, [www.cevaz.com]. Native speakers given pre-service training.

Iowa Institute, Avenida Cuatro con Calle 18, Mérida Edo. Mérida; 011-58-74-526404; iowainst@ing.ula.ve, [www.ing.ula.ve/~iowainst]. Teaching opportunities for trained TEFL teachers and for Americans with camp counseling experience to teach children.

Wall Street Institute, a. Francisco de Miranda, Torre Lido, piso 11 Torre C, ofic. 111C, 113C El Rosal, Caracas; 011-58-2-953 7102; wsiven@cantv.net.

Perspective

Work in Chile

ESL Teachers Needed in Santiago

By Edward Carpenter

If you are a North American traveler or teacher looking for work, dozens of institutes in Santiago, Chile, will employ you for your language skills. But to insure success, contact the language schools five or six months in advance of your arrival. Many are on the Internet. Send a resume to those you find most interesting. Highlight any English training, including university studies, and teaching experience. Don't forget volunteer work. Include information on traveling, living, and studying abroad, as well as exposure to foreign cultures. Schools want to hire adventurous people, not those easily put off by inconveniences. If you know the language and the culture, flaunt it.

In a letter of introduction explain why you are interested in the position, what makes you qualified, what your goals are, and how you see your position with the institute will contribute to those goals. Finally, set out clearly, though not bluntly, why the institute should hire you—what position you will fill and why you can do it better than the person whose resume they read next. The idea is to stand out.

The school year starts at the end of March. Don't expect replies until the New Year. Once you receive positive responses, you'll have about a week to decide. Some of the institutes have contracts, which are used to justify their sponsorship of your visa. Others hire on the spot. In this case, you'll have to leave the country to renew your tourist visa every three months. Paperwork sometimes demands patience but is not usually a problem. The institutes know how to deal with it or get around it.

Most schools have a two- to three-week unpaid training program. Salaries range from 200,000-400,000 pesos per month (approximately $400-$500). You won't be able to afford many luxuries in addition to travel, but it's not an uncomfortable wage. Some institutes provide basic insurance; other benefits are rare.

Classes range from one to 12 students. A full-time schedule requires odd hours. Most teachers work split shifts between mornings and evenings. Afternoons are free for napping, tutoring (which can be profitable), or other activities.

Santiago has much to offer: museum and gallery shows, opera, classical music, jazz and popular singing, and Latin dancing in theaters around the city. The hundreds of markets and malls in the city—many of which are hidden in buildings downtown that look like offices—sell everything from artisanal work to Gucci. The pedestrian walks are filled with entertainers—from musicians to preachers to mimes. Parque Forestal, especially around the Museo National de Ballas Artes, is a free-for-all meeting place for amateur jugglers and clowns and musicians every Sunday. In fact, there are so many things to see and do in the city it's impossible to know them all. Half the fun is stumbling onto something as you walk along.

The night life in Santiago can only be described as "something else." After warming up over a few drinks and maybe dinner, the clubs and dance pubs start jumping around midnight. No matter where you are, don't plan on going home until five or six in the morning.

From simple beer dives to Cuban, Reggae, or Brazilian clubs, every culture and subculture is represented with its own style of food and drinks, dancing, and music. Later, you can press on to the ritzier side of town in Providencia on Avenida Suecia. The locals call it Gringolandia and with good reason—it's the place where the "professionals" hang out. Expect to pay twice what you paid in Bellavista.

Santiago is a city that never ends, that never stops growing. It's a culture of borders and conflicts. That's what makes it interesting.

Teaching English Abroad
The Key Print Resources
Selected and Reviewed by William Nolting

Teaching English may not require any special credentials other than having English as your native language and a year's commitment (and usually a college degree). Typical locations: Eastern Europe and Asia. Apply as early as December prior to the fall you want to start. *Essential; *Outstanding and of broad interest.*

For ordering information, if not included below, see Key Publishers, Page 13.

The ELT Guide. 1999. 9th ed. 271 pp. TESOL. (Order #683GAZ). $28.95 (member $24.95). Comprehensive reference for English language teaching worldwide. Primarily intended for ESL teachers with credentials. Country-by-country guide with recruitment information, school listings, and courses.

** **French Cultural Services: English Teaching Assistant Program.** Applications available from: Cultural Services of the French Embassy, 972 5th Ave., New York, NY 10021; fax 212-439-1455; [http://info-france-usa.org/culture/education/index.html]. Several hundred academic-year positions available for Americans under 30 with a college degree and working knowledge of French. Stipend covers living expenses.

* **Fulbright English Teaching Assistantships.** Applications free from USIA Fulbright, U.S. Student Programs Division, 809 United Nations Plaza, New York, NY 10017-3580; 212-984-5330, [www.iie.org/fulbright]. Enrolled students must apply through own college; graduates apply "at-large" to regional IIE offices. English teaching options for graduates in Belgium/Luxembourg, France, Germany, Hungary, Korea, Taiwan, and Turkey. Application deadline for current students is in mid-September (or mid-October "at-large" applicants) the following year.

** **Japan Exchange Teaching Program** (JET). Free applications from Office of the JET Program, Embassy of Japan, 2520 Massachusetts Ave. NW, Washington, DC 20008; 800-INFO-JET or 202-939-6772, [www.jet.org], or contact Japanese consulate. The largest program for teaching English abroad, with more than 6,000 participants annually. Offers 2 types of paid positions in Japan: English-teaching assistantships in secondary schools or Coordinator for International Relations (latter requires Japanese proficiency).

* **Make a Mil-¥en: Teaching English in Japan.** by Don Best. 1994. 176 pp. $14.95 plus $3 (book rate) or $3.95 (first-class) shipping from Stone Bridge Press, P.O. Box 8208, Berkeley, CA 94707; 800-947-7271, fax 510-524-8711;

sbp@stonebridge.com, [www.stonebridge.com]. Guide has information on everything from the job search to settling in. The experts at O-Hayo Sensei consider this to be the best book on Japan from an American perspective currently available.

* **More Than a Native Speaker: An Introduction for Volunteers Teaching Abroad** by Don Snow. 1996. 321 pp. (Order #641). $29.95 (member $24.95) plus $4.50 shipping from TESOL. Covers classroom survival skills for teaching English as a second or foreign language from lesson planning to adaptation to life in a new country, with details on how to teach listening, speaking, reading, writing, grammar, vocabulary, and culture.

Native Speaker: Teach English and See the World by Elizabeth Reid. 1996. 96 pp. In One Ear Publications. $7.95 plus $3 s/h from Book Clearing House, 46 Purdy St., Harrison NY 10528, 800-431-1579. A basic guide to teaching English as a second language, finding a position, and setting up private classes, by an American who taught in Latin America.

* **O-Hayo Sensei: The Newsletter of Teaching Jobs in Japan** edited by Lynn Cullivan. Twice-monthly by email, $12 for 12 issues. Single issue free, check web site. To subscribe, send check or money order payable to: O-Hayo Sensei, Subscription Dept., 1032 Irving St., PMB 508, San Francisco, CA 94122; fax 415-731-1113; editor@ohayosensei. com, [www.ohayosensei.com]. Lengthy lists of current job openings for English teachers, university-level teachers and others. Classifieds, Japan info and list of school.

Opportunities in Teaching English to Speakers of Other Languages by Blythe Camenson. 1999. 160 pp. $20 hardcover/$11.95 paperback from VGM Career Horizons (see Key Publishers). Overview of the professional field of Teaching English as a Foreign/Second Language.

** **Peace Corps.** Peace Corps, 1111 20th St., NW, Rm. 8436, Washington, DC 20526; 800-424-8580; [www.peacecorps.gov]. Peace Corps sends substantial numbers of teachers of English and other subjects such as math, science and business to regions including Africa, Asia, Eastern Europe and Russia, Latin America, Middle East and the Pacific Basin. See Peace Corps entry in the Volunteer section for more details.

* **Teaching Abroad Without Certification** by William Nolting. Available free on the Univ. of Michigan web site, [www.umich.edu/~icenter/overseas]. A well-researched listing of U.S.-based placement organizations .

** **Teaching English Abroad: Talk Your Way Around the World** by Susan Griffith. Vacation Work (U.K.). 1999. 415 pp. $16.95 from Peterson's. The only book with extensive worldwide coverage (including Western and Eastern Europe, the Middle East, and other regions left out of other guides), this outstanding volume gives in-depth information on everything from preparation to the job search. Many first-hand reports from teachers. Extensive directories of schools.

* **Teaching English in Asia: Finding a Job and Doing it Well** by Galen Harris Valle. 1995. 178 pp. $19.95 plus $3 s/h from Pacific View Press, P.O. Box 2657, Berkeley, CA 94702; 510-849-4213, fax 510-843-5835; pvp@sirius.com. Detailed overview of teaching English in Asia, with comprehensive teaching tips, by a professional teacher. However, it provides few job search addresses.

TESOL Placement Bulletin. TESOL members: $28/year, nonmembers $38/year. Monthly bulletin lists position openings for qualified ESL/EFL teachers and administrators. TESOL, 700 South Washington St., Suite 200, Alexandria, VA 22314; 703-836-0774, fax 703-836-6447; info@tesol.org, [www.tesol.org].

Teaching English as a Second Language

Directory of Training and Placement Programs

By Transitions Abroad Editors

If you lack experience or credentials, you may want some formal study before heading overseas in search of an English language teaching position. Virtually all positions require only a bachelor's degree. However, candidates with advanced training and either a certificate or a master's degree in TESOL will have greater flexibility and command more pay. For the most current information see the *Transitions Abroad* web site [www.TransitionsAbroad.com] or contact the program directors. And please tell them you read about their programs in this book. Organizations in more than one country are listed under "Worldwide."

CANADA

RSA Cambridge CELTA

The Certificate in English Language Teaching to Adults (CELTA) is the world's most widely recognized entry-level certificate for teaching English as a second or foreign language and is the credential employers ask for by name. CELTA at ILI is now offered as a 4,000 level university credit.
Dates: Jun 2-26, Jan 29-Feb 23, Feb 26-Mar 23, Mar 26-Apr 20, Apr 23-May 18, May 22-Jun 15, Jun 18-Jul 13, Jul 16-Aug 10, Aug 13-Sep 7, Sep 10-Oct 5, Oct 9-Nov 2, Nov 5-30. **Cost:** Registration fee $75. Course fee $1,500. **Contact:** Registrar, International Language Institute, 5151 Teminal Rd., 8th Fl., Halifax, NS, B3J 1A1, Canada; 902-429-3636, fax 902-429-2900; study@ili-halifax.com, [www.ili-halifax.com].

CENTRAL EUROPE

Bridges for Education

Bridges for Education sends volunteer teachers to teach conversational English in summer. Three weeks teaching, 1 week travel. Educated adults (including families) and college students pay roundtrip airfare and BFE administrative expenses. Since 1984, about 650 teachers to 8 countries, serving 6,000 students in 26 countries with Ministry of Ed, UNESCO. **Dates:** Summer, Jul and Aug. **Cost:** Approx. $2,000, depending on departure and destination points. **Contact:** Margaret Dodge, Applications Coordinator 8912 Garlinghouse Rd., Naples, NY 14512; 716-524-9344; mdodge@frontiernet.com, [www.bridges4edu.org].

Cambridge/RSA CELTA

Four-week intensive course for those wishing to enter ELT or experienced teachers seeking recognized qualification. Highly practical, including seminars and workshops, observed teaching practice, and feedback. Assessment of teaching and written work throughout course. Help provided with accommodations.
Dates: Aug 2001. **Cost:** £590 course fee (including RSA/Cambridge registration fee). **Contact:** Elisa Jaroch, International House, ul. Leszczynskiego 3, 50-078 Wroclaw, Poland; Tel/fax 011-48-71-7817-290; ttcentre@id.pl.

Central European Teaching Program

Teach conversational English (or German, French, and other subjects) in schools in Hungary, Poland, and Romania. Live and work for a year in this rapidly changing part of the world, and immerse yourself in a new culture. Salary, housing, and health insurance are provided. Program support services.
Dates: Sep-Jun or Jan-Jun. **Cost:** Placement fee: $2,000. **Contact:** Alex Dunlop, CETP, Beloit College, 700 College St., Beloit, WI 53511; 608-363-2619; dunlopa@beloit.edu, [www.beloit.edu/~cetp].

CHINA

China Teaching Program

A training and placement program for those wanting to teach at institutions of higher education or at secondary schools throughout the P.R.C. Most opportunities are in TEFL, some in business or law. Five-week summer training session held on WWU campus. Participants study Chinese language and culture, TEFL methodology, etc. Minimum requirements: BA, native speaker of English. (Placement-only option may be possible.)
Dates: Application deadline for Summer Session 2001 is Feb 9. **Cost:** Approx. $1,200 (includes tuition and placement). **Contact:** Catherine Barnhart, Director, China Teaching Program, Western Washington Univ., OM 530, Bellingham, WA 98225-9047; 360-650-3753; ctp@cc.wwu.edu, [www.wwu.edu/~ctp].

CZECH REPUBLIC

ITC International TEFL Certificate

Internationally recognized 4-week TEFL course in Prague and Barcelona. Sessions are year round on a monthly basis. The course is designed for individuals with little or no teaching experience. Trainees receive extensive supervised teaching practice with foreign students during the course. ITC has graduated over 1,500 teachers who are now working around the globe and has onsite EFL school.
Dates: Jan 8-Feb 2; Feb 12-Mar 9; Mar 19-Apr 13; Apr 23-May 18; May 28-Jun 22; Jul 2-27; Aug 6-31; Sep 10-Oct 5; Oct 15-Nov 9; Nov 19-Dec 14. **Cost:** $1,500 tuition. Includes 4-week TEFL certificate course, course manual, lifetime job guidance worldwide, job guarantee in Eastern Europe. Housing and work visa assistance is available. Optional lodging: $450. **Contact:** ITC, Kaprova 14, 110 00 Prague, Czech Republic; 011-420-2-2481-4791. In U.S.: 800-915-5540, fax 509-561-5827 or 815-550-0086; info@itc-training.com, [www.itc-training.com].

EGYPT

The American Univ. in Cairo

Graduate Master's degree program and fellowship for teaching English as a foreign language are offered at the American Univ. in Cairo. Courses essential for effective teaching are given by a supportive, skilled faculty. The master's degree program requires 2 years and the intervening summer for completion. Program starts in September only.
Dates: Sep-Jun; Jun-Aug. **Cost:** Without fellowship: year $11,525; summer $2,858. **Contact:** Matrans Davidson, American Univ. in Cairo, 420 5th Ave., 3rd Fl., New York, NY 10018-2729; auc-egypt@aucnyo.edu, [www.aucegypt.edu].

EUROPE

English Language Teaching

Certificate and diploma courses for English language teaching to adults and younger learners, certified by Cambridge Univ. Part-time and intensive courses available.
Dates: Intensive Jan 25-Feb 21; May 31-Jun 27; Jun 28-Jul 25; Sep 3-28; part-time Sep 27-Dec 18; Feb 27-May 29. **Cost:** LIT2,500,000 plus Univ. Cambridge fee LIT230,000. **Contact:** Teacher Training Dept., International House, Viale Manzoni 22, 00185 Rome, Italy; 011-390-6-70476894, fax 011-390-6-70497842.

FRANCE

French in France

Among the ways to learn French, total immersion is the most enjoyable and effective. School has been running for 25 years in a small historical city located in Normandy (west of Paris). Any age and any level welcome in 1- to 10-week programs, intensive or vacation type, from mid-Mar to mid-Nov.
Dates: Spring: Mar-May; summer: Jun-Aug; fall: Sep-Nov. **Cost:** From $525 per week (tuition, room and board, and excursions). **Contact:** Dr. Alméras, Chairman, French American Study Center, 12, 14, Blvd. Carnot, B.P. 4176, 14104 Lisieux Cedex, France; 011-33-2-31-31-22-01; centre.normandie@wanadoo.fr, [http://perso.wanadoo.fr/centre.normandie/].

JAPAN

Japan Exchange and Teaching (JET) Program

Sponsored by the Japanese Government, the JET Program invites over 1,300 American college graduates and young professionals to share their language and culture with Japanese youth. One-year positions are available in schools and government offices in Japan. Apply by early December for positions beginning in July of the following year.

Dates: One-year contracts renewable by mutual consent not more than 2 times. **Cost:** Participants receive approx. ¥3,600,000 per year in monthly payments. **Contact:** JET Program Office, Embassy of Japan, 2520 Massachusetts Ave. NW, Washington, DC 20008; 202-238-6772, fax 202-265-9484; eojjet@erols.com, [www.mofa.go.jp/j_info/visit/jet/index.html].

Teaching English in Japan

Two-year program to maximize linguistic and cultural integration of participants who work as teachers' assistants. Placements twice yearly in Apr and Aug. Most positions are in junior high schools in urban and rural areas. Bachelor's degree and willingness to learn Japanese required.

Dates: Hiring for positions every Apr and Aug. Applications accepted year round. Potential applicants are encouraged to submit applications between Oct-Feb. **Cost:** No application fees. **Contact:** Institute for Education in Japan, Earlham College, 801 National Rd. West, D-202, Richmond, IN 47374; 888-685-2726, fax 765-983-1553, [www.earlham.edu/~aet].

MEXICO

New World Teachers

Accelerated 4-week TEFL/TESL Certificate course in Puerto Vallarta. Integrates established European Direct Method with contemporary teaching techniques. Developed by internationally-experienced trainers and aimed at trainees with an American education, this course requires no second language. Includes supervised practice teaching foreign students, permanent access to job placement guidance and information. Extensive Internet resources. Two-day seminar in Teaching English to Young Learners also available with every course.

Dates: Four-week intensive courses begin: Feb 21, Apr 24, Jun 12, Jul 24, Sep 4, Oct 23. **Cost:** $2,750. Includes deposit, registration, books, course materials, and lifetime job placement assistance. Accommodations: single room with private bath, 5 minutes walk from the beach, $300. *Transitions Abroad* readers receive free accommodations package. **Contact:** New World Teachers, 605 Market St., Suite 800, San Francisco, CA 94105; 800-644-5424; teachersSF@aol.com, [www.goteach.com].

SPAIN

International Career Center

Four week, 100-plus hour TEFL Certification Program offered in Barcelona. Direct access to the European job market. Lifetime job assistance, initial work visa assistance, course manual (all included in registration fee). Housing, orientation, airport greeting available. No prior teaching experience necessary.

Dates: Monthly starting in Feb. **Cost:** $1,200. **Contact:** Jo Ruoss, ICC International Career Center, P.O. Box 94, Winthrop, WA 98862; Tel./fax 888-256-2519 or 509-996-2583. In Spain: Calle Sant Pere Mes Alt, 59bis, 3-1, 08003 Barcelona, Spain; Tel./fax 011-34-93-268-3283.; info-icc@explora.edu, [www.teflbarcelona.com].

Univ. of Cambridge/RSA CELTA

CELTA (Certificate in English Language Teaching to Adults) is an initial training course in the teaching of English as a foreign language. The course gives a thorough basic grounding in all areas of modern EFL (U.S. ESL), and is the minimum required qualification of many EFL schools. Accommodations arranged by the center.

Dates: May 8, Jul 3, Aug 28, Sep 25, Oct 23, Nov 20. **Cost:** Approx. $1,350 tuition and accommodations. Meals not included. **Contact:** Teacher Training Dept., CLIC International House, Albareda 19, 41001 Sevilla, Spain; 011-34-954-502131, fax 011-34-954-561696; clic@clic.es, [www.clic.es].

TAIWAN

Hess Educational Organization

Largest private children's language school in Taiwan specializing in Teaching English as a Foreign Language (TEFL). Over 100 schools and 40 kindergartens island-wide offer 3 contract options. The curriculum has been tried, tested, and constantly updated to provide the most successful programs for teaching English to learners of all ages. Requirements: a bachelor's degree, a passport from an English-speaking country, a 1-year commitment, and being a native English speaker. For an application form, check out the web site.

Dates: Application deadlines are Jan 31 for Jun 1; Apr 30 for Sep 1; Jul 31 for Dec 1; and Oct 31 for Mar 1. **Cost:** No fee. We recruit only for our own schools. **Contact:** North Americans contact Hess Educational Organization, 4 Horicon Ave., Glens Falls, NY 12801; Tel./fax 518-793-6183. Citizens of all other countries contact Hess Educational Organization, English Human Resource Dept., 419 Chung Shan Rd., Sec. 2, Chung Ho City 235, Taiwan, ROC; 011-886-2-3234-6188 ext. 1053, fax 011-886-2-2222-94-99; hesswork@hess.com.tw, [www.hess.com.tw].

Overseas Service Corps YMCA

BAs to PhDs placed in ESL teaching positions in community-based YMCAs. No Chinese language necessary. Preference given to applicants with teaching experience, either general or ESL, or degree in teaching. Conversational English program provides an opportunity for cultural exchange. Must reside in North America and be a citizen of an English-speaking country. Twenty to 30 openings.

Dates: Call anytime for a brochure and application. Placement end Sep through following Sep, 1-year commitment. **Cost:** $50 application fee. Benefits include: housing, health insurance, return airfare, paid vacation, bonus, orientation, sponsorship for visa, and monthly stipend. **Contact:** Jann Sterling, Program Assistant, International Group, YMCA of the USA, 101 N. Wacker Dr., Chicago, IL 60606; 800-872-9622 ext. 167, fax 312-977-0884; sterling@ymcausa.org, [www.ymca.net].

UNITED KINGDOM AND IRELAND

Cambridge/RSA CELTA and DELTA Courses

CELTA 4-week preparatory certificate in teaching English, the most widely accepted qualification for teaching English in the world. Also DELTA, an 8-week intensive course for teachers with a minimum of 2 years experience teaching English as a second/foreign language (vital for more responsible posts e.g., D.O.S., Director, etc.).

Dates: CELTA every 6 weeks; DELTA Jul/Aug every year. **Cost:** CELTA £895; DELTA £1,400. **Contact:** Trevor Udberg, Director, International House Newcastle, 14-18 Stowell St., Newcastle Upon Tyne; NE1 4XQ, England; 011-44-191-232-9551, fax 011-44-191-232-1126; ihnew@compuserve.com.

WORLDWIDE

CTEFL and Advanced CTEFL

Transworld Schools is approved by the state of California to offer both the CTEFL and Advanced CTEFL courses. All courses include teaching practicum, language awareness, business English, teaching children, computer assisted language learning, and job training. We provide job placement assistance through our worldwide network of schools, universities, and corporations.

Dates: Year round. Full-time every 2 weeks from Jan 10, part-time every 6 weeks from Jan 11. **Cost:** Comprehensive CTEFL $1,800, CTEFL $1,600 all materials included. **Contact:** Ceri Rich-Odeh, Owner/Director, Transworld Schools, 701 Sutter St., 2nd Fl., San Francisco, CA 94109; 415-928-2835, fax 415-928-0261; transwd@aol.com, [www.transworldschools.com]

English Teaching, Conservation, and Work Experience

Voluntary jobs teaching English, conserving the environment and internships placements in Asia, Latin America, Far East, Russia, and Australia. Intensive TEFL training U.K., online TEFL courses from Dec 99.

Dates: Fully flexible, TEFL courses every weekend, also online. **Cost:** $1,500-$2,500 (1-3 months). **Contact:** i to i International Projects, 1 Cottage Rd., Headingley, Leeds LS6 4DD, U.K.; 011-44-870-333-2332, fax 011-44-870-052-5760; travel@i-to-i-com, [www.i-to-i.com].

ESL Intensive Institute

Learn English pronunciation, listening comprehension, conversation, reading and writing. Includes an orientation to American culture and weekly field trips. By Univ. of New Hampshire in Durham. For students wanting to learn English before college or who want to improve TOEFL scores (3-10 credits, 4 hours per day).

Dates: Sessions run year round; 4-, 8-, 12-, 16-, and 20-week study. **Cost:** Tuition varies depending on length of study. Room and board available at additional cost. **Contact:** L. Conti, UNH Continuing Education, ESL Institute, 24 Rosemary Ln., Durham, NH 03824; 603-862-2069; learn.dce@unh.edu, [www.learn.unh.edu/ESL].

Goal Recruiting

Goal Recruiting works with private language schools in Taiwan, Korea, and Thailand providing them with ESL teachers. Should be available soon in Latin America. Applicants must have a university degree; prior experience is helpful but not necessary. No fees charged to the applicant.

Dates: Year round demand for teachers. Cost: Free. Contact: Goal Recruiting, 307 Glebemount Ave., Toronto, ON, M4C 3V3, Canada; 888-772-7203, 416-696-2344, fax 416-423-0195; apply@goalasia.com, [www.goalasia.com].

Hamline TEFL Certificate Course

The Graduate School of Education at Hamline Univ. offers an internationally recognized TEFL Certificate Course to prepare individuals to teach English overseas. An interactive approach enables participants to discover the practices of language teaching. Courses include lectures, workshops, and practice teaching. Career counseling provided. Graduates can complete 3 additional online courses for an Advanced TEFL Certificate, or apply their course work to an MA in ESL.

Dates: Three 1-month intensives: Apr, Jul, and Aug; 8-week semi-intensive: Jan-Mar; Evening extensive: Oct-Mar. On-campus room and board available except in Aug. Cost: All courses are $2300.00 beginning June 2001. Participants receive 8 graduate semester credits upon completion of the program. Materials: approx. $80. Rates valid through June 2002. Contact: Betsy Parrish, Associate Professor/Coordinator, TEFL Certificate Program, Graduate School of Education, Hamline Univ., 1536 Hewitt Ave., St. Paul, MN 55104; 800-888-2182, fax 651-523-2489; bparrish@gw.hamline.edu.

IELI at Humboldt State Univ.

Intensive English with part-time university courses in a congenial community in northern California. Small classes, personalized instruction. Housing in homestays, student apartments and on campus. Complete recreational and activity program. Airport pickup and assistance in getting settled.

Dates: Jan, Mar, May, Aug, and Oct—8-week sessions. Cost: Tuition $1,440 for 21 hours per week. Room and board $1,320 for 8 weeks. Contact: IELI, Humboldt State Univ., Arcata, CA 95521-8299; 707-826-5878, fax 707-826-5885; ieli@humboldt.edu, [www.humboldt.edu/~ieli].

International Schools Services

Learn about teaching opportunities in private American and international schools around the world and discover how you can carry your education career overseas. The Educational Staffing program of International Schools Services has placed over 17,000 K-12 teachers and administrators in overseas schools since 1955. Most candidates obtain their overseas teaching positions by attending our U.S.-based International Recruitment Centers (IRCs) where ISS candidates interview with overseas school heads seeking new staff. Applicants must have a bachelor's degree and 2 years of current K-12 teaching experience. The experience may be waived for those who have overseas living or working experience, teaching certification, and a motivation to work in the developing world. IRC registration materials are provided upon approval of your completed ISS application. See web site for more information or to fill out an application.

Dates: International Recruitment Centers in Feb, Mar, and Jun. Cost: $150; International Recruitment Center registration: $200. There are no placement fees charged to candidates who are placed through the work of ISS. Contact: Educational Staffing, ISS, P.O. Box 5910, Princeton, NJ 08543; 609-452-0990 or 609-452-2690; edustaffing@iss.edu, [www.iss.edu].

Lado TEFL Certificate

Four-week intensive, 10-week night/Saturday classes. Highly successful placement services. Recognized by ACE (American Council on Education).

Dates: Year round. Cost: $1,750 includes registration fee, textbooks, and other materials. Contact: Bill Stout, Lado TEFL, 2233 Wisconsin Ave., NW, Washington, DC 20007; 202-333-4222, fax 202-337-1118; teachertraining@ladoent.com, [www.lado.com/home_t.htm].

Midwest Teacher Training Program

Earn a TEFL certificate in a 5-week intensive training program that prepares trainees to teach English worldwide. Hands-on approach incorporates course work, practice teaching, and ESL observation in a unique observation theater. No foreign language or teaching experience required. Job placement assistance and career workshops included.

Dates: Jan 22-Feb 23, Mar 19-Apr 20, May 14-Jun 15, Jul 9-Aug 10, Sep 17-Oct 19, Nov 12-Dec 14.

Cost: $2,200 includes books. Contact: Renee Lajcak, Program Director, Midwest Teacher Training Program, 19 N. Pickney St., Madison, WI 53703; 800-765-8577, fax 608-257-4346; info@mttp.com, [www.mttp.com].

New World Teachers

Largest TEFL/TESL Certificate school in the U.S. Accelerated 4-week courses in San Francisco, Puerto Vallarta (Mexico), Budapest (Hungary), and Phuket (Thailand). Integrates established European Direct Method aimed at trainees with an American education. Course requires no second language. Includes supervised practice teaching foreign students, access to job placement guidance and information. Extensive Internet resources, 2-day seminar in Teaching English to Young Learners available with every course.

Dates: Four-week intensive courses begin in San Francisco: Jan 10, Feb 14, Mar 20, May 29, Jun 26, Jul 24, Aug 28, Sep 25, Oct 23, Dec 4. Ten-week Tuesday evening and Saturday courses begin Feb 8, Jun 6, Oct 3. In Puerto Vallarta: Feb 21, Apr 24, Jun 12, Jul 24, Sep 9, Oct 23. In Budapest: Apr 24, Aug 23. In Phuket: Jan 10, 2000. Cost: San Francisco $2,200; Puerto Vallarta $2,750; Budapest $2,950; Phuket $3,200. Includes deposit, registration, books, course materials, and lifetime job placement assistance. Accommodations: San Francisco $575 per month in the New World Guest House near Union Square (walk to the school). Shared room, maid service and cooking facilities. Accommodation packages available at all overseas course locations $300 per month. Contact: New World Teachers, 605 Market St., Suite 800, San Francisco, CA 94105; 800-644-5424; teacherssf@aol.com, [www.goteach.com].

RSA/Univ. of Cambridge CELTA

The most widely recognized initial qualification for teaching English as a foreign language to adults, the CELTA is offered at our Portland, San Francisco, and Santa Monica centers year round. You need to be at least 20 years old, have a good standard of education and recent foreign language learning experience to be qualified.

Dates: Jan-Nov year round. Cost: $2,150. Contact: John Myers, International House-Portland, 200 SW Market St., Suite #111, Portland, OR 97201; 503-224-1960, fax 503-224-2041; teachertraining@ih-portland.com.

School of Teaching ESL

Online and onground classes. Since 1985, a pioneer of intensive ESOL training. Prepare to teach in the U.S. and overseas. Receive 900-level education credits and the Certificate in Teaching English as a Second or Foreign Language. Credits also apply to Washington State Additional Endorsement in ESL and to Seattle Univ's. M-TESOL program. (Onground classes only). Graduates currently teaching and administrating in the U.S. and more than 58 other countries. On-site ESL class. Qualified and experienced instructors. Lifetime job information. Internet discussion list. International applicants welcome (I-20s available). We work with VISTA, Americorps, and other government agencies for tuition. Dates: Eleven starting dates per year for the 4-week intensive sessions. Evening non-intensive program and online classes are on the Seattle Univ. quarterly schedule. Cost: $2,340 for the 12-credit certificate training. Low-cost housing on-site. Contact: School of Teaching ESL, 2601 NW 56th St., Seattle, WA 98107; 206-781-8607, fax 206-781-8922; hasegawa@seattleu.edu, [www.seattleu.edu/soe/stesl].

St Giles Language Teaching Center

Training courses leading to the prestigious, internationally recognized Cambridge RSA Certificate in English Language Teaching to Adults (CELTA). The CELTA is the TEFL qualification required by many employers worldwide. Successful candidates also earn a graduate credit recommendation of 6 hours toward an MA TESOL. Each course is externally moderated by Cambridge Univ. We also offer lifelong job guidance to our graduates. Dates: Jan 8, Feb 19, Mar 26, Apr 30, Jun 4, Jul 9, Aug 6, Sep 10, Oct 15, Nov 26. Cost: $2,695 ($2,495 in Jan and Feb). Contact: St Giles Language Teaching Center, 1 Hallidie Plaza, Suite 350, San Francisco, CA 94102; 415-788-3552, fax 415-788-1923; sfstgile@slip.net, [www.stgiles-usa.com].

TESOL Career Services

TESOL Career Services is the place to find the best ESOL teaching positions worldwide. The TESOL *Placement Bulletin* has worldwide job listings and job searching resources for ESOL professionals. Subscriptions include 10 issues per year, by mail, and email. The Employment Clearinghouse at TESOL's annual convention and exposition in March is the world's largest ESOL job fair. Jobs will be posted and interviews are conducted on site. More than 100 schools will be recruiting. March 15-18 at the Vancouver Convention and Exhibition Center. **Dates:** Call for details. **Cost:** Contact TESOL for more information. **Contact:** TESOL, 700 South Washington St., Suite 200, Alexandria, VA 22314; 703-836-0774, fax 703-836-6447; career@tesol.edu, [www.tesol.edu/].

WorldTeach in Africa, Asia, and Latin America

WorldTeach is a nonprofit, nongovernmental organization which provides opportunities for individuals to make a meaningful contribution to international education by living and working as volunteer teachers in developing countries. **Dates:** Year round. **Cost:** $3,990-$5,990. Includes international airfare, health insurance, extensive training, and in-country support. **Contact:** WorldTeach, Center for International Development, Harvard Univ., 79 John F. Kennedy St., Cambridge, MA 02138; 800-4-TEACH-0 or 617-495-5527, fax 617-495-1599; info@worldteach.org, [www.worldteach.org].

The Best Web Sites

Internet Resources for Teaching English Abroad

Selected and Reviewed by William Nolting

Teaching abroad is one of the most accessible options for longer-term work abroad, typically for a year, though some programs offer short-term placements. Teaching English as a second or foreign language (TESL, ESL, TEFL, EFL) may be an option for college graduates without TESL credentials. Alternatively, other options are strictly for professionals with at least a Masters in Teaching English. ** *Essential* * *Outstanding and of broad interest.*
(I) Informational site with directories or databases listing many programs
(P) Site for a specific work abroad program
(S) Scholarships or fellowships

** **(I) Dave's ESL Café** [www.eslcafe.com] by Dave Sperling. This site has a staggering amount of well-organized information about teaching English as a second language, either abroad or in the U.S., as well as job databases. Useful for those with or without TESL credentials. A highly recommended resource for anyone interested in working abroad.

** **(P) Fulbright English Teaching Assistantships, Fulbright Student Programs, Institute of International Education** [www.iie.org/fulbright]. Program for recent university graduates to serve as English Teaching Assistants in Belgium/Luxembourg, France, Germany, Hungary, Korea, Taiwan and Turkey. The Fulbright Student Program also offers scholarships for study abroad.

** **(P, I) Japan Exchange and Teaching Program (JET)** [www.jet.org]. JETAA site by Michael McVey. The Japan Exchange and Teaching Program, administered by the Japanese government, is the largest program for teaching English. Graduating seniors and university degree holders eligible. Offers positions for those who have studied Japanese as Coordinators of International Relations. This site, by the JET Alumni Association (JETAA), has links to the JET program site. It also has extensive information about international jobs (great links to job search sites worldwide [www.jet.org/job]) and a good discussion about career choices after teaching abroad. You can subscribe to JET-L, a discussion group by participants (returned, current and prospective), from this site—useful for anyone interested in teaching abroad.

(I) O-Hayo Sensei [www.ohayosensei.com]. Listings of ESL and other types of teaching positions in Japan.

** (P, I) Peace Corps [www.peacecorps.gov]. Sometimes overlooked because of its designation as a volunteer program, Peace Corps is one of the largest work-abroad programs for U.S. citizens. It provides some of the best-paid teaching opportunities in less-wealthy regions such as Africa, Latin America, South and Southeast Asia, and even Eastern Europe and the former USSR.

* (I) Teachers of English to Speakers of Other Languages (TESOL) [www.tesol.edu]. Web site of the largest U.S. professional association for ESL teachers. An essential resource for qualified professionals, though less useful for students.

** (I) Univ. of Michigan, International Center's Overseas Opportunities Office [www.umich.edu/~icenter/overseas]. See article on "Teaching Abroad Without Certification" which lists U.S.-based programs for teaching abroad that do not require professional TESL credentials.

* (I) US State Department, Office of English Language Programs [http://e.usia.gov/education/engteaching]. Official information about U.S.-sponsored programs for teaching English abroad. Includes links to job search sites, of use especially to qualified ESL teachers (MA in TESL).

CHAPTER 7

K-12 AND UNIVERSITY TEACHING

Teachers with K-12 certification have a wide range of options for teaching abroad. The types of schools can be viewed in terms of the amount of integration into the host culture that the teacher is likely to experience. The following are listed in an order that proceeds from cul-turally less-integrated to more-integrated settings.

Key Programs and Organizations
Teaching K-12 and University

By William Nolting

Department of Defense Schools. Located at military bases in 19 countries around the world, some 200 DOD schools employ around 13,000 U.S. citizens. The teaching environment is roughly similar to that of U.S. public schools. Contact with host-country nationals is relatively limited. Contact: **Department of Defense Dependents Schools**, 4040 North Fairfax Dr., Arlington VA 22203-1634; (703) 696-3269; [**www.state.gov**]. Publishes free brochure *Overseas Employment Opportunities for Educators*. Available from Department of Defense, Office of Dependent Educational Activity, Office of Personnel, Dependents Schools, 4040 N. Fairfax Drive, Alexandria, VA, 22203; 703-696-1352. Includes application.

The **U.S. Dept. of State** publishes the free brochure *Overseas American-Sponsored Elementary Schools Assisted by the U.S. Department of State.* Order from Office of Overseas Schools, U.S. Dept. of State, Rm. 245, SA-29, Washington, DC, 20522; 703-875-7800, fax 703-875-7979. Information on 192 private schools.

Private International Schools. Located worldwide, nearly 1,000 private English-language K-12 schools educate the children of diplomats and businesspeople and of wealthy host country nationals. The teaching environment is similar to that of elite U.S. private schools. Although one can apply directly, the most efficient way to apply is through recruitment fairs in the U.S (see below), most of which take place in February (apply early since some fill up by December).

Volunteer Organizations. Despite the name, most volunteer placements, if long

173

term (two years), usually cover expenses and provide a stipend. Options range from the government-sponsored Peace Corps to religious organizations (from non-proselytizing to traditional missionaries).

Unlike private schools, pupils in these schools will be the children of ordinary people from the host country. Contact: **Peace Corps,** Room 8500, 1990 K St. NW, Washington DC 20526; 800-424-8580; [www.peacecorps.gov]. Contact religious organizations directly; some recruit at the teaching abroad fairs already mentioned.

Fulbright Teacher Exchange (K-12 and Community Colleges). This program is unique in two respects: it is a one-for-one exchange of teachers between schools, and teachers are fully integrated into regular host-country schools. Applicants must currently have a full-time teaching or administrative position. Application deadline is in October for the following academic year. Contact: **Fulbright Teacher Exchange Program,** U.S. Information Agency, 600 Maryland Ave. SW, Room 235, Washington, DC 20024-2520; 800-726-0479.

University Teaching

Nearly all university positions require a PhD (or at least "ABD") or other terminal professional degree.

Teaching for Study Abroad Programs. This is generally a tough market since U.S.-sponsored programs tend to use home-campus faculty or hire local professors. One organization sometimes hires resident directors (802-258-3114) and also publishes two-page resource lists on teaching and internship opportunities abroad ($2 each): Professional Development Resource Center, **School for International Training,** Box 676, Kipling Road, Brattleboro, VT 05302-0676; 802-258-3397, fax 802-258-3248; [www.sit.edu].

Fulbrights. Information on Fulbright grants to support an academic year of teaching in an overseas university is available from the **Council for International Exchange of Scholars** (CIES), 3007 Tilden St. NW, Suite 5M, Washington, DC 20008-3009; 202-686-4000; info@ciesnet.cies.org, [www.cies.org]. Application deadlines are May or August 1997 for academic year 1998-99. Grants also available for international education administrators.

Special Placement Programs Most of the organizations listed in Teaching English Abroad Key Resources (page 162) can offer university-level positions for those who are qualified. Worth special mention are: **The Civic Education Project** (CEP), P.O. Box 205445, Yale Station, New Haven, CT 06520-5445; 203-781-0263, fax 203-781-0265; cep@minerva.cis.yale.edu, [http://cep.nonprofit.net]. CEP offers positions in Eastern Europe for PhDs and PhD candidates in economics, history, international relations, political science, sociology, public administration, and law. Application deadline: February 1.

Colorado China Council, 4556 Apple Way, Boulder, CO 80301; 303-443-1108, fax 303-443-1107; alice@asiacouncil.org, [www.asiacouncil.org]. CCC offers placements in universities in the People's Republic of China, especially in English, TESL, journalism, business, sciences, and engineering.

Regular Faculty Positions See such standard academic job listings as those in the *Chronicle of Higher Education* (U.S. 800-347-6969 or [www.chronicle.merit/edu])

the *Times Higher Education Supplement* (U.K. [www.timeshigher.newsint.co.uk]) or the *Guardian* (U.K.), found in most university libraries.

Find a Teaching Job Abroad
Recruitment Fairs Are the Places to Get Jobs
By Clay Hubbs

The bulk of teaching opportunities abroad are for English teachers. You can obtain formal credentials in Teaching English as a Foreign (or Second) Language (variously called TEFL, TEFOL, TESL, TESOL, or ESL) in a one-month course or a two-year MA program. (See Directory of Training and Placement Programs, page 164.)

Qualified K-12 teachers have another range of options: Scattered around the world are at least 800 U.S.-style international elementary and secondary schools which employ around 35,000 American educators. To find a position in one of these schools you can either conduct your own job search—using the resources at the end of this chapter—or sign up for one of the recruiting fairs listed below.

The Employment Connection (*The Source*), an online service provided by The College of Education, Placement Services, The Ohio State Univ. (address below), contains all postings received through its offices. Subscriptions cost $25 per quarter. Other web sites that catalog teaching jobs abroad (both ESL and K-12) are listed on page 179, and are updated annually in the September/October issue of *Transitions Abroad* [www.TransitionsAbroad.com].

Recruiting Fairs

Attending a recruiting fair is probably the easiest way to find a teaching job overseas. Some fairs charge fees; others are free. Most charge a fee if you are offered a job. Some restrict the number of participants or have early registration deadlines.

Assn. Of American Schools in South America, AASSA-Teachers Search, 14750 NW 77th Ct., Suite 210, Miami Lakes, FL 33016; 305-821-0345, fax 305-821-4244; aassa@gate.net, [www.aassa.com]. **Fair dates:** usually late November or December; write in September for exact dates. Openings for schools in Central and South America, Mexico, and the Caribbean.

European Council of International Schools, 21B Lavant St., Petersfield, Hampshire Gu32 3EL, U.K.; 011-44-1730-68244, fax 011-44-1730-267914; staffingservices@ecis. org, [www.ecis.org]. **Fair dates:** Melbourne, AUS, usually early January; Vancouver, Canada, usually mid-February; London, England, usually early February and early May. Very early deadline. Contact early.

International Schools Services, Educational Staffing, P.O. Box 5910, Princeton, NJ 08543; 609-452-0990, fax 609-452-2690; iss@iss.edu, [www.iss.edu]. **Fair dates:** Washington D.C in February; Miami, FL, in early March; Philadelphia, PA, in late June. Credential files must be received six weeks before fair dates.

Michigan State Univ., Career Services and Placement, Michigan State Univ., 113 Student Services Bldg., E. Lansing, MI 48824; 517-355-9510, fax 517-353-2597; [www.csp.msu.edu]. **Fair date:** Mid-February.

National Assn. Of Independent Schools (NAIS), 1620 L St., NW, Washington, DC 20036; 202-973-9705, fax 202-973-9700; [www.nais.org]. **Fair date:** February 24-28. NAIS primarily serves independent schools in the U.S.

Ohio State Univ., Office of Placement Services, 110 Arps Hall, 1945 N. High St., Columbus, OH 43210-2741; 614-292-2581, fax 614-688-4612; [www.coe. ohio-state.edu/placement]. *The recruiting fair has been discontinued, however they provide a useful resource packet on teaching jobs abroad.*

Queen's Univ., Placement Director, Faculty of Education, Queen's Univ., Kingston, ON K7L 3N6, Canada; 613-967-4902, fax 613-967-8981; [www.queensu.ca]. **Fair date:** Early February.

Search Associates, P.O. Box 636, Dallas, PA 18612; 717-696-5400, fax 717-696-9500; In Canada: 613-967-4902, fax 613-967-8981; [www.search-associates.com]. **Fair dates:** February in Cambridge, MA; Carmel, CA; Houston, TX. June in Bethesda, MD. Also 10 other locations worldwide.

Teacher Recruitment Int'l., P.O. Box 177, Tumby Bay, Australia; 011-618-86-88-4260, fax 011-618-86-88-4222. **Fair dates:** Sydney, usually early January; Melbourne, usually late March and mid-April.

TESOL, 1600 Cameron St., Suite 300, Alexandria, VA 22314-2751; 703-836-0774, fax 703-836-7864; conv@tesol.edu, [www.tesol.edu]. **Fair date:** February or March. Primarily a convention for ESL (English as a Second Language) teachers. All levels. Good placement opportunities worldwide.

University of Calgary, Faculty of Education, Univ. of Calgary, 2500 University Dr., NW, Calgary AB T2N 1N4, Canada; Tel./fax 403-220-5627, fax 403-282-7574; [http://external.educ.ucalgary.ca]. **Fair date:** Summer; call for details.

University of Northern Iowa, Overseas Placement Center for Educators, SSC-19, Univ. of Northern Iowa Career Center, Cedar Falls, IA 50614; 319-273-2083, fax 319-273-6998; overseas.placement@uni.edu, [www.uni.edu/placemnt/student/internat.html]. **Fair date:** Cedar Falls, IA, usually in late February.

Perspective

Travel and Teach

Trade Your Concrete Jungle for a Real One

By T.J. Fournier

As I gather my books for my day at school, I look out the window at the snow-capped Andes. Smoke curls from the chimneys of houses some 1,000 feet below and church bells ring in the barrio. On the bus to work I eat a warm, buttered *arepa* while we twist through the hills.

Trading my U.S. classroom in the concrete jungle for one in mountainous Colombia was not a hard choice for me. For many educators, though, teaching abroad seems only something to dream about because they may not be aware of the real opportunities to travel and teach.

"Many foreign schools have a very significant need for well-trained North American teachers," says Joe Fuchillo of International Educators Cooperative (IEC), an agency whose goal is to match teachers and administrators with South American schools. "Most U.S. teachers are unaware of the opportunities available worldwide for both short- and long-term contracts."

"Traditionally, the contracts for foreign teachers run from two to five years," he notes, "so there is constant turnover, a constant demand for new staffing."

IEC is one of the smaller headhunting agencies serving international schools. (See list of recruitment agencies and fairs above.) Most fairs are held in late February while large numbers of North American schools are closed for vacation. Attendees include administrators, teachers, and school service professionals. Many are veterans of international education. Others, like my wife and I were, are novices.

Just recently married, my wife and I began our journey over a cup of coffee. We are both former Peace Corps volunteers and perpetually afflicted with wanderlust; we were discussing whether to continue teaching in the Detroit public schools or to take a leave of absence and travel. It was evident before the coffee got cold what we were going to do.

We began by canvassing university schools of education, the Peace Corps office in Washington, and our colleagues for information regarding international schools: where they are, who hires, who gets hired, the average salary, etc. We were sent brochures, pamphlets, and applications.

The choices seemed endless. Instead of pursuing every lead, we decided what region of the world we wanted to focus on and what type of population we wanted to work with (urban or rural, native or expatriate, poor or wealthy). Our choice was South America, partly because I am fluent in Spanish. We were determined not to teach in a capital city as we were already accustomed to large populations in small spaces. Finally, we preferred teaching a native population.

Selecting an Agency

These criteria allowed us to hone our choices to a few selected agencies that deal specifically with South American schools. IEC, as a small agency, was very accommodating in responding to our questions and concerns. With our resumes and dossiers in hand, we flew to Houston for a weekend of interviewing, trading information with other applicants, and undergoing intense soul searching.

The fair began on Friday evening with an ice-breaking cocktail hour. We mingled with teachers, administrators, and conference coordinators. We were fascinated with our competition—attendees came from all parts of the world. On Saturday morning we met in a large conference room in which each school had its own table. The school directors had already reviewed our applications and posted the names of potential applicants at their stations. We were to find our names and wait in line to be interviewed. If our names were not posted anywhere, or if the school in which we were interested didn't post our names, we became second priority and were to stand in line until the preliminary interviews were finished. We were each given six interviews and received as many job offers.

Upon deciding on the Colegio Granadino in Manizales, Colombia, we returned to Detroit with new contracts in hand. Our principals accepted our announcement with good cheer, pleased that their staff members were looking to broaden their experiences. We were both offered unconditional leaves of absence and support in linking our schools in Detroit with Colombia through e-mail pen pal exchanges.

As we begin our second term teaching at elementary schools in Manizales, we can hardly believe our luck. New experiences, new challenges, and a new perspective are benefits we find here that even the strongest of unions back home could not bargain into our contracts. Do yourselves and your classrooms a favor. Take a risk and do what few dare to do: teach abroad.

Teaching K-12 and University
The Key Print Resources
Selected and Reviewed by William Nolting

International teaching jobs in K–12 schools usually require a teaching credential. Jobs in universities often require a PhD. Major K–12 job fairs are held in February (apply in November).

** Essential; *Outstanding and of broad interest.
For ordering information, if not included below, see Key Publishers, page 13.

Friends of World Teaching, P.O. Box 84480, San Diego, CA 92138-4480; 800-503-7436, fax 619-224-5363; details@fowt.com, [www.fowt.com]. Maintains updated listings of English-speaking schools and colleges in over 100 foreign countries where educators may apply throughout the year. For a free brochure, send a self-addressed stamped envelope.

* Fulbright Scholar Program: Grants for U.S. Faculty and Professionals. Free information from Council for International Exchange of Scholars, 3007 Tilden St. NW, Suite 5L, Washington, DC 20008-3009; 202-686-7877; fax 202-362-3442; scholars@cies.iie.org, [www.iie.org/cies]. Program offers university-level opportunities for lecturing and research abroad; most positions require doctoral degrees and/or equivalent professional experience. Application deadlines are Aug 1 (lecturing and research awards); Nov 1 (international education administrators); Jan 1 (NATO scholars).

* Fulbright Teacher Exchange: Opportunities Abroad for Educators. Free application from the U.S. Department of State, Fulbright Teacher Exchange Program, 600 Maryland Ave. SW, Suite 320, Washington, DC 20024-2520; 800-726-0479; fulbright@grad.usda.gov, [www.grad.usda.gov/International/ftep.html] Program descriptions and application for direct exchanges in over 30 countries for currently employed K-12 and community college faculty and administrators. Application deadline for 2001-2002: Oct 15.

* The ISS Directory of Overseas Schools edited by Gina Parziale (revised annually). 560 pp. International Schools Services. $34.95 from Peterson's. The most comprehensive and up-to-date directory to over 580 overseas American and international K-12 schools. International Schools Services, 15 Roszel Rd., P.O. Box 5910, Princeton, NJ 08543; 609-452-0990, fax 609-452-2690; iss@iss.edu, [www.iss.edu]. Available directly from ISS: NewsLinks, $20/year, a bimonthly magazine for international school community; and Teaching and Administrative Opportunities Abroad, free, application to ISS job fairs for

teaching overseas.

Overseas Academic Opportunities. Monthly bulletin. $42/year from Overseas Academic Opportunities, 72 Franklin Ave., Ocean Grove, NJ 07756; Tel./fax 732-774-1040. Openings primarily for new teachers in K-12 subject areas for jobs where the only language needed is English and state certification not required.

Overseas American-Sponsored Elementary Schools Assisted by the U.S. Department of State. Free pamphlet available from the Office of Overseas Schools, U.S. Department of State, Rm. 245, SA-29, Washington, DC 20522-2902; 703-875-7800, fax 703-875-7979, [www.state. gov]. Information on 192 private overseas K-12 schools. *Fact Sheets* provide more detailed information. Complete information free on web site [www.state.gov/www/about_state/schools/index.html].

Overseas Employment Opportunities for Educators (Department of Defense schools). Annual. Free from Department of Defense, Office of Dependent Educational Activity, Office of Personnel, Dependents Schools, 4040 N Fairfax Dr., 6th Fl., Alexandria, VA 22203; 703-696-1352; [www.odedodea.edu]. Application for K-12 employment opportunities in over 200 schools worldwide serving U.S. military bases. Minimum academic requirement is a BA or BS with at least 18 hours of education courses.

* **Overseas Placement Service for Educators, Univ. of Northern Iowa (UNI).** To order registration materials for the oldest and one of the largest U.S. international recruiting fairs for K-12 teachers, send $5 to Overseas Placement Service for Educators, Univ. of Northern Iowa, SSC #19, Cedar Falls, IA 50614-0390; 319-273-2083, fax 319-273-6998; overseas.placement@uni.edu, [www.uni.edu/placemnt/overseas]. The Fair, held each February, attracts over 100 American international schools. Fact book and newsletters are included with registration (also available as separate purchases).

The Best Web Sites
Internet Resources for K-12 and University Teaching Abroad

Selected and Reviewed by William Nolting

Teaching in international K-12 schools usually requires teaching certification. Teaching at the university level usually requires a PhD or terminal professional degree, though there are some options available for advanced graduate students. ** *Essential;* * *Outstanding and of broad interest.*
(I) *Informational site with directories or databases listing many programs*
(P) *Site for a specific work abroad program*
(S) *Scholarships or fellowships*

TEACHING ABROAD K-12

* (P) Fulbright Teacher Exchange: US State Department, Bureau of Educational and Cultural Affairs [www.grad.usda.gov/International/ftep.htm]. Teaching exchanges (reciprocal) for currently employed K-12 and community college teachers.

* (P, I) International Schools Services (ISS) [www.iss.edu]. Nonprofit organization publishes a directory of international K-12 English-language schools and organizes job fairs for certified teachers for these schools.

** (I) Ohio University, Employment Resources for Language Teachers [www.ohio.edu/esl/teacher] by John McVicker. A comprehensive collection of web sites for finding language teaching positions and courses, both abroad and in the U.S. Site also has a guide to web resources for those studying foreign languages.

* (I) Overseas Teachers Digest and Expat Exchange For Americans [www.overseasdi-

gest.com]. Not a job bank, this site contains valuable information for Americans working abroad. Be sure to see the *Better Business Bureau* article made available by this site, "Overseas Job Scams," [http://overseasdigest.com/scams.htm].

* (I) Univ. of Northern Iowa's Overseas Placement Service for Educators [www.uni.edu/placemnt/overseas]. This university-sponsored service organizes an annual job fair for certified teachers for international K-12 English-language schools, and publishes information about these schools.

* (I) U.S. Department of State, Teaching Overseas [www.state.gov/www/about_state/schools]. Site describes English-language K-12 schools abroad, opportunities for teaching, and gives links to relevant organizations.

** (I) Univ. of Michigan, International Center's Overseas Opportunities Office [www.umich.edu/~icenter/overseas]. See article on "Teaching Abroad for Qualified Teachers," which lists options for K-12 and university-level teaching.

UNIVERSITY TEACHING

** (I) Chronicle of Higher Education [http://thisweek.chronicle.com/jobs/]. For academicians the *Chronicle* is the best source of job listings. Much of site accessible only to subscribers. Also check with discipline-specific professional associations.

** (P) Fulbright Scholar Program, Grants for U.S. Faculty and Professionals, Council for International Exchange of Scholars (CIES) [www.iie.org/cies]. Overseas teaching and research positions for those qualified to teach or to do research in universities, as well as study tours for international education administrators.

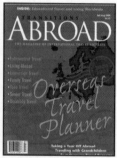

About the Contributors

Editors

CLAY HUBBS is the founder, editor, and publisher of *Transitions Abroad*. He taught Modern European and American literature and served as Director of International Studies at Hampshire College from 1972-1998.

SUSAN GRIFFITH is the author of *Work Your Way Around the World* and *Teaching English Abroad: Talking Your Way Around the World*, both available from Peterson's Guides.

WILLIAM NOLTING is the Director of the Univ. of Michigan Overseas Opportunities Office and International Education Editor for *Transitions Abroad*.

Contributors

EDWARD CARPENTER writes from Santiago, Chile.

LORI CLOUTIER is a 1999 graduate of the Univ. of Michigan. She participated in BUNAC's Work in Britain program during the summer of 1996.

KATE DOYLE is an English teacher and writer currently based in Barcelona, Spain.

BRYAN J. ESTEP founded a trading company with offices in Mexico City, San Francisco, and Santiago, Chile. He is the coauthor of the guide *Exporting to Mexico*.

T.J. FOURNIER writes from Manizales, Colombia.

ANTHONY HAND is a graduate student in the School of Information at the Univ. of Michigan. He is a JET program alum.

ROBERT HEIN is author of *Travel the South Pacific on Private Yachts*, based on more than 20 years as a yacht sailor and captain.

LAURA HIGGINS was a Fulbright scholar in French Polynesia and will spend next year in France. She is a doctoral student in romance languages at Duke Univ.

KELLY BEMBRY MIDURA writes from Springfield, VA.

KARA C. McDONALD works at the Center for Democracy and Governance at USAID in Washington, DC. She has participated in three missions to Bosnia and was involved with efforts in Kosovo. She holds a Masters degree from the Fletcher School of Law and Diplomacy.

CHARLIE MORRIS is a writer and computer consultant. He has worked throughout Europe and lived in Switzerland, Norway, and England.

DEBRA PETERS-BEHRENS is a career counselor at the Univ. of California, Santa Barbara.

HEATHER POWERS is Program Coordinator, Field Service and Regional Affairs for NAFSA: Association of International Educators, Washington, DC.

CHARITY RYABINKIN spent a semester in Moscow and landed a job teaching English at the American Home in Vladimir after graduating from Carleton College. She currently lives with her Russian husband and works as an editorial assistant at the Association of Governing Boards of Universities and Colleges (AGB) in Washington, DC.

MISHELLE SHEPARD is a freelance writer currently living in Thailand. She served as a Peace Corps Volunteer in the Czech Republic from 1994–1996.

BRIAN THORNTON, originally from Clifden, Ireland, had his first teaching abroad experience in Thailand. He presently works at the Galway Cultural Institute in Ireland as a general English teacher.

CHRISTINE VICTORINO has volunteered in Sri Lanka, Costa Rica, and India, and was formerly the Director of the International Volunteer Programs Association (IVPA). Christine currently works for VIA, a cross-cultural exchange and public service program based at Stanford University.

DANIEL WALFISH graduated from Yale in 1998 and then spent the summer studying Chinese in Beijing. There he found a job teaching English at Nankai Univ. in nearby Tianjin. He now lives in New York and works at *American Lawyer* magazine.

ERIKA WEIDNER lives in San Mateo, CA.

DANIEL WEISS received his PhD in Educational Policy from the Univ. of Minnesota. He is the executive director of Amizade, Ltd., based in Deerfield, IL.

BECKY YOUMAN moved to Mexico City where, through a chain of contacts, she landed a job as country manager for a U.S. company in Mexico.

Index

A

Africa
Key Employers 74
Short-Term Jobs 74-76

Argentina
English Schools 157

Asia
English Schools 149-151
Short-Term Jobs 76-77
Teaching English 142-149, 163

Au Pairing 90
Placement Agencies 93-95
Austria 90, 93
Belgium 90, 93
Denmark 92, 93
Finland 92, 94
France 91, 93
Germany 91, 94
Greece 91, 94
Iceland 92, 94
Israel 91, 94
Italy 92, 94
Netherlands 92, 94
North American Agencies 93
Norway 94
Portugal 94
Spain 92, 94
Sweden 92, 94
Switzerland 93, 94

B

Baltic States
Teaching English 135

Bolivia
English Schools 157

Brazil
English Schools 157

Britain
Short-Term Jobs 46

C

Canada
ESL Training and Placement 164

Central and Eastern Europe
English Schools 138-139
Teaching English 133-137
ESL Training and Placement 164

Central and South America
English Schools 157-160
ESL Training and Placement 159

Chile
English Schools 157
Teaching English 161

China
English Schools 149
Teaching English 143
ESL Training and Placement 164

Colombia
English Schools 158

Czech Republic
Teaching English 135
ESL Training and Placement 165

E

Ecuador
English Schools 158

Egypt
Language Schools 133
Teaching English 132
ESL Training and Placement 165

El Salvador
English Schools 158

ESL Training and Placement Programs
Canada 164
Central Europe 164
China 164
Czech Republic 165
Egypt 165
Europe 165
France 165
Japan 165
Mexico 166
Spain 166
Taiwan 166
Teaching English 164

Worldwide 167-170

Europe
ESL Training and Placement 165
Teaching English 123-131, 133
Work Permits for Professionals 23
Work Permits for Short-Term Jobs 23

F

Finding a Job 19-22

France
ESL Training and Placement 165

G

Germany
Teaching English 126

Greece
Teaching English 127

Guatemala
English Schools 159

H

Hungary
Teaching English 137

I

India
Internships 65

Indonesia
English Schools 149
Teaching English 143

International Careers
Foreign Service 24
Key Print Resources 26-30
Key Web Sites 30-36
Preparation 17-19
Western Europe 22

Internship Programs
AIESEC 41, 55, 72, 96
AIPT 42, 53, 55, 60, 62
American-Scandinavian Foundation
40, 55, 60, 87, 97
Australia 63
Belize 63
CDS 40, 42, 43, 53, 55, 60, 72, 81

Costa Rica 64
Czech Republic 64
Directory of Programs 62-68
Ecuador 64
Educational Organizations 57
Europe 64
France 65
Germany 65
IAESTE 40, 41, 53, 55, 60, 62, 72, 96
India 65
International Education 58
International Organizations 55
Internships International 55, 114
Key Print Resources 60-61
Latin America 64, 66
Mexico 66
Non-Government Organizations 57
Poland 66
Private Enterprise 57
Private Voluntary Organizations 57
Public Multinationals 57
Russia 66
Spain 66
Types of 55
United Kingdom 67
United States 68
U.S. Government 56
Web Sites 69-70
When to Apply 40
Worldwide 62-63

Italy
Teaching English 128

J

Japan
English Schools 150
Teaching English 144
ESL Training and Placement 165

K

K-12 and University Teaching
Key Print Resources 178-179
Key Programs 173-175
Recruitment Fairs 175
Web Sites 179-180

Key Print Resources
International Careers 26-30
International Internships 60-61

International Job Listings 29-30
K-12 and University Teaching 178-179
Key Publishers 13-14
Short-Term Work for Students and
Recent Graduates 49-54
Regional Work and Study Abroad 51-53
Short-Term Paid Work 53-54
Study Abroad 49-51
Teaching English 162-163
Volunteering 107-109
Work Placement Programs 43-44

Korea
English Schools 150
Teaching English 145

M

Mexico
English Schools 159
ESL Training and Placement 166

Morocco
Language Schools 133
Teaching English 132

P

Peru
English Schools 159

Poland
Teaching English 136

Portugal
Teaching English 128

R

Recruitment Fairs 175

Russia
Teaching English 134

S

Scholarships 38, 50, 56, 68-70, 104

**Short-Term Jobs for Students
and Recent Graduates**
Exchange Programs 40
Key Print Resources 49-54
Work Abroad Checklist 44
Work Permits 37, 41

Short-term Work
Africa 74
Antarctica 76
Asia 76
Australia 77-78
Austria 81
Belgium 87
Central and Eastern Europe 78
France 80
Germany 81
Italy 82
Key Employers 71-90
Latin America 83
Luxemborg 87
Mediterranean 85
Middle East 86
Netherlands 87
Portugal 88
Scandinavia 87
Spain 88
Switzerland 81
United Kingdom 88
Worldwide Employers 71-74

Spain
Teaching English 127, 129
ESL Training and Placement 166

T

Taiwan
English Schools 151
Teaching English 146
ESL Training and Placement 166

Teaching English
Baltic States 135
Central and Eastern Europe 133
China 143
Czech Republic 135
Directory of Programs 164-170
Eastern Mediterranean 131
Europe 123-131
France 125
Freelancing 124
Germany 126
Greece 126
Hungary 137
Indonesia 143
Italy 128
Japan 144

Key Print Resources 162-163
Korea 145
Overview 119
Poland 136
Portugal 128
Preparing 121
Russia 134
Slovak Republic 135
South Asia 148
Spain 127, 129
Taiwan 146
Thailand 147
Turkey 131
Ukraine 135
Web Sites 170-171

Thailand
English Schools 151
Teaching English 147

Turkey
Language Schools 132
Teaching English 131

U

Ukraine
Teaching English 135

United Kingdom
Key Employers 88-90

V

Volunteering 44
Australia 110
Canada 110
Caribbean 110
Central America 110
Coping With Potential Problems 101
Cost of 99
Costa Rica 111
Directory of Programs 110-116
Ecuador 111
Europe 112
Funding Your Experience 100
International Monitoring 104
Japan 112
Key Print Resources 107-109
Latin America 112
Mexico 112
Nepal 112

Overview 39, 99
Pacific Region 113
Romania 113
Taiwan 113
United States 113
Web Sites 34, 117
Why Volunteer? 99
Workcamps 44
Worldwide 114-116

W

Web Sites
Africa 34
Asia 35
Australia 35
Canada 34
Central and Eastern Europe 35
International Careers 30
International Education 33
Internships 69
K-12 and University Teaching 179
Latin America 34
Middle East 34
New Zealand 35
Profession-Specific (Careers) 32
Region Specific (Careers) 34
Scholarships 69
Short-Term Work
Teaching English 170-171
Volunteering 34, 117
Worldwide Work Abroad 15

Work Permits 23

Workcamps 44

Worldwide
ESL Training and Placement 167-170
International Careers 17-36
Internship Programs 62-63
Short-Term Jobs 71-74
Short-Term Work for Students and Recent Graduates 49
Volunteering 114

Index to Advertisers

Alternative Travel Directory	70
BUNAC	171
Cross-Cultural Solutions	118
International SOS	6
International TEFL Certificate	48
TEFL International	140
Transitions Abroad Magazine	180
Transworld Schools	98
Worldwide Teachers	172

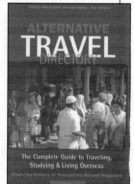

Reader Response Page

Transitions Abroad relies on its editors for the best available information on alternative travel resources and programs. It relies on readers for first-hand reports. Please use the space below (or a separate sheet) to describe you own alternative travel and work abroad discoveries. The most useful reports will be published in Information Exchange in *Transitions Abroad*.

Send to Information Exchange, Transitions Abroad, P.O. Box 1300 Amherst, MA 01004-1300; fax 413-256-0373; info@TransitionsAbroad.com. For longer submissions, please read our Writers' Guidelines, available on our web site at [www.TransitionsAbroad.com/information/writers].